SHAKESPEARE'S THEATRES AND THE EFFECTS OF PERFORMANCE

THE ARDEN SHAKESPEARE LIBRARY

SHAKESPEARE'S THEATRES AND THE EFFECTS OF PERFORMANCE

Edited by

FARAH KARIM-COOPER
AND TIFFANY STERN

Bloomsbury Arden Shakespeare
An imprint of Bloomsbury Publishing Plc

B L O O M S B U R Y
LONDON • NEW DELHI • NEW YORK • SYDNEY

Bloomsbury Arden Shakespeare
An imprint of Bloomsbury Publishing Plc

Imprint previously known as Arden Shakespeare

50 Bedford Square	1385 Broadway
London	New York
WC1B 3DP	NY 10018
UK	USA

www.bloomsbury.com

BLOOMSBURY, THE ARDEN SHAKESPEARE and the Diana logo are trademarks of Bloomsbury Publishing Plc

First published in 2013 by Bloomsbury Arden Shakespeare
Paperback edition first published in 2014
Reprinted 2014

British Library Cataloguing-in-Publication Data
A catalogue record for this book is available from the British Library.

ISBN: HB: 978-1-4081-4692-7
PB: 978-1-4725-5859-6
ePDF: 978-1-4081-7464-7
ePUB: 978-1-4081-5705-3

Library of Congress Cataloging-in-Publication Data
A catalog record for this book is available from the Library of Congress.

Printed and bound in Great Britain

CONTENTS

ACKNOWLEDGEMENTS   vii
PREFACE   ix
Andrew Gurr
LIST OF ILLUSTRATIONS   xiii
LIST OF CONTRIBUTORS   xv

Introduction   1
Farah Karim-Cooper and Tiffany Stern

Part One: The Fabric of Early Modern Theatres

Chapter One
'This Wide and Universal Theatre': The Theatre as
Prop in Shakespeare's Metadrama   11
Tiffany Stern

Chapter Two
Storm Effects in Shakespeare   33
Gwilym Jones

Chapter Three
Performing Materiality: Curtains on the Early
Modern Stage   51
Nathalie Rivere de Carles

Part Two: Technologies of the Body

Chapter Four
'*They eat each other's arms*': Stage Blood and
Body Parts   73
Lucy Munro

Chapter Five
Cosmetic Transformations   94
Andrea Stevens

Chapter Six
Costume, Disguise and Self-display   118
Bridget Escolme

Chapter Seven
Character Acting   141
Paul Menzer

Part Three: The Sensory Stage

Chapter Eight
Within, Without, Withinwards: The Circulation of
Sound in Shakespeare's Theatre   171
Bruce R. Smith

Chapter Nine
'As Dirty as Smithfield and as Stinking Every Whit':
The Smell of the Hope Theatre   195
Holly Dugan

Chapter Ten
Touch and Taste in Shakespeare's Theatres   214
Farah Karim-Cooper

Chapter Eleven
'Sight and Spectacle'   237
Evelyn Tribble

NOTES   253
INDEX   289

ACKNOWLEDGEMENTS

The editors would like to thank everyone at Bloomsbury / Arden who worked on this book, and in particular, Margaret Bartley, Claire Cooper, Judy Tither and Emily Hockley for their support and enthusiasm throughout. Grateful thanks are also due to all of the contributors for their patience and energy, and to Ben Higgins for creating the index. Thank you to David Bellwood of Shakespeare's Globe for providing the Globe images.

Farah Karim-Cooper would like personally to thank her collaborator, Tiffany, for making this project so easy and pleasurable; her family, Jerry Cooper, Sabreena Cooper, Fazal and Fawzia Karim, Charles and Barbara Cooper; and her colleagues Patrick Spottiswoode, Dominic Dromgoole, Neil Constable, Chris Stafford, Fiona Banks, Paul Shuter, Alex Massey, Jo Luck, Ruth Frendo, Amy Kenny and Gordon McMullan. She dedicates her contribution to Claire van Kampen.

Tiffany Stern would like to thank her amazing collaborator, Farah, and her wonderfully supportive colleagues Nicholas Halmi and Laura Varnam. She dedicates her contribution to Daniel Grimley.

ACKNOWLEDGMENTS

PREFACE
by Andrew Gurr

How sophisticated was early modern staging? The bloodily realistic parcel of guts and phials of blood used for three onstage disembowellings listed in the 'plot' of *The Battle of Alcazar* in 1600 stand at quite a distance from such special effects as Prospero appearing on the '*top*', reflecting the staging of Jonson's masque *Hymenaei*, or Ariel dressed as a winged harpy dangling downwards till he could touch the banquet table. That was Ariel's third disguise in *The Tempest*, with more to follow – later he seems to have appeared as Ceres, in place of Hymen, in the masque. In one of Shakespeare's shortest plays, Prospero adopts almost as many changes of dress as does his chief spirit. Costume, like blood, had a massive visual impact in the original stagings of these plays. The range of senses impacted by a playgoing experience was far broader then than the experiences we expect today. In this remarkable book, each chapter expands the possibilities of early staging, touching (and feeling) all the human senses.

We may have become too preoccupied with most of the inexhaustible elements in the experience of going to plays. A lot has been written lately, particularly about actor–audience relations, but very little has really gone into the evident sophistication of the scenic, visual and sensory aspects of early staging. As yet, we do not even have much idea of how or whether acting fashions changed over the years. There must surely have been major changes introduced through the great decades up to the closure of 1642. We might expect such innovations as direct conversation with the crowd in the yard falling away gradually, as the clown's exchanges with his audience became stale, but did the later plays that ignore the presence of the audience show a change in public tastes? Was it, perhaps, that such plays reflect a shift in writers' concerns? Why should the spectacle of gruesomely realistic visions and horror effects in the earlier plays, even the brazen head used for scenes of magic in *Alphonsus of Aragon* and *Friar Bacon and Friar Bungay*, have fallen out of use, ignored in later years except for the occasional revivals of the by-then-already-golden classics? Did Jonson really expect to find that his own scorn, expressed in *Bartholomew Fair*, over the now outdated preference for *The Spanish Tragedy* and *Titus Andronicus*, would be widely replicated in his first audiences at the new Hope playhouse in 1614? Did Tamburlaine never return in his chariot drawn by four still-crowned kings, after Alleyn retired from the stage in 1603? We might expect the play of *Doctor Faustus* had to be rewritten over the years with different conclusions according to current shifts in religious inter-pretation, as Leah Marcus has suggested,[1] with drastic effects on the staging. But if so, which of its three or more versions should we prefer to have reproduced on modern stages?

That is an enduring and unanswerable question. Editors, asked to choose a single ideal play-text, have still not found any comfort-able way of choosing between the desire to have the version of a play-text closest to what left the author's mind, as against the worked-on and adapted version that first reached the stage, or even a later version, sharpened and polished as it might be by years of performance. Performance criticism is still at odds with literary criticism, as the seminar on 'the return of the author' with W. B. Worthen's lengthy response in a recent *Shakespeare Quarterly*, will indicate.[2] Performance criticism is quite enough at odds with its own practices, between the scholarly attempts to ascertain just what the plays were originally designed to show, museum theatre, and what modernising productions actually show now, either on stage or on screen.

We can agree, though, on a few features of early staging without too much risk of contradiction. We recognise that agility and athleticism was a constant, and not only for messengers rushing on or off stage.[3] Speed of movement, given the size of the known outdoor stages, is one invariable in the early performances, although the smaller size of the indoor stages that became dominant in later years must have altered those practices more than a little. The slick use of costume changes for disguise, and the use of props for such things as the complex language of hats, is another. Too many of the early social mannerisms are lost to us. In Massinger's *The Picture*, the counsellor Eubolus tells his monarch 'I must tell you, 'tis ill manners in you, / Having depos'd your selfe to keepe your hat on.'[4] For most readers, and even directors and actors, understanding this joke entails at the very least an explanatory footnote. But how could we accept it on stage?

Worst of all, because most insidious, we still too readily think of staging as a two-dimensional exercise, ruled by the assumption that audiences sat in 'front' of the players, not all around them, as the chief evidence from the time declares. 'My throne stood like a point in midst of a circle' (1.1.214) laments Marston's deposed Duke Altofront (the malcontent of his play).[5] So did Richard III's, when he assumed the crown, this change of position turning him into everyone's target, instead of being the free troublemaker he was before, prowling the outer margins of the stage and fooling the characters in centre stage. The 'round Globe' was not made round by accident.

And there are many more such issues raised in this book. It is more than a scholarly generation now since I introduced (with an article in 1984 and a book in 1987) the question why, given the priority that Jonson and others gave to the ear over the eye, a priority defeated for ever in 1660, we still prefer to use the aural term, audience, rather than the visual, spectator, for the experience of going to a play. This volume does wonders at pushing forward our sense of what early modern audiences might have brought to the plays they experienced, and how extensive was the wealth of tacit information their authors laid on for them. Besides augmenting what have become the two most familiar senses in a playhouse, seeing and hearing, the chapters here make wonderful use of all five senses to augment our understanding of the plays. They can even develop our sense of what is called here the 'smellscape' that early audiences (and spectators) experienced.

LIST OF ILLUSTRATIONS

Figure 1   Tiring-House – front view, with 'heaven' above and 'hell' below. Architectural detail of Shakespeare's Globe, photograph by Pete Le May. With kind permission of The Globe Theatre. Page 16

Figure 2   Wenceslas Hollar's *A View from St Mary's, Southwark*. The 'lantern' in the Globe's double gabled roof may have housed a bell. Yale Center for British Art, Paul Mellon Collection. Page 30

Figure 3   Mark Rylance as Duke Vincentio in disguise (as friar), in *Measure for Measure* at Shakespeare's Globe, photograph by John Tramper. With kind permission of The Globe Theatre. Page 123

Figure 4   Title-page detail from John Cooke's *Green's Tu Quoque, or the Cittie Gallant* (1614). The Bodleian Library, University of Oxford, 4° T.36 (4) Art. Page 152

Figure 5   Detail from the title page of *The Spanish Tragedy* (1615). Title page of Q7 with the woodcut showing scenes 2.4 and 2.5 (© The British Library Board, C.117.b.36). Page 153

Figure 6   Text detail from *The Spanish Tragedy* (1615), D2r (© The British Library Board, C.117.b.36). Page 154

Figure 7   Mark Rylance (Vincentio) in *Measure for Measure*, Shakespeare's Globe (2004), photograph by John Tramper. With kind permission of The Globe Theatre. Page 243

Figure 8   *Titus Andronicus*, drawing by Henry Peacham. © Reproduced by permission of the Marquess of Bath, Longleat House, Warminster, Wiltshire, Great Britain. Page 245

LIST OF CONTRIBUTORS

Farah Karim-Cooper is Head of Courses and Research at Shakespeare's Globe and Visiting Research Fellow, King's College London. Her publications include: *Cosmetics in Shakespearean and Renaissance Drama* (2006); *Shakespeare's Globe: A Theatrical Experiment*, co-editor Christie Carson (2008); *Shakespeare and the Hand* (forthcoming). In addition to a number of articles and reviews, she has published essays, including, 'Literary Heritage: Stratford and the Globe', in conversation, Farah Karim-Cooper and Kate Rumbold, *Authors at Work: The Creative Environment*, ed. Ceri Sullivan and Graeme Harper (2009); 'Performing Beauty on the Renaissance Stage', *Shakespeare in Stages: New Directions in Theatre* History, ed. Christie Carson and Christine Dymkowski (2009); 'Props and the Construction of History at Shakespeare's Globe', in *Shakespeare and the Making of Theatre*, ed. Bridget Escolme and Stuart Hampton-Reeves (2012); 'Playing, Disguise, and Identity', in *Middleton in Context*, ed. Suzanne Gossett (2010); '"Non-Shakespeare" at Shakespeare's Globe', in *Performing Early Modern Drama Today*, ed. Kathryn Prince and Pascale Aebischer (2012).

Tiffany Stern is Professor of Early Modern Drama at Oxford University, and the Beaverbrook and Bouverie Fellow and Tutor in English Literature at University College, Oxford. She specialises in Shakespeare, theatre history from the sixteenth to the eighteenth century, book history and editing. Her monographs are *Rehearsal from Shakespeare to Sheridan* (2000), *Making Shakespeare* (2004), *Shakespeare in Parts* (2007, co-written with Simon Palfrey, and winner of the 2009 David Bevington Award for Best New Book in Early Drama Studies), and *Documents of Performance in Early Modern England* (2009, winner of the 2010 David Bevington

Award for Best New Book in Early Drama Studies). She has edited the anonymous *King Leir* (2001), Sheridan's *The Rivals* (2004), Farquhar's *The Recruiting Officer* (2010), and has written upwards of thirty articles and chapters exploring bibliographical, editorial, theatrical and architectural concerns from the sixteenth century to the eighteenth. Currently completing an edition of Brome's *Jovial Crew*, Tiffany is also a general editor of the New Mermaids play series, and is on the editorial board of the RSC *Shakespeare*, the new *Oxford Complete Works of Shakespeare*, the Greenwood *Shakespeare Encylopedia*, and the journals *Shakespeare Bulletin*, *SEDERI* and *Shakespeare Yearbook*.

Holly Dugan is an Associate Professor of English at the George Washington University. She received her PhD in English and Women's Studies from the University of Michigan, Ann Arbor, and her BA from the Rutgers University. Her publications include *The Ephemeral History of Perfume: Scent and Sense in Early Modern England*, forthcoming with Johns Hopkins University Press, and articles in *Literature Compass* (2009), *The Journal of Medieval and Early Modern Culture* (2008), and essays in the collections *Metropolis of Vice: London, 1550–1750* and *Working Subjects in Early Modern England*. She is a co-editor of a special issue of *Postmedieval* (forthcoming in 2012) on the intimate senses of taste, touch and smell.

Bridget Escolme is a Senior Lecturer in Drama at Queen Mary University of London. Her published work, particularly *Talking to the Audience* (2005), has explored the relationship between performer and audience in Shakespeare production. She is currently completing a monograph, *Emotional Excess on the Shakespearean Stage: Passion's Slaves* (c. 2013) which examines the ways in which theatre reflects, produces, regulates and celebrates extremes of emotion. She is also researching *Shakespeare and site-specific performance* for the new Palgrave series *Shakespeare in Practice*, eds. Escolme and Stuart Hampton-Reeves, and is co-editor, with Hampton-Reeves, of the edited collection *Shakespeare* *and the Making of Theatre*, for which she has written the contribution on costume. Her research is underpinned by theatre practice: she has published work on her promenade production of *Coriolanus* in *Shakespeare Survey*, has worked as a dramaturg, a director and a Theatre in Education practitioner.

Gwilym Jones is Lecturer in English Literature at Queen Mary, University of London. He has been a Lecturer and research assistant for several years at Shakespeare's Globe. His book, *Shakespeare's Storms*, will be published in 2013 by Manchester University Press.

Paul Menzer is an Associate Professor at Mary Baldwin College, where he is Director of the MLitt/MFA Program in Shakespeare and Performance. He is the author of *The Hamlets: Cues, Qs, and remembered texts* (2008), editor of *Inside Shakespeare: Essays on the Blackfriars Stage* (2006), and his articles on textual transmission, theatre history and performance have appeared in such journals as *Shakespeare Quarterly*, *Renaissance Drama* and *Shakespeare Bulletin*. His plays, *Anonymous*, *Shakespeare on Ice* and *The Brats of Clarence* have been produced at Staunton's Blackfriars Playhouse and elsewhere.

Lucy Munro is Senior Lecturer in English at Keele University. Her publications include a monograph, *Children of the Queen's Revels: A Jacobean Theatre Repertory* (Cambridge University Press, 2005), editions of Edward Sharpham's *The Fleer* (Nick Hern Books, 2006), Shakespeare's *Pericles*, in *William Shakespeare: Complete Works*, ed. Jonathan Bate and Eric Rasmussen (Palgrave Macmillan, 2007), Richard Brome's *The Queen and Concubine* and *The Demoiselle*, in *Richard Brome Online*, gen. ed. Richard Cave (2009) and John Fletcher's *The Tamer Tamed* for New Mermaids (A&C Black, 2010), and more than twenty essays in journals and edited collections. She was recently awarded a Leverhulme Trust one-year fellowship for her monograph project, *The English Archaic: Materialising the Past in Early Modern Literature and*

Culture, and she is also working on editions of James Shirley's *The Gentleman of Venice*, for *The Works of James Shirley*, gen. ed. Eugene Giddens, Teresa Grant and Barbara Ravelhofer (Oxford University Press), and Thomas Dekker, John Ford and William Rowley's *The Witch of Edmonton* (Arden Early Modern Drama).

Nathalie Rivere de Carles is Lecturer in Early Modern Studies (University of Toulouse Le Mirail). She is the Deputy Head of the Research Group on Drama within the English Department Research Centre, Cultures Anglo-Saxonnes, EA 180 and the General Editor of the collection *Nouvelles Scènes*, Presses Universitaires du Mirail. Some of her publications include: 'Staging Shakespeare's exoticism on the continent', in *Twelfth Night: New Critical Essays*, ed. Philip C. Kolin and James Schiffer (Routledge, 2010); 'Acceptable Amazons? Female Warriors on the English and French Early Modern Stage (1580–1650)', *Anglophonia*, 27 (2010); '"Her breath will mist or stain the stone": Confusing visions in King Lear', in *The true blank of thine eye: approches critiques de* King Lear, ed. Pascale Drouet and Pierre Iselin (Presses de l'Université Paris Sorbonne, 2009); '"Seest thou not what a deformed theefe this fashion is?" le costume-piège dans le théâtre renaissant', in *Costume et déguisement dans le théâtre de Shakespeare et de ses contemporains*, ed. Pierre Kapitaniak and Jean-Michel Déprats (Société Française Shakespeare, 2008).

Bruce R. Smith is Dean's Professor of English at the University of Southern California. A former president of the Shakespeare Association of America, he is the author of five books on Shakespeare and early modern culture, most recently *The Key of Green* (2009) and *Phenomenal Shakespeare* (2010), and is general editor of the Cambridge World Shakespeare project.

Andrea Stevens is an Assistant Professor of English and Theatre at the University of Illinois at Urbana-Champaign, where she teaches courses on Shakespeare and early modern literature, culture and drama. Her published research focuses on theatre history, methods of original practices staging, early modern materiality, performance studies and body studies. She is currently completing a book MS (*Inventions of the Skin*) on the early modern special effects and materials most closely related to the body in performance, in particular theatrical paint.

Evelyn Tribble is Donald Collie Chair at the University of Otago, Dunedin, NZ. Her most recent book is *Cognition in the Globe: Attention and Memory in Shakespeare's Theatre*. She is at work on a new project entitled 'Ecologies of Skill in Early Modern England'.

INTRODUCTION
FARAH KARIM-COOPER AND TIFFANY STERN

In *The Historie of Justine*, George Wilkins, thought to be Shakespeare's co-author on *Pericles*, writes of the pleasure of 'sitting as it it [sic] were in the Theater and stage of mans life' which he describes as 'most exquisitely furnished in all points'.[1] Man's life here is not depicted as a stage play, as might be expected, but as a playhouse – a playhouse, moreover, characterised by the fact that it is beautifully appointed. According to sermon writer John Stoughton, however, 'The Church of God is an honourable stage'; 'God, and Men, and Angels, are judicious spectators'; and 'you' are the actors. 'You', writes Stoughton, are enjoined to 'bethinke your selves of all the helps and ornaments that may either grace or expedite your function'.[2] In both instances, performance is glorious for the staging. In the first, however, it is the space and its accoutrements that are relished; in the second, it is the theatrical 'helps' or props that populate the space which make performances graceful. Physical artefacts – the theatre and its props – together with the smell, sound and touch created by and for the environment, collectively made up the effects of performance; together with text, the medley was able to 'ravish the beholders with varietie of pleasure'.[3] It is the way physical and sensual theatre contributed to textual theatre that is the subject of this book.

The Globe playhouse, in particular, was known for its extra-textual effects. Indeed, when Scottish Commander General Alexander Leslie, in a letter dripping with irony, invited John Suckling to write a play for the army, he jeered: 'Though wee cannot accommodate our Actors with such Properties, as you sometimes bestowed on the Globe, yet shall wee suite them with such Habilliments, as may sort.'[4] The actors and clothes he refers to here are army men in army garb; Leslie's comparison, however, suggests that the Globe, in which Suckling's actual plays were clearly mounted (they are known to have been put on at the company's other playhouse, the Blackfriars), was particularly famous for the accoutrements with which it embellished its performances. The Globe's performance legacy, like the Blackfriars', will have been shaped by Shakespeare the actor-writer; more than any other playwright, he had, financially and artistically, contributed to the style and practices of these thrilling spaces. Indeed, as will be shown here, Shakespeare's plays, like the plays of other early modern writers, regularly and repeatedly batten on stage effects as well as verbal ones.

In what follows, the contributors to this collection will consider the materiality of the playhouses, showing that, for early modern playgoers, attending theatre performances was a fully embodied, sensuous experience, its emotions arising as much from the physical environment as from inscribed textual moments. Working upwards from the fact that the appeal of early modern playhouses resided in their architecture, their furnishings, their props, their clothes, their smell, their look, their sound and their 'feel', this collection considers the playhouses' material contributions to the sensation of performance – and performances' contributions to text.

A book on the subject of theatrical effect is timely for a number of reasons. Up until recently, 'performance' and the practicalities of staging were the preserve of theatre historians, despite the fact that all modern critical editions contain a section on early modern staging, and much literary criticism touches on performance issues. While a lot of important books on theatre history provide and collate data, the *impact* of the material they have gathered together on play-texts, actors or audiences has not been fully addressed. In particular, no study to date has considered performance effects on Shakespeare or early modern drama, though informed critical discussions of the staging of early modern drama – and Shakespeare in particular – are increasingly in demand.

The essays collected here are all interested in theatrical effects as an extension of textuality; all, in one form or another, put theatrical effects in the context of the language of the plays. Collectively, these essays address certain fundamental critical questions: how did Elizabethan and Jacobean acting companies create their multi-faceted effects and how did this shape the plays written for them? What materials and technologies were available to early modern players, and how did these impact on staging? What role did the senses play in the reception of theatre and in what ways did texts acknowledge them? How was being the audience in the early modern theatre a multi-sensory experience, and where can that experience be traced in the plays that survive?

This collection is designed to be read alongside Shakespeare's plays and those of other early modern playwrights. It situates itself within critically informed theatre histories as well as materialist studies of early modern theatre and culture, broadening perceptions about what 'special effects' and 'technologies' mean. But the essays here also provide methods of thinking about these effects, examining the illusionistic principles that define the parameters of early modern performance. Using the lens of performance, these chapters explore how materiality affects poetic and theatrical language, allowing for fresh readings of Shakespeare's plays and those of his contemporaries.

The book is divided into three sections, all of which highlight the importance of its central premise: that for Shakespeare and his contemporary playwrights, there was no binary between the materiality of theatre and the emotional, metaphorical and poetic registers of the plays themselves. For the playwrights explored here, the written word is itself a kind of technology: perhaps as much a technology as stage architecture or actor's voice.

Part One considers 'the fabric of early modern theatres' – the theatrical buildings and their structure – and the stage's props, in particular, hangings, squibs and thunder runs. That the stages were bare or 'blank canvases' is an idea that can be put to rest by this section, which considers not only the innovative technologies with which theatres were equipped, but also what each part of the playhouse conveyed to its audiences. Chapter 1, '"This Wide and Universal Theatre": The Theatre as Prop in Shakespeare's Metadrama' by Tiffany Stern, identifies the highly symbolic role of each part of the theatre, its metadramatic function and its 'prominence' in the audience's experience. By examining the titles of parts of the stage's architecture – 'heaven', 'hell', and perhaps 'earth' – and comparing them to other facets of the physical stage, like the 'scene', which has a meaning conflating literature and stage, Stern asks how the theatrical space was used by authors, and 'read' by the audience. Considering the function of the stage's tiring-house, its balconies, ladders and internal bell, she suggests that the stage's background features – with which the tiring-house is connected – have a different meaning from its foregrounded features; she suggests that, perversely, the stage may be at its most metatheatrical when it avoids metatheatrical terminology. In Chapter 2, 'Storm Effects in Shakespeare', Gwilym Jones explores thunder and lightning effects in *Julius Caesar* (1599), comparing the use of visual and aural 'storm' indicators with those more subtly employed in *The Tempest* (1610–11): how did the outdoor Globe and indoor Blackfriars convey the storm effect, and how did Shakespeare's approach to staging storms change over theatres? In exploring these questions, Jones illustrates Shakespeare's staging developments, and outlines the effect they have on his dramatic poetry. Chapter 3, 'Performing Materiality: Curtains on the Early Modern Stage' by Nathalie Rivere de Carles, examines the unique vocabulary of onstage curtains and hangings. Showing that curtains vary not only in name – hanging, arras, canopy – but also in form and function, she explains how curtains produce literal divisions on the theatrical stage, and metaphorical divisions on tone or mood. Ultimately, as she illustrates, curtains effect and extend characterisation itself. Highlighting the impact of stage hangings on the actor's performance and body, Rivere de Carles analyses the way material elements shaped the playwright's imagination.

Part Two turns to the 'technologies of the body', or props

pertaining to the actor – stage blood, prosthetic body parts, cosmetic paints, clothing for disguise – and the written 'character' out of which an actor's part was made. So in Chapter 4, '"*They eat each other's arms*": Stage Blood and Body Parts', Lucy Munro examines the interplay between language and specific props associated with gory special effects. Exploring how prop heads, skulls, legs, arms, hands, fingers and hearts were deployed on stage, Munro asks whether techniques for creating or using prop body parts differed between the indoor and outdoor playhouses, and what impact they had on playhouse audiences. This involves a consideration of the contribution made by props to issues such as genre, gender, agency or interiority. On stage, Munro suggests, blood and dismemberment scenes not only raise questions about what precisely a prop is, but also ask where 'character' itself starts and stops. In Chapter 5, 'Cosmetic Transformations', Andrea Stevens focuses on what she refers to as the early modern theatre's most ubiquitous and frequently unruly prosthetic: stage paint. Not portable or detachable like other stage props – beards, costumes or masks – paint, as Stevens shows, was a body-transforming prop used to produce a wide range of effects, including race, femininity, bloodshed and even death. Although this chapter includes a range of examples, Stevens takes as her primary case studies the use of blood as a disguise device in the anonymous *Look About You* (1593); blackface disguise in William Berkeley's *The Lost Lady* (1637); beauty and ugliness in Thomas Heywood's *Love's Mistress* (1634); and, finally, death and statuary in Shakespeare's *The Winter's Tale* (1611).

Seeing disguise as a specific technology of theatre, Bridget Escolme, in Chapter 6, 'Costume, Disguise and Self-Display', discusses costume's distinctive relationship to identity. Escolme argues that early modern spectators were willing to accept the premise that wearing someone else's clothes made one look like that person, because their expectations about mimesis, identity and recognition differed from those of modern playgoers. Considering the ways in which the technology of disguise works on poetic language to construct dramatic meaning, she addresses the audience's historically specific understanding of clothing and identity, looking, in particular, at three plays that feature rulers who disguise themselves: Shakespeare's *Measure for Measure* (1604), John Marston's *The Malcontent* (1603) and Shakespeare's *Antony and Cleopatra* (1606–07), whose 'ruler' has a penchant for self-display.

Chapter 7, 'Character Acting', by Paul Menzer, examines the early modern title pages that show actors or characters uttering hand-lettered scrolls from their mouths, designed to represent speech. This familiar graphic convention, he argues, raises questions about the way early modern actors accessed the linguistic materials of performance: should we imagine them speaking 'in print' or 'in script', and what does this say about the actual words they enunciated? Refocusing attention from print practices to scribal ones, Menzer considers the technologies of player preparation that are obscured by printed codex editions of early modern plays. Methods of characterisation – a term that conflates performance and the written 'character' or letter – can be reconceived by investigating the actor's relationship to his part and to text in all its forms.

Finally, in Part Three, 'the sensory stage', the book asks how the senses are deliberately engaged through performance. Recent work on Shakespeare and the senses recognises the materiality and historicisation of literary and theatrical cultures. Yet this section challenges the idea that theatrical effects were designed purely for aural and visual pleasure. Chapter 8 of this volume, 'Within, Without, Withinwards: The Circulation of Sound in Shakespeare's Theatre', by Bruce R. Smith, analyses the circulation of sound in the theatre and the materiality of air itself within its three containers: the tiring-house, the theatre auditorium and the human body. Studying sound in terms of theatrical location, Smith analyses sounds 'within' that are heard but not seen; sounds 'without' that have a visible source; and sounds 'withinwards' in which the producers of sound and the recipients of sound are caught up together in an experiential space, obliterating the distinction between producers and recipients, between 'there' and 'here'.

Sounds – verbal as well as non-verbal – are focused on as cues to bodily motion. Smith's fresh understanding of the movement of sound within amphitheatres, which depended upon embodying the experience of the aural and visual components of performance, shows how plays need to be understood not just in a series of multi-sensory ways, but as a series of multi-sensory prompts.

Holly Dugan, in Chapter 9, asks the reader to imagine the smell of early modern London, and more specifically of the Hope Theatre, and conducts an olfactory reading of Ben Jonson's *Bartholomew Fair* (1614). Early modern productions often involved olfactory props, made from leeks, dung squibs, distilled rosewater, incense and perfumed leather gloves. Yet little has been written about how the smell of the theatre itself might have influenced stage productions and the phenomenological experience of playgoing. By interrogating the relationship between the smell of the Hope playhouse – known for its unique and terrible stench – and the re-creation of Smithfield market in Jonson's *Bartholomew Fair*, Dugan gestures towards a forgotten part of the historical phenomenology of early modern playgoing: its smellscape.

Chapter 10, 'Touch and Taste in Shakespeare's Theatres', explores how the senses are not only effects but also conditions of early modern performance. Farah Karim-Cooper identifies three ways in which touch is at work in the playhouse: contact, onstage touching and affective touch; it was feared that plays could touch spectators both in reality and metaphorically – emotionally or morally – perhaps changing them for ever. This chapter examines instances from Shakespeare's plays where the language of touch and moments of touching appear to be objectified as theatrical experiences, before exploring taste in literal and figurative terms – literal in that there is ample evidence that eating was a popular commercial activity that accompanied playgoing; figurative in that taste was linked by some dramatists to the opinions of audiences. Investigating the ways in which plays were said to enter into the body, Karim-Coooper shows how powerfully the ear and the eye were viewed as points of entry for early modern dramatic language.

In the final chapter of this volume, 'Sight and Spectacle', Evelyn Tribble argues that regardless of the critical commonplace that early modern audiences went to 'hear a play', there is more than enough evidence to show that seeing was a crucial priority in Shakespeare's theatres. Tribble establishes the anti-theatrical and anti-sensory anxieties about sight and seeing in the period – that they were founded upon the vulnerability of the eyes to deception and corruption. Despite this, she shows that the visual elements of performance had the ability to arouse emotion and impact positively on playgoers in this period. Considering the visual parsimony of the playhouses, Tribble demonstrates how the theatres nevertheless exploited their own structural features, highlighting the importance of symbolic metadrama in, for example, the prologue to *Henry V*.

This volume, then, aims to do more than simply enumerate or qualify the sensational and provocative functions of props and theatre technologies. It argues that performance effects were not merely *for* effect, but that they worked together with language; we need to understand both in order to comprehend dramatic meaning fully. This book suggests that the multi-sensory devices of theatre were as imperative to dramaturgical structure as language itself; its chapters explore why and how.

PART ONE

THE FABRIC OF EARLY MODERN THEATRES

CHAPTER ONE

'THIS WIDE AND UNIVERSAL THEATRE':
THE THEATRE AS PROP IN
SHAKESPEARE'S METADRAMA
TIFFANY STERN

It is sometimes said that the early modern playhouse was a hearing, rather than a seeing, space. 'Audience', or 'auditors', or 'hearers', words regularly used for the people who attended plays, are said to indicate that the theatre was a place where language flourished, perhaps in the face of the visual.[1] Up to a point, this is true: when Moth, preparing to perform young Hercules in Shakespeare's *Love's Labour's Lost*, suggests 'if any of the audience hiss, you may cry, "Well done, Hercules"!' (5.1.129–30), he is indicating a trick he will play on a group of people who are not only intently listening to the production but also responding to it with sound. If they hiss him, says Moth, he will pretend the sound they make issues from his property snake: he will embrace and reinterpret the audience's noise within the aural world of his performance. Less complicatedly, when the Chorus to *Henry VIII* calls the audience 'gentle hearers' he unites the people before him as noble listeners; his stress on the aural is linked to a request that the 'hearers' 'think ye see / The very persons of our noble story' (Prologue, 17, 25–6), and allow imagination to prevail over aspects of the theatre's pretence.

Yet concentration on the auditory has led to a neglect of other and contrary references. Shakespeare, like many writers of his time, also called his audience 'spectators'. The Chorus to *The Winter's Tale* specifically reverses the terminology used in *Henry VIII*, addressing the audience as 'gentle spectators', even though similarly begging them to heighten the experience with their imaginations: 'imagine [. . .] that I now may be / In fair Bohemia' (4.1.20–1). As it seems, then, the audience might equally be conceived of as, primarily, devoted to 'hearing', or devoted to 'seeing' – but, either way, the expectation is that on occasion they will bolster their physical experiences with imagination.

Imagination was requested because hearing and, even more obviously, seeing, were dictated by the theatrical spaces in which they took place. The visual vitality of London's theatres was such that they repeatedly, and confidently, conveyed one and the same thing, imposing it on to all plays: themselves. With their painted ceilings, pillars and stage background they offered an unchanging backdrop for every play mounted within them; with their universal lighting, they imposed the same mood on to every drama. The fixed features of these theatres could not be substantially remoulded for specific performances, and few efforts seem to have been taken to change general ambiance from one production to another. Though references suggest that genre-specific hangings might be employed – black hangings signalling a tragedy (so making a literary rather than a 'realistic' statement) – general staging seldom acknowledged the separation of one play from another. It is the fact that every play had, essentially, the same staging, that explains that repeated plea for imagination found throughout Shakespeare: imagination was required not to flesh out the empty stage, but to override or reshape the permanent features that playhouses imposed on every production. Yet often, as this chapter will show, what 'imagination' actually consisted of was more rooted in the theatre than Shakespeare may have realised.

One indication of how prominent the playhouse's appearance was to the theatrical experience is the fact that the round, outdoor playhouse in which Shakespeare's early plays had been performed was named 'The Theatre'. As writers of the time knew, 'theatre' was 'Greek [. . .] derived from a verb that signifies to *See* [. . .] Whence a noun that signifies a *Theater*, where persons are brought forth to be shown unto people.'[2] Watching and being watched, observing and being observed, and showing and being shown were activities heralded by the space – and the other round theatres that imitated it. Plays always had to fit around, utilise or add to what the stage was, visually, offering; all of the major theatres, round and square, for which Shakespeare wrote, are described as being stunning not to perform in (or watch performances in) but to look at: 'the gorgeous Playing place erected in the fieldes [. . .] as they please to have it called, a Theatre'; 'the Globe, the glory of the banke'; 'the new Globe [. . .] which is saide to be the fairest that ever was in England'; and the theatre for which 'great charge and troble' was spent, the mysterious 'Torchy [Black]friars'.[3]

It is only to be expected that Shakespeare would call attention to the visually charged theatrical environments his plays continually negotiated. He did so in a series of pointed theatrical references to actors, theatres and staging; references that were examined collectively in book-length form by Anne Righter (later Anne Barton) in her influential *Shakespeare and the Idea of the Play* of 1962. Like others after her, Righter saw Shakespeare's theatrical allusions as compensatory and, often, subversive: the theatre was, thought Righter, what was left behind when imagination failed. Shakespeare, Righter argued, learned to hate his stage; 'shortly after the turn of the century [. . .] the actor, all his splendour gone, became a symbol of disorder, of futility, and pride': Hamlet's references to actors as 'robustious periwig-pated fellow[s]' (3.2.9) were, Righter felt, Shakespeare's attempts to do down an environment he now despised.[4] Yet, when Hamlet is made to criticise players who 'tear a passion to tatters' and 'split the ears of the groundlings' (3.2.10–11), he may equally be expressing the quiet confidence of a playwright assured of the Chamberlain's Men's acting superiority. For *Hamlet*, performed in 1601 when Shakespeare's company was at the height of its success, and had recently built its new Globe theatre, is filled with references to playing, to staging, and, as will be discussed, to the Globe itself. Given that Shakespeare had a hefty financial stake in the Chamberlain's Men, it seems more likely that *Hamlet* is drawing attention to the company's unassailable performing superiority and its unmatched stage than critiquing it: not least because, as a 'sharer', Shakespeare probably oversaw the building of – and perhaps even helped design – the Globe itself.

Shakespeare's many self-conscious gestures towards his theatre are, these days, often described as 'metatheatrical' or 'metadramatic' – vocabulary derived from Lionel Abel's 1963 *Metatheatre: A New View of Dramatic Form*.[5] Both words are used particularly for the moments when Shakespeare's theatre comments on itself in some way: by staging plays-within-plays, or by referring to the playhouse's physical structure. But the nomenclature of 'metatheatre' and 'metadrama' comes with interpretative baggage. Sometimes Shakespeare's recourse to metatheatre is said to show that his plays are *about* dramatic form: that Shakespeare in his plays repeatedly and worriedly reflects on what drama means, how reality can be moulded theatrically, and how to elevate the stage as an art.[6] Alternatively Shakespeare's metatheatre is said to prefigure Brecht's *'verfremdungseffekt'* or 'alienation-effect': thus Shakespeare's plays are said to be 'subversive' in their 'level of anti-realism' because they need to palliate 'the dangers . . . in the deceptions of realism'.[7] Both approaches to Shakespeare's metatheatre share with Righter a sense that theatrical reference is negative. The first imagines that Shakespeare was conflicted about his art – an idea voiced by Hazlitt and Lamb in the nineteenth century, but not necessarily true of a period before English literature was sub-divided into 'high' and 'low', with theatre falling into the 'low' category. The other imagines that Shakespeare, like Brecht, set out to alarm his audience with stage references. But while it is true that Brecht's emphasis on the theatrical will have been shocking to spectators used to staged 'realism', Shakespeare, writing for a non-illusionistic stage, would hardly surprise spectators by telling them that they were in the theatre.[8] Indeed, Shakespeare's reference to a theatre that was so visually a part of performance could be seen as the reverse of alienation: it celebrated the space, while letting the spectators off the hook, allowing them the relaxing option of not, for once, having to add imaginative fancy to what they see in order to believe.

Against writers who, from Righter onwards, have found Shakespeare's theatrical references alienating or artful, this chapter will argue that, on the contrary, such references are proud acknowledgements of staging possibilities. Examining Shakespeare's approach to the visual and aural aspects of his play-houses, it will concentrate on the many moments when Shakespeare, for all his requests to overcome stage limitations through 'imagination', carefully worked with what was in front of him; it will suggest that early modern theatres were, as props, enthusiastically, if complicatedly, employed.

As few structural features beyond that of the stage itself have been written about, the argument will look at what surrounded the stage from below (the 'hell' with its 'trap'), from above (the 'heaven[s]'), on the stage level itself ('earth' and its 'pillars'), and from behind (the 'scene' with its 'balcony' and 'ladders'; and the 'tiring-house' with its stage 'bell'). In doing so, it will investigate the various statements, metaphors and analogies the stage made for and about itself, and their interpretative ramifications for Shakespeare. So the first section will discuss the broad 'theatrum mundi' construction of Shakespeare's theatres, with their 'heaven', 'hell' and 'earth'. The second section will turn to the stage when it is frank about its architecture, considering the factual and fictional use of the pillars. The third section will explore ways in which the stage might exploit its literary geography, considering the literal and metaphorical function of the backstage 'scene'. The fourth section will investigate the theatre at its most functional and realis-tic, examining use made of the (tiring) house and balcony. Finally the stage's most fixed aural prop, the stage bell or clock, will be explored. Shakespeare's complexity, and his profoundest 'metath-eatre', this chapter will suggest, is angled to the ways in which the physical reality of the stage met the fictions enacted upon it. Exploring the meaning of stage space as location and prop, this chapter will suggest that Shakespeare used his theatre's construc-tion itself as a prime locus of imaginative power.

THE STAGE AS WORLD: HEAVEN, HELL, EARTH

It is often pointed out that Shakespeare's regular references to the world as a stage – 'all the world's a stage' (*As You Like It*, 3.1.139),

Figure 1 Tiring-House – front view, with 'heaven' above and 'hell' below.
Architectural detail of Shakespeare's Globe, photograph by Pete Le May.
With kind permission of The Globe Theatre

'I hold the world [. . .] but as [. . .] a stage' (*The Merchant of Venice*, 1.1.77), 'let this world no longer be a stage' (*2 Henry 4*, 1.1.155) – refer to the ancient classical motif of 'theatrum mundi' (literally, 'the world as stage'). This has even been said to be 'the master-metaphor' of Shakespeare's canon: a metaphor Shakespeare used to remind the spectators that they themselves were not much different from actors, with movements and will prescribed by God, or the Devil, or the King.[9] That, though partly true, is to forget that the very theatrum mundi metaphor was complicated by stage terminology. For when the wood that had made up what was named 'the Theatre' was reused to make what was named 'the Globe', Shakespeare's 'stage' literally became his 'world' in a way that blatantly appropriated the master-metaphor. As, in both cases, the stage remained a stage, however, the power of the metaphor was reduced. This was a problem that beset other playhouses of the time in one form or another, for parts of the stage had been given names so reflective of the theatrum mundi motif – in particular, 'heaven' and 'hell' – as to turn plays into conceits protected from reality by their obviously fictional universe.

'Am I in earth, in heaven, or in hell?' (*Comedy of Errors*, 2.2.211) asks Antipholus of Syracuse. Titus declares that 'sith there's no justice in earth nor hell, / We will solicit heaven' (*Titus Andronicus*, 4.3.50–1); Hamlet exclaims upon the same three options 'O all you host of heaven! O earth! What else? / And shall I couple hell?' (*Hamlet*, 1.5.92–3). While these characters are referring to early modern ideas about the structure of the universe, with heaven above, earth in the middle, and hell below, they are also all, simultaneously, making references to the structure of the theatres in which they perform. For as Thomas Dekker makes clear when he describes how tailors '(as well as Plaiers) have a hell of their owne, (under their shopboard)', the area under the stage was known as 'hell' in playhouses – a leftover from the religious staging adopted for Medieval Mystery plays.[10] Likewise, as Heywood articulates when he writes of 'the coverings of the stage, which wee call the heavens', the roof that overhung the performers was, conversely, known as 'heaven' or 'the heavens'.[11] The stage where the actors performed, with heaven above and hell below was, as a consequence, the earth itself. Analogies comparing the theatre to the progress of man's life, regularly equate the stage with earth for this reason, and there is a possibility that the stage space was sometimes entitled 'earth' to match its 'heaven' and 'hell' counterparts: 'hee thinkes hee is placed in this world as in a royall Theatre: the Earth, the Stage, the Heavens the Scaffolds round about'; 'The Earth's the stage, heaven the spectatour is / To sitt and judge what ere is done amisse'.[12]

Each of the three Shakespearean characters named above, then, is speaking lines that seem metatheatrical, both verbally and visually, but that are also literal. The literal will have been highlighted by the fact that references to the spaces surrounding the actor came with a clear gestural referent. A famous classical joke, regularly related in the period, told the story of 'a ridiculous Player, who when in a Tragedy he had cried out, *ô Coelum!* ['O Heaven!'] he put forth his *Hand* to the earth: and againe pronouncing, *ô Terra!* ['O Earth!'] erected his face towards Heaven'.[13] Shakespeare's actors, suiting correctly, as Hamlet had it, 'the action to the word' and 'the word to the action' (*Hamlet*, 3.2.18–19) are, in the examples given, asked to acknowledge by gesture the heaven and hell defined by the contours of the theatre. As a result, at the very moment when the *characters* appeal beyond the limits of the world, the *players* resituate the words back in the theatre.

For the audience, this will have reinforced the world/stage conceit while also making clear that the staged events belonged to the realms of fiction. An epitaph on Richard Burbage, the principal actor and chief player in Shakespeare's dramas, shows the effect this could have. Comparing the 'real' heaven and hell of the world, to the fictional heaven and hell of the actor, the epitaph wonders by which of the two the dead player will ultimately be judged. It decides that Burbage belongs to the world of the stage; that, rather than God, will adjudicate for him:

> when a player dies [. . .]
> What need hee stand at the judgement throne
> Who hath a heaven and a hell of his owne?[14]

Metatheatre involving heaven and hell, then, is 'safe': the audience is 'outside' the stage's metaphorical heaven–earth–hell sandwich, and is not necessarily implicated in what it sees.

As 'hell' and 'heaven' were such insistently 'fictional' spaces in the theatre, they could be used to highlight obvious dramatic points. Shakespeare regularly exploited these features of stage geography. He positioned in 'hell' bad or demonic sounds, for instance. 'Hoboys', an earlier form of oboe, are heard playing under the stage in *Antony and Cleopatra*: they signify that 'the god Hercules, whom Antony loved / Now leaves him' (4.3.21–2), spreading Antony's hellish fatalism to fictional soldiers and factual audience alike. It is also from hell that the ghost of Hamlet's father in *Hamlet* cries 'swear' (2.1.157): thus, though Hamlet questions whether the man he has seen is his father in Purgatory or a 'goblin damn'd' (1.5.40) tempting him to wrong, the audience, knowing the ghost's location, has an answer, though one it cannot convey to Hamlet.[15]

As the trapdoor supplied an exit to or entrance from hell, it was equally readable, and was equally often used: '*Hell* being under everie one of their *Stages*, the Players [. . .] might with a false Trappe doore have slipt him downe,' explains Dekker.[16] Thus when Hamlet and Laertes jump into the 'grave' to assert their violent love for Ophelia, they 'tell' the audience they are flirting with damnation; they closely resemble, in staging terms, Quintus and Martius who briefly visit a metaphor for hell itself when, in *Titus Andronicus*, they fall into this 'loathsome pit' (2.2.176) and find it to be the damned hole in which Lavinia has been raped and Bassianus murdered. Likewise properties that arose from or went down to the trap had hellish connotations: the witches' cauldron in *Macbeth* 'sinks' (4.1.106) into the trap, showing Macbeth's future, like the pot from which he learned it, descending to hell; while the 'gold' that Timon digs up from the trap, in *Timon of Athens*, visually makes clear the play's point about money's hellish origins (4.3.26).

The 'heavens' were equally employed by Shakespeare to illustrate good. There are few 'heavenly' entrances, and all in late plays – the God Jupiter '*descends*' on the back of an Eagle in *Cymbeline* (5.4.90), Juno likewise '*descends*' to bless the marriage of Ferdinand and Miranda in *The Tempest* (4.1.73) – which may suggest that only Shakespeare's last theatre, Blackfriars, had a mechanism for a descending 'heavenly' chair. Nevertheless the heavenly entrance made clear and unambiguous statements about good intent: the theatre thus gave Shakespeare a way of adding 'easy' explanations on to his drama through telling use of stage location.

A difference, however, was that the look of the stage heavens also moulded Shakespeare's literary perception. Perhaps because he was writing plays to be performed beneath them, or perhaps because he had so often performed under them himself, he consistently associated the concept of 'heavens' with the concept of stars. This was reflective of the fact that the stage heavens were decorated with symbols of night: Drummond describes the world as 'a sable Stage / Where slave-borne Man playes to the scoffing Starres'; Middleton explains in his world/stage analogy how 'heaven is hung so high, drawne up so farre, / And made [. . .] fast, naylde up with many a Starre'.[17] This accounts for some of Shakespeare's regular appeals to astronomy: the stars pointedly overhung the stage and all plays were performed beneath them anyway. Pericles demands 'cease your ire, you angry stars of heaven!' (*Pericles*, 2.1.1); the Captain observes 'meteors fright the fixed stars of heaven' when the king dies (*Richard II*, 2.4.9); Belarius, returning the two princes to their father Cymbeline, inveighs: 'The benediction of these covering heavens / Fall on their heads like dew, for they are worthy / To inlay heaven with stars' (*Cymbeline*, 5.5.351–3). For the audience, however, these are further theatrum mundi references with factual locations; the plays in which they occur, locating themselves under a fictional, yet painted and hence factual, night sky, had events shaped by a supernatural belonging not in the real heaven but in an actorly one.

Thus even Hamlet's world-weariness is oddly theatrically located. Shakespeare, perhaps because of his excitement over the new Globe theatre, or even simply because he was enthralled by the way staging could reinterpret a reference, places Hamlet's sorrow firmly in the playhouse:

> I have of late, but wherefore I know not, lost all my mirth, [. . .] this goodly frame the earth, seems to me a sterile promontory, this most excellent canopy the air, look you, this brave o'erhanging firmament, this majestical roof fretted with golden fire, why, it appeareth nothing to me but a foul and pestilent congregation of vapours.
>
> (*Hamlet*, 2.2.297–304)

For Hamlet the 'earth' *seems* a sterile promontory, but *is* a 'goodly frame'. 'Frame' as well as 'earth' was a way of describing the stage – Thomas Nashe portrays a 'Theater of pleasure' as having 'an artificial heav'n to overshadow the faire frame'.[18] The 'canopy', meanwhile, *seems* a congregation of vapours, but *is* a 'brave ore-hanging [. . .] roof, fretted with [. . .] fire' – a stage-heavens was fretted ('embossed') with stars. Even the congregation of vapours may give Hamlet an excuse to gesture towards the 'groundlings' standing below the stage in an area congruent to

'Hell'. Thus the real world that Hamlet is not able to appreciate is undercut by being, anyway, a gorgeous staged one, 'goodly', 'excellent' and 'brave'. Hamlet is trapped in the story of *Hamlet* enacted on the beautiful stage of what is tellingly named, in *Hamlet*, 'this distracted globe' (1.5.97). In these moments, the theatre pointedly abstracts itself from the audiences' reality in order to praise itself: Hamlet's grief is not that he cannot enjoy the beauty of the world, but that he cannot enjoy the obvious beauty of the stage on which he stands.

An alternative use of these 'readable' locations was when they offered – but then denied – theatrum mundi uses. When Othello intones 'Arise, black vengeance from the hollow hell' (*Othello*, 3.3.450) (that last word is sometimes amended to 'cell', but is clearly the reverse of the 'heaven' to which appeal has just been made) the possibility is raised that a ghost might emerge from below the stage, as had happened in other Shakespeare plays. But no such 'vengeance' in ghost form – or in terms of a meaningful sound from below stage – comes to help him. The options offered by staging are, here, purposefully ignored: Othello is not relieved, and the audience is not, as in *Hamlet*, allowed to distance itself by and through the theatricality of the story.

THE STAGE AS ARCHITECTURE: PILLARS

Yet as all heaven/hell references kept plays theatre-bound, it was parts of the stage that lacked metaphorical names that participated more 'realistically' in the dramas enacted around them. The very pillars or posts, for instance, which joined hell to heavens, and which were present at the Globe, and probably the Theatre (it is less clear that Blackfriars had pillars, perhaps because a separate stage roof to protect actors' clothes will have been unnecessary in an enclosed theatre) hovered between necessary structural features, points of reference and stage props.

From stage directions such as that in Barnes' Globe play *The Divils Charter*, 'he stands behind the post', it is obvious the pillars could be used as sites for concealed characters, who, hidden from their fellow characters, were visible to the audience.[19] So when Romeo is on stage but hidden from his friends (*Romeo and Juliet*, 2.1.), he is probably behind such a post; the posts will equally have provided locations in which Polonius and Claudius could 'hide' in *Hamlet*. But the posts may also have enhanced and complicated the scenes in which they were utilised. For one of their practical uses in the theatres was as alternative stocks: they were public sites where playhouse felons, once caught, could be attached for public ridicule. William Kemp, long-time fool for Shakespeare's company, describes 'a noted Cut-purse' as 'such a one as we tye to a poast on our stage, for all people to wonder at, when at a play they are taken pilfering'.[20] These negative connotations may have added ambiance to the stage posts; certainly some variety of post – though archaeology suggests not one supporting the heavens in this instance – was negatively exploited to add to the fiction when, in the Rose playhouse of 1587, the players had 'a devyse in ther playe to tye one of their fellows to a poste and so to shoote him to deathe'.[21] Did Shakespeare exploit his own posts because they came with associations with punishment? Gloucester in *King Lear*, bound by servants, and awaiting the removal of his eyes, describes being, like a performing bear, or a man about to be burned to death, 'tied to the stake': this suggests that he is attached to a stage post (3.7.53), with all the shame and public cruelty that implies. And, though it would be simplistic to suggest that posts always have potential tragedy attached to them, they often come with associations of humiliation or embarrassment. The verses that Orlando attaches to trees in *As You Like It* – almost certainly the posts again – seem to be mocked by location itself. Yet as the posts, unlike 'hell' or 'heaven', were 'real' in name, even if fictionally they might be used as trees or towers, they were sites of interpretative conflict in a way that the features they linked together were not. The audience had to decide whether the posts were always, or only sometimes, bleak through association; authors, writing for stages with posts, had to make the same decision.

THE STAGE AS LITERATURE: SCENE

Unlike pillars/posts, named for what they were, and heaven and hell, named for what they represented, there was a structure inside the theatre that confusingly mingled the representational with the real and that raised an entirely separate series of interpretative questions. The 'scene', these days often discussed under its Latin title, *frons scenae*, was the back of the visible stage: the wall through which actors made their entrances and exits. When 'A vast and stately Theater' is described as being 'adorn'd with a Scene magnificently drest', the 'scene' is shown to be a crucial aspect of the theatre's sumptuous visual life; while, when backstage actors are said to 'put their heads through the hangings of the Scene' in order to see the audience, the scene is shown to straddle a crucial divide – its curtained entrances allowed actors to be partially in the fictional world of the stage, and partially out of it in the factual backstage world of the tiring-house.[22]

The recent habit of calling the scene *'frons scenae'* has hidden the import of the location's name itself. As Blount described it in his *Glossographia*, 'scene' was used for 'the front or forepart of a Theatre or Stage, or the partition between the Players Vestry, and the Stage', as discussed, but also stood for a more familiar definition, 'the division of a Play into certain parts, [. . .] which sometimes fall out more, sometimes fewer in every Act'.[23] 'Scenes', then, were units of play in two forms: stage and page. As actors entered through the physical scene and filled the stage, so a new literary scene was perceived to have begun; as they exited back through the physical scene and emptied a stage, so a literary scene was perceived to have ended. The play's structure, then, was both a manifestation and a consequence of the theatre's structure; it was described in terms that were as physical as they were conceptual. When, in *A Midsummer Night's Dream*, Puck describes how Bottom was rehearsing his part of Pyramus and 'Forsook his scene and enter'd in a brake', he both explains that Bottom forsook the physical scene through which he was supposed to enter, and forsook the fictional scene in which he was supposed to play – allowing an 'ass's nole' to be 'fixed on his head' (3.2.15–17). The design of the theatre, in that instance, shaped the way Shakespeare wrote his lines and intended them to be interpreted.[24]

Shakespeare, alert to the complexities of the stage's backdrop, seems, like other writers, to have used the stage's physical 'scene' for a particular purpose that in itself further muddied the divide between writing and staging. There had long been a habit, often confined to private theatres, of writing the name of a play's location on a 'scene-board' – an inscribed plank that was hung on the 'scene'. Sir Philip Sidney, for instance, refers to the practice of using scene-boards when he asks derisively, 'What childe is there, that comming to a play, and seeing *Thebes* written in great letters on an old Doore doth believe that it is Thebes?'[25] Several Shakespeare plays open on clear reference to scene locations – 'in Troy, there lies the scene' (*Troilus and Cressida*, Prologue, 1), 'in fair Verona [. . .] we lay our scene' (*Romeo and Juliet*, Prologue, 2); one play makes a reference to changing scene locations: 'The king is set from London [. . .] Unto Southampton do we shift our scene' (*Henry V*, 1.2.34–42). These are obviously not references to the scenes that collectively make up acts, for they provide permanent or semi-permanent features of the drama; moreover, several other Shakespeare plays indicate fictional locations as 'scenic' facts aside from the words of the drama – 'The Scene Vienna' is written just above 'The names of all the Actors' at the end of the folio of *Measure for Measure*; 'The Scene, an un-inhabited Island' is written just above the 'Names of the Actors' at the end of the folio *The Tempest*. As all these Shakespearean uses of 'scene' for what is in fact place make clear, Shakespeare associated location with 'scene', presumably because he sometimes hung fictional place, in a board, on to that part of the theatre. If so, then several more of his demands for imagination were delimited by words and situated firmly in the theatre: when Shakespeare wished, he could use the theatre's structure to dictate just what 'imagination' should consist of.

THE STAGE AS FACT: (TIRING-)HOUSE, BALCONY

Shakespeare also made regular, separate, use of the dramatic possibilities offered by the 'scene'. For the structure of the 'scene' as a
whole contained not just doors of entrance on stage level, but a
further entrance above, which was protected with a railing – as a
window or balcony might be. Collectively, then, the 'scene' resem-
bled, in appearance, the face of a house; it even fronted what was
generally called the 'tiring-house'. So the space was simultaneously a pretend front to a pretend house, and a real front to a real,
if particular, kind of house.

The tiring-house within the 'scene' was a practical necessity. It
was, at all times, filled with backstage people: the dressers (known
as 'tiremen' and 'tirewomen') who stayed 'in the Tyring-house' to
'dis-robe' the actors; 'The Booke-holder' or prompter, who 'stands
in the Tyring-house' to prompt the players; the author who, if an
actor performs badly, 'is forc'd to send one to pull him into the
Tiring-Room'; players' 'boys', or servants, who might, from 'the
Tyer-house', be bid to go on stage with a forgotten property; and
performers.[26] Within its room or rooms was also storage and other
space: accounts mention the 'Ward-robe' where 'when the Play is
ended, the Conquerour must put off his Crown . . . where the Fool
puts off his Cap'; the boxes where 'all the *Maskes*, the *Visards*, and
Disguises' of 'the [. . .] Tiring-roome' are contained; the social
space, where actors who 'lye stretcht stark dead upon the stage'
can, 'once drawn off, find themselves well and alive, and [. . .]
ready to tast a cup of wine with their friends in the attiring room'.[27]
The tiring-house, then, was made up, when possible, of several
rooms; indeed, when William Davenant projected in 1639 building a new theatre, he stated that it needed to contain 'necessary
tyring & retyring roomes': the backstage area could have more
than one partition, the word 'tiring' here showing its duel function
of 'attiring' (getting dressed) and 'retiring' (relaxing). The
tiring-house was, in terms of its sub-divided and heavily utilised
spaces, a 'house' indeed.[28]

Shakespeare seems to have used the fact of this backstage house
as a way of layering his fiction. Sometimes the tiring-house as itself

made its way into his plays, so that the fiction itself became disconcertingly real. So at what might seem to be a particularly
metatheatrical moment, when the mechanicals in *A Midsummer
Night's Dream* determine that a hawthorn brake behind their
'stage' will be 'our tiring-house' (3.1.3–4), for instance, they are
backed by an actual tiring-house. This confuses the fiction; now a
real tiring-house stands in for a fictional hawthorne brake standing
in for a tiring-house. This moment seems to be *about* the theatre
and its constitutional playfulness. Alternatively, when the players
in *Hamlet* are sent off to 'make [them] ready' (3.2.46), it is to the
tiring-house that they will factually and fictionally go; here the fact
becomes one with the fiction – though the play is notionally drawing distinctions between performer and real person ('this player
here [. . .] Could force his soul [. . .] to his own conceit [. . .] For
Hecuba! / [. . .] What would he do / Had he the motive and the
cue for passion / That I have?', 2.2.552–62), the theatre makes the
reverse point, bringing them all together. In both instances,
performance takes place in the 'reality' of the staged space – a
space dedicated to fiction. On one level, this raises questions about
drama and reality; but on another it wilfully draws attention to the
physical construction of the stage itself, featuring it, lionising it
but using it to query the fiction's very fictionality.

More ambiguously still, the tiring-house was used in disconcertingly house-like ways. Any reference to leaving the stage by
entering a house – and, equally, any reference to exiting to a 'room',
as 'tiring-room' was as an alternative to 'tiring-house' – embraced
the theatre's structure, not by calling attention to what it was not,
but to what it was. When Bertram says 'Now will I lead you to the
house and show you / The lass I spoke of' (*All's Well*, 3.7.103–4),
he leads his fellow actor to the tiring-house where the boy playing
the 'lass' will literally be located; likewise when Hamlet deter-
mines to 'lug the guts' of Polonius 'into the neighbour room'
(*Hamlet*, 3.4.214), he will be seen to be doing precisely that. In
such instances the audience must eschew too much imagination: it
is to understand what it sees literally, as Shakespeare reminds the
audience that plays have their own reality. For this reason, an exit

to a house or room is entirely different from an exit to a fictional place like a battlefield, or the sea. Exits that confounded story with actuality introduce a richly complex form of metadrama. Writers on metatheatre, who concentrate on the idea of theatre as metaphor, neglect moments when theatre rejects metaphor for fact, with all the tensions that dragging fiction into 'reality' can produce.

Sticking out of the tiring-house midway up the scene was the place for entrances 'above': a recessed room with a balcony, as is suggested by the drawing of the Swan theatre, or perhaps a protruding balcony over which the actors could look down. That space is, then, balcony or room 'factually'; fictionally it might stand in for city walls, lookout posts or other places located above. Most interesting is its relationship to the stage ladder. For though from the tiring-house this balcony could be accessed from behind, from the stage a special theatrical prop was needed when a character was to rise from ground to upper level in view of the audience. It appears to have been normal to bring a rope or, more usually, a rope-ladder on stage – which accounts for the large number of rope-ladders fictionally called for in drama of the time. The balcony's needs were shaping writing. In Middleton and Dekker's *Blurt Master-Constable*, 'a ladder made of roapes' is lowered from Simperino's 'window' up which Frisco climbs; likewise in Marston's *Insatiate Countess*, Mendoza '*throwes up a ladder of cords, which she makes fast to some part of the window, he asends, and at top fals*'.[29] In Fletcher's *Maid in the Mill* the dialogue explains that it is with a 'ladder' that Antonio ascends to the window; in Chapman's *May-day* Lodovico brings on a '*ladder of ropes*' for Aurelio, but Aemelia 'above' only consents to fasten it 'so [. . .] your selfe will come up'; in Tailor's *The Hogge hath Lost his Pearle* 'Albert ascends, and being on the top of the ladder, puts out the candle'; in *The Partiall Law* Lucina is 'at the window' and, 'at the watch-word given throwes downe the rope, & [Philocres] climbes up'.[30]

Shakespeare sometimes shapes his fiction around this playhouse necessity, particularly when asserting that the tiring-house is a house. In *Two Gentlemen of Verona*, Valentine intends to fetch Silvia from her room using 'a ladder quaintly made of cords' which can be 'cast up, with a pair of anchoring hooks' (3.1.117–18), a literal description of a prop that notionally could 'really' be used; in *Romeo and Juliet*, the Nurse is bribed to carry cords to Juliet's chamber from which Romeo can climb down: after entering 'above' he uses this ladder, for having said 'one kiss and I'll descend' (3.5.42), he goes down, finishing the scene on stage level. These references show Shakespeare fitting his plot to the design of the stage and, again, promoting the one by promoting the other. Such situations are different, then, from occasions when the stage ladder is employed, but is fictionalised as something else. Though instances when this is the case can only be guessed at, it is likely that Pindarus in *Julius Caesar* used the ladder in order, while on stage, to ascend 'higher on that hill' (5.3.18) from where he can then comment from 'above':

PINDARUS
   O my lord!
CASSIUS
   What news?
PINDARUS
   Titinius is enclosed round about
   With horsemen, that make to him on the spur;
   Yet he spurs on. Now they are almost on him.
   Now, Titinius! Now some light. O, he lights too.
   He's ta'en.

                                     (5.3.25–30)

Pindarus' narrative is about motion: Titinius spurs his horse along through other horses as they are spurred towards him – finally he 'lights' (alights) from his horse. If Pindarus approaches and then rises up a ladder while making this speech, that places his motion in apposition to Titinius', his 'up' ironising the way Titinius has been forced down; while the fact that he is on a hill that is not a hill draws attention to the way things are not as they seem. The same theatrical prop can hold two different functions: when it is part of the story, it worryingly literalises the tale; when it is a metaphor for something else, it queries the drama's reality but, by calling attention to seeming and being, can intensify the meaning of the poetic or dramatic language used around it.

THE AURAL STAGE: THE STAGE BELL

One final stage feature introduces yet another complexity into Shakespeare's use of metatheatre. There were few built-in props in this largely functional stage – but there was one and it was heard rather than seen: the stage bell. Located possibly in the gable over the stage but, more likely, above the tiring-house, from where it could be rung backstage, the bell stood in for two objects: the public bell that stated alarm or ceremony; and the clock bell that stated time (see Figure 2). Shakespeare made use of it as the 'alarum bell' that rang out warnings in *Othello* and *Macbeth*, for instance. But as the bell was not 'real', it was easy to confuse what it stood in for with what it was. Clock and bell were, at the time, closely connected (public clocks 'rang' the hour from church towers); the word 'clock' indeed descends from the French 'cloche', meaning bell. Perhaps for this reason, or perhaps because of the stage bell, Shakespeare often wrote 'bell' when 'clock' was intended, as when, in *Hamlet*, Bernardo relates how the ghost came when 'the bell' was 'then beating one' (1.1.42); or when, in *Antony and Cleopatra*, the heroes will 'mock the midnight bell' (3.13.181); or when John in *King John* asks Hubert whether

> the midnight bell
> Did, with his iron tongue and brazen mouth,
> Sound one into the drowsy race of night.
>
> (3.2.47–9)

These slips, which may be intentional, call into question real-world time's relationship to dramatic time – as actual London time will have been audible hourly when the church clocks rang.

When the bell was unambiguously to be understood as a clock, characters would, as people did at the time, count the strokes, slowing the pace of the play, telling the audience when fictionally this moment was taking place, and, of course, ensuring that time

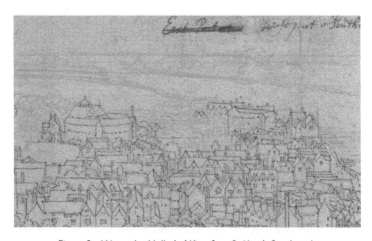

Figure 2 – Wenceslas Hollar's *A View from St Mary's*, Southwark.
The 'lantern' in the Globe's double gabled roof may have housed a bell.

was a subject as well as a device. In *Richard III* a '*Clock striketh*', after which Richard demands 'Tell [count] the clock there' (5.3.277); Iachimo in *Cymbeline* is heard doing so: 'One, two, three: time, time!' (2.2.51). But this bell, hovering already between bell and clock, was so ambiguous that, by design or error, it could start as a stage bell but be recalled as a clock by Shakespeare's characters – and perhaps Shakespeare himself. Prop was, in this instance, moulding drama. So in *Macbeth*, Macbeth asks his servant to 'bid thy mistress, when my drink is ready, / She strike upon the bell' (2.1.31–2); when the bell is then rung, Macbeth comments on its true meaning: 'The bell invites me. / Hear it not, Duncan; for it is a knell / That summons thee to Heaven, or to Hell' (2.1.62–4). The next bell heard is the 'alarum bell' announcing the fact that Duncan is now dead. So Duncan's murder is sandwiched between two bell strokes. Yet when Lady Macbeth goes mad, she starts 'telling' or counting the remembered bell strokes, reconceptualising them as hours: 'One; two: why, then 'tis time to do't' (5.1.36–7). Of course, this is a play where concepts of time are highly important, and the encapsulation of the action into two strikes of the bell

– together with the movement from 'alarm' to 'time', and from heralding the need to kill Duncan to the memory of his death – underscores the slippage of meaning that is such an important feature of the play; use of the stage bell allows or perhaps brought this about.

CONCLUSION

Because of the different names, functions and uses of various bits of the theatre, metatheatre could be located either 'safely' in the theatrum mundi aspects of the stage, questionably, as with the pillars and bells, and disconcertingly, as when theatre appeared to offer a form of 'reality' in house, balcony or ladder – or a form of 'unreality' when those features were reimagined as something 'literary', like the 'scene'. There was not, then, one form of metatheatre that Shakespeare used with one effect, but nor does metatheatre seem to have been adopted hesitantly, angrily or wearily. Rather, the early modern playhouse seems to have repeatedly been used as a way of interpreting and heightening the words and, sometimes, as a way of querying or undercutting them.

Against this, Shakespeare's calls for imagination need to be reconceptualised. True, there are moments when Shakespeare wants not to be constrained either by the overarching metaphors of his stage, or its crude realism. But a look at the way he locates a poet's imagination in *A Midsummer Night's Dream* shows just how fundamentally organised it was by and around the stage:

> The poet's eye, in fine frenzy rolling,
> Doth glance from heaven to earth, from earth to heaven;
> And as imagination bodies forth
> The forms of things unknown, the poet's pen
> Turns them to shapes, and gives to airy nothing
> A local habitation and a name.

(5.1.12–17)

Consciously or unconsciously, the poet here is described as glancing between two aspects of the stage, 'heaven' and 'earth', in order to come up with his visions; what he then sees is given habitation and a name – as the 'scene' enclosed both actors' habitat and location's name. Imagination seems, for Shakespeare, to be scarcely distinguishable from its theatrical home and ultimately located there.

What is clear throughout Shakespeare's writing is that, as is to be expected, he wrote for the places in which his plays were performed, sometimes wrapping their features into his fictional world, sometimes wrapping his fictions around their features. Even at the moments when Shakespeare begged his audience to make imaginative additions to his text, he exploited the metaphor and reality wrapped in the structure of his playhouse. A fixed prop, the playhouse itself dictated and circumscribed imaginative space for Shakespeare's audience, not in an overtly literary fashion – though the result is literary – but by its locational, visual and aural presence; in so doing, this chapter has argued, it prescribed the imaginative world of Shakespeare himself too.

CHAPTER TWO

STORM EFFECTS IN SHAKESPEARE
GWILYM JONES

> How ere you understand't, 'Tis a fine Play:
> For we have in't a Conjurer, a Devill,
> And a Clowne too; but I feare the evill,
> In which perhaps unwisely we may faile,
> Of wanting Squibs and Crackers at their taile.
> But howsoever, Gentlemen I sweare,
> You shall have Good Words for your Money here.[1]

The Prologue of *The Two Merry Milke-Maids* (c.1619) satisfies the requirements of his generic job description. He is deferential to his audience, stakes his case for the forthcoming play – it has, after all, 'a Conjurer, a Devill / And a Clowne' – and makes clear that he understands the financial commitment the listening crowd has made, with his promise that it 'shall have Good Words'. And, within the promise of all that is fine in the play he, like many prologues, raises the possibility of failure: opting for the play not to have 'Squibs and Crackers' – types of fireworks – may, it is feared, be unwise on the part of the playwright.

Unwise, and perhaps also unexpected, for *The Two Merry Milke-Maids* was performed at the Red Bull in Clerkenwell, a playhouse known for its raucousness and spectacle.[2] The Prologue, however, speaks at, and in response to, a time of transition in this particular amphitheatre. After a period of some tumult, and following the death of their patron, Queen Anne, a number of the Red Bull players had formed a new theatre company, the Company of the Revels – and with their new name had come a new, muted acoustic aesthetic. With 'the Stage being reform'd, and free /

From the low'd Clamors it was wont to be', the Red Bull audience were prompted to change their wonted habits and 'expect no noyse of Guns, Trumpets, nor Drum, / Nor Sword and Targuet; but [. . .] Sence and Words'.[3]

Squibs and crackers, guns and drum would be lacking. Yet these had hitherto comprised the sound of theatre in early modern London: as the Prologue's lines suggest, these devices could be utilised in a number of ways depending on the effect required. They were part of the arsenal of multi-sensory effects with which companies embellished their staging of large battles and they accompanied the entrance of devils and gods. However, it was in their guise as thunder and lightning that these effects reached their full potential. Shining rockets shooting across the stage, cannonballs trundling in the echoing wooden heavens, drums rolling and ordinance discharging: the new Company of the Revels must indeed have had a high opinion of their newfound 'Sence and Words' to forgo the possibilities offered by all of this.

While the actors at the Red Bull adopted a quieter approach to drama, rival outdoor playhouses continued to use pyrotechnics to enthral the crowd. John Melton, in 1620, refers to Marlowe's still-popular *Doctor Faustus* in his refutation of the claims of 'astrologasters' (those who use astrology to predict the weather, among other things):

> Another will fore-tell of Lightning and Thunder that shall happen such a day, when there are no such Inflamations seene, except men goe to the *Fortune* in *Golding-Lane*, to see the Tragedie of Doctor *Faustus*. There indeede a man may behold shagge-hayr'd Deuills runne roaring over the Stages with squibs in their mouths, while Drummers make Thunder in the Tyring-house, and the twelve-penny Hirelings make artificial Lightning in their Heavens.[4]

Even as Marlowe's play approached its thirtieth birthday, the staging of it was still something to 'behold'. Melton's writing, moreover, shows how natural it was to conflate dramatic pyrotechny with genuine thunder and lightning. While the effects in amphitheatres might not have been realistic by modern standards, there is no question that in the play they represented storms.

This chapter is largely about the way in which Shakespeare writes thunder and lighting into his plays. So it will open by outlining the stage effects that would have been available to Shakespeare and his contemporaries,[5] noting that while *lightning* is a visual effect – usually produced through some kind of pyrotechnics – *thunder* is an auditory effect, made in the tiring-house and the heavens.[6] I will then outline the ways in which knowledge of these effects can be brought upon a reading of *Julius Caesar*. In the second half of the chapter I will argue that spectacular effects are not always necessary to stage a storm, and that the opening of *The Tempest* relies on those effects being kept to a minimum.

THUNDER AND LIGHTNING: STAGE EFFECTS

As I have suggested, through the extracts from J.C.'s *The Two Merry Milke-Maids* and John Melton's *Astrologaster*, fire effects could be used for several purposes; devils, for example, often entered to the accompaniment of squibs. But it is in the technique used in the staging of a storm that they were at their most spectacular. The main way of creating lightning on the stage was through using what was known as, or at least subsequently came to be called, a swevel. This device is similar to a modern firework rocket, though, as John Bate made clear in 1634, it also had a guiding mechanism:

> Swevels are nothing else but Rockets, having instead of a rod (to ballast them) a little cane bound fast unto them, where through the rope passeth. Note that you must be carefull to have your line strong, even & smooth, and it must be rubd over with sope that it may not burn. If you would have your Rockets to returne againe, then binde two Rockets together, with the breech of one towards the mouth of the other, and let the stouple that primeth the one, enter the breech of the other.[7]

Bate, like his fellow firework writers, markets his book for those interested in 'Triumph and Recreation'; fireworks had become a form of niche theatre in their own right.[8] The companies of the public playhouses, however, were certainly aware of the technique for using swevels. Thus, in Thomas Dekker's *If this be not a good Play, the Diuell is in it* (1612), when the stage direction calls for '*Fire-workes on Lines*', swevels would have been ignited by somebody off stage.[9] When lightning was being created, the line presumably ran from the heavens down to the stage.[10] As with several examples of theatrical pyrotechny of the period, the effect is mirrored in the language of characters: indeed in Dekker's play, a character directs the swevels. Ruffman, a disguised demon in the court of Naples, is asked by the King for a wonderful display. Ruffman dismisses the efforts of the human courtiers – 'the toyes they bragged of (Fire-works / and such light-stuffes)' – before offering his own:

RUFFMAN

you shall see

At opening of this hand, a thousand Balles
Of wilde-Fire, flying round about the Aire – there.
Fire-workes on Lines

[ALL]

Rare, Rare.[11]

An extensive storm, then, such as that in Shakespeare's *Julius Caesar*, which I discuss below, would have included quite a display of fireworks to represent lightning. Thunder, however, was heard and not seen. The chief means for producing the effect was with a heavy cannonball.[12] At its most simplistic, the method involved rolling the ball on the floor of the heavens, to vibrate the wood and produce a thundering sound. Also available was the 'thunder run', nomenclature which post-dates the drama, though early evidence for the mechanics of the 'run' is well established.[13] The device is a very simple one. A wooden trough, either on a fulcrum or sloping along the floor, contains a cannonball which, when see-sawed or released, rolls. Different levels may be built into the trough, to enable separate thunderclaps to be sounded when the ball drops.[14] In early modern texts, the reference to use of the run is usually confined to a 'rolling bullet', as in the prologue to Ben Jonson's *Every Man In His Humour*: the 'rolled bullet [is] heard, / To say, it thunders, or tempestuous drum / Rumbles to tell you that the storm doth come'.[15] The effect is pleasingly convincing,[16] although perhaps less so when, as Jonson suggests, drums contributed to the noise. The stage machinery that represented the storms in early modern playhouses, then, is easy to create, whether or not the totality of spectacle it must have produced is easy to imagine. Of greater interest than the machinery itself, though, is the way it coloured the dramatic poetry of the plays in which it appeared.

POETRY AND STAGE EFFECTS: *JULIUS CAESAR*

Shakespeare's first major depiction of a storm is in *Julius Caesar*. As I have argued elsewhere, the date of this play – coinciding with the opening of the Globe in 1599 – suggests that Shakespeare would have been particularly conscious of commercial values.[17] The storm in the play, I have suggested, is part of Shakespeare's attempt to promote the Globe as an exciting playhouse that stages the spectacular. How, then, does this affect the language of the play? Following the stage direction for *Thunder and Lightning*, Caska meets Cicero in the storm:

> O, Cicero,
> I have seen tempests when the scolding winds
> Have rived the knotty oaks, and I have seen
> Th'ambitious ocean swell and rage and foam
> To be exalted with the threatening clouds;
> But never till tonight, never till now,
> Did I go through a tempest dropping fire.
> Either there is civil strife in heaven,
> Or else the world, too saucy with the gods,
> Incenses them to send destruction.
>
> (1.3.4–14)[18]

An audience watching *Julius Caesar* at the Globe might think that Caska is right to be worried. Thunder and lightning effects in early modern drama tend to occur alongside the depiction of supernatural events, whether of gods descending from the heavens or devils rising from the traps. This has led Leslie Thomson to argue that '[i]n the case of *thunder and lightning*, the audience was almost invariably prompted to expect the supernatural – and got what it expected'.[19] Shakespeare, however, is rather more subtle with his effects. Caska fears the 'gods [may] send destruction', but no such gods appear.

Instead, in relation to special effects heralded by the stage direction '*Thunder and Lightning*', a striking detail emerges. The fieriness of Caska's description matches the effects of the swevels. The focus of Caska's speech – and of Cassius' when he enters – is fire, quite reasonably, as fire is indeed 'dropping' around the actors. There is no reference to rain in the play. Caska's lines do not, however, suggest that the stage effects are a convincing simulation of a storm; instead, they revel in their unusualness: 'never till tonight, never till now / Did I go through a tempest dropping fire'. Throughout the scene, moreover, references to the pyrotechnics continue. The phrases of Cassius, which depict the 'very flash of it' (52), the 'sparks' (57) and 'all these fires, all these gliding ghosts' (63) draw attention to the stage effects. If Shakespeare is advertising the new playhouse as a venue for spectacular effects, then he is also writing into the play images which draw attention to those effects. This dramatic irony is surely comic. When Brutus, in the following scene, claims that 'The exhalations whizzing in the air / Give so much light that I may read by them', the irony persists, even if the rockets do not (2.1.44–5). Similarly, when the fireworks appear again, with the *thunder and lightning* of the next scene, so too does the metadramatic language, this time through the medium of Calphurnia: 'Fierce fiery warriors fight upon the clouds' (2.2.19), 'ghosts [. . .] shriek and squeal' (19), 'The noise of battle hurtle[s] in the air' (22).

The language of the play, then, brazenly refers to the stage effects of the new playhouse. And yet there are subtler poetic resonances in the lines. For example, a transition takes place from supernatural judgment – that feared by Caska – to human punishment by vigilantes. Just as Cassius has 'bared [his] bosom to the thunder-stone' (1.3.49), so Brutus, attempting to swear his constancy, says:

> When Marcus Brutus grows so covetous,
> To lock such rascal counters from his friends,
> Be ready gods with all your thunderbolts,
> Dash him to pieces!
>
> (4.3.79–82)

Brutus' lines recall the rallying cry of the vigilante Plebeians who set upon Cinna the Poet in 3.3. 'Tear him to pieces', says one, 'Tear him, tear him!' another, and 'Come, brands, ho! Firebrands! To Brutus', to Cassius', burn all!' say all together (3.3.28, 35, 36). Thunderbolts and fire have been physically – visually – conflated on the stage, to the extent that one may stand for the other. Thus Brutus and Cassius, in calling upon the storm to prove their justifiability, slip into a category error: the thunder they invoke is explicitly supernatural, yet there is a viscerally functional human thunder in the frenzied crowd. Caska is frightened about what the storm portends, and Cassius is empowered: each crucially misreads the environment as something other than natural. The dramatic irony noted above is therefore deeper than it first appears. In a play that is often strikingly aware of the potential of theatre, the conspirators, though explicitly aligned with the creation and the action of the drama, are represented through a naïve and basic audience response: storm equals supernatural. *Julius Caesar*, as well as delighting in, and drawing attention to, its own special effects, is a comment on this response, its crudity and its dangers.

STAGE EFFECTS: *THE TEMPEST*

If *Julius Caesar* revels in the theatricality of its pyrotechnics, then *The Tempest* does something quite different. Written for the indoor Blackfriars theatre,[20] fire effects, I will argue, were absent in the staging of the opening scene, leaving the storm to be represented through sound alone:

> *A tempestuous noise of thunder and lightning heard;*
> *enter a Shipmaster and a Boatswain.*

MASTER

Boatswain!

BOATSWAIN

Here master. What cheer?

MASTER

Good, speak to th' mariners. Fall to it yarely or we run ourselves aground.

> *Exit.*

BOATSWAIN

Heigh, my hearts; cheerly, cheerly, my hearts!
Yare! Yare! Take in the topsail. Tend to the
master's whistle! Blow till thou burst thy wind, if
room enough.

$$(1.1.0–8)^{21}$$

In his essay '*The Tempest*'s Tempest at Blackfriars' (1989), Andrew Gurr discusses the various possibilities for staging the play's first scene.[22] Although, as with any attempted explication of early modern staging, Gurr is necessarily speculative, his closing remarks are persuasive: 'If *The Tempest* truly was the first play Shakespeare planned for the Blackfriars, his opening scene was a model of how to *épater les gallants* [startle the fashionable gentlemen]. The shock of the opening's realism is transformed into magic the moment Miranda enters.'[23] As with *Julius Caesar* and the Globe, the notion that the storm could define the character of the playhouse is an attractive one. Gurr's approach to *The Tempest* and the Blackfriars may appear to reflect this notion, but a crucial difference is that the indoor theatre already had an established mode of practice when Shakespeare's play was staged there. The Children of the Queen's Revels had played at the Blackfriars from

1600 until 1608. As Sarah Dustagheer has shown, 'the Children of the Queen's Revels' repertory at the Blackfriars did *not* contain extensive and integral use of sound effects. The plays written for the indoor theatre between 1600 and 1608 are remarkably quiet in comparison to the Globe's repertory.'[24] Hence the impact of the storm in Shakespeare's play is as much to do with surprise as with impressive spectacle. It is less a matter of the play determining an aesthetic for a *new* playhouse (as was the case in *Julius Caesar*); more a matter of subverting the expectations of an audience who were familiar with the pre-existing character of Blackfriars performances.

The stage direction for '*A tempestuous noise of thunder and lightning heard*' (1.1.0sd) is probably written by the scrivener Ralph Crane, who seems to have prepared the script of *The Tempest* for publication in the 1623 Folio.[25] If we are to take the stage direction literally, as 'the earliest evidence we have of how the play was staged by the King's Company', then it is unusual in specifying lightning as an *auditory* effect.[26] As Gurr notes, 'Fireworks [were] unpopular at the halls because of the stink', and so the offstage noise of the stage direction was unlikely to include pyrotechnics.[27] Given that lightning is a visual effect elsewhere in the contemporary drama, it is more likely that Crane himself opted to use 'thunder and lightning' as a phrase to depict casually the noise of a storm. 'Thunder and lightning' was a commonplace phrase for an aural effect in early modern English: a pamphlet of 'strange newes' roughly contemporaneous with *The Tempest*, for example, describes 'a horrible noyse of both of thunder and lightning'; John Foxe writes of a 'warre [. . .] presignified by terrible thundering and lightning heard all England over in the moneth of march' and Leo Africanus describes a mountain that 'is called by the name of the lyon in regard of the dreadfull thunders and lightnings which are continually heard from the top thereof'.[28] 'Thunder' and 'lightning' – as outlined above – are different theatrical effects, but 'thunder and lightning' is a compound phrase synonymous with 'storm'.[29] There is, then, no decisive contradiction in the stage direction that maintains that '*thunder and lightning*' are '*heard*'. In light of this, and the unpopularity of indoor fireworks, the '*tempes-tuous noise*' is likely to have been *only* a noise. This might, in the context of the spectacular pyrotechnics described above, seem disappointing. However, while lightning effects are a visual extrav-agance, the noise of a rolling cannonball to represent thunder is convincing and accurate. As I will argue below, this realistic quality is necessary for the aesthetic of the play; if the play's language, as well as the stage effects, is considered, it becomes obvious that accuracy of representation is a priority of the opening scene.

As in *Julius Caesar*, Shakespeare is careful to complement the staging of the storm effects with the dramatic language of his char-acters. Although the storm is an illusion, the actions and diction of the crew are firmly grounded in Jacobean reality. Shakespeare seems to have paid great attention to the accurate portrayal of contemporary nautical procedures in his writing of the scene. The Boatswain's instructions to the crew reveal a determination on the part of the playwright to be as precise as possible: 'Take in the topsail', 'Down with the topmast', 'Bring her to try with the main course' and 'Set her two courses off to sea again! Lay her off!' are all valid instructions (1.1.6, 33, 34, 48). In fact, the extent to which Shakespeare deals in nautical technicalities is remarkable, as A. F. Falconer, in *Shakespeare and the Sea*, has explained. In response to the commands of the Boatswain, Falconer writes:

> The ship is sound, the seamen are disciplined, the right orders are given. Some of the newer manoeuvres of the day, even one that was debateable, have been tried, but all without success. [. . .] Shakespeare could not have writ-ten a scene of this kind without taking great pains to grasp completely how a ship beset with these difficulties would have to be handled.[30]

This detail of the scene is indicative of the authenticity at which Shakespeare is apparently aiming. Why the playwright would adhere to such specifications is puzzling: it is certainly highly unusual in Jacobean drama.[31] Perhaps the possibility that there would be, among the audience, some who had been to sea and absorbed some knowledge of shipping, was important. Whatever the reason, it is apparent that the scene draws attention away from its aesthetic framework by evoking valid nautical commands in a correct and justifiable order. We might fruitfully contrast this with Shakespeare's anachronisms elsewhere, not least his notorious propensity to insert coastlines and seaports on landlocked countries and inland towns.[32] While Shakespeare is so often casual with the factual accuracy of his details, *The Tempest*'s opening scene has a precision perhaps unmatched in the rest of his work. In this precision lies the singular aesthetic of the play: the minutely detailed storm that echoes over in subsequent scenes.

The scene, then, depicts a ship in a storm by using nautical terminology, rather than relying on conventions of stage practice. Its phrases do not even descend from printed literature; Falconer makes clear that the shipping manoeuvres to which *The Tempest* refers are only described in print in nautical texts that post-date the play.[33] The first of such texts, Henry Mainwairing's *Seaman's Dictionary*, published in 1623, when Shakespeare had been dead for seven years, advertises its novelty even at that late date:

> To understand the art of navigation is far easier learned than to know the practice and mechanical working of ships, with the proper terms belonging to them, in respect that there are helps for the first by many books [. . .] but for the other, till this, there was not so much as a means thought of, to inform any one in it.[34]

Shakespeare was employing language that was not, then, found in other plays or printed texts. Whether he learned the manoeuvres from a private manuscript, or from conversation, the point is the same: the scene effectively broadcasts that it is not taken from drama, is not taken from books, is not the descendant of any kind of artificial world and that therefore what you are watching is real. Timothy Morton has defined this kind of realistic writing as 'rendering': 'All signals that we are in a constructed realm have been minimized.'[35] The success of rendering depends not on the illusion's exactitude but on the ease, facilitated by *The Tempest*'s use of stage effects, with which the audience is enabled to accept it as reality. It is for this reason, I believe, that convincing noises are heard, but extravagant fireworks are absent.

For the scene minimises 'signals that we are in a constructed realm' through its use of stage effects and its unprecedented nautical precision. This rendering is found in the accuracy of the Boatswain's commands and their expression. Figurative language barely makes an appearance for the majority of the Boatswain's speech, and the imagery he uses when speaking to the nobles, or to the Mariners when his orders have failed, is pointedly contrasting with the direct diction he uses in the rest of the scene: 'What cares these roarers for the name of king?' and 'What, must our mouths be cold?' (16–17, 51). The only time when the Boatswain uses figurative language, then, is in this rhetorical question just quoted; the nautical imperatives have no answer but action; the imagery no answer at all. In the Boatswain's speech, the survival of those onboard is dependent on the absence of metaphor: the language of his commands is therefore direct and unambiguous. Figurative language, then, is portrayed in the scene as an extravagance, which has the result of making the storm as convincing as possible: by prioritising the technical terms and by isolating the imagery, the Boatswain's language conceals the aesthetic framework of the drama as a whole, and its special effects.

In order to illustrate this further, it is helpful to compare the scene with its counterpart in John Fletcher's *The Sea Voyage* (1622). Although Fletcher's work alludes repeatedly to *The Tempest*, the difference in terms of the figurative language of the two plays is clear in the first speech. As in Shakespeare's play, there are stage directions for a storm and the Master speaks first:

> *A Tempest, Thunder and Lightning.*
> *Enter Master and two Saylors.*

MASTER

> Lay her aloofe, the Sea grows dangerous,
> How it spits against the clouds, how it capers,
> And how the fiery Element frights it back!

> There be devils dancing in the aire, I think
> I saw a Dolphin hang ith hornes of the moone
> Shot from a wave: hey day, hey day,
> How she kicks and yerks?
> Down with'e main Mast, lay her at hull,
> Farle up all her Linnens, and let her ride it out.[36]

Despite the concern, expressed by Gurr, that 'Fletcher's scene is designed to be an immediately recognisable echo and development of Shakespeare's and therefore cannot be compared too closely with it', this speech in fact embellishes the language of its predecessor.[37] As in *The Tempest*, the nautical commands are evident, but here they merely bookend the speech rather than dominate it. For the majority of the speech, the imagery of the sea, the clouds, the dolphin and the fiery element give the lines an entirely alternative focus. *The Sea Voyage*, then, uses elaborate conceits to portray the storm while *The Tempest*, as Christopher Cobb has remarked, 'withholds poetic descriptions of both the storm and the suffering of those caught in it'.[38] This is not to dismiss Fletcher's scene, merely to point out that it is inherently different from the scene on which it is based. *The Tempest*'s opening keeps the extravagant stage effects to a minimum, and this is reflected in its unadorned, practical language. The stylised language of Fletcher's Master is precisely the sort avoided by Shakespeare's Boatswain.

Implicit in all of the above arguments is the recognition that the aesthetic of the opening of *The Tempest* is dependent upon the language of the scene more than upon the stage effects of thunder and lightning, which, to some extent, exists in all of Shakespeare's storm scenes. With any of Shakespeare's storms the stage effects – however realistic are drums, cannonballs and fireworks – have a necessarily limited contribution to the overall effect of the scene. The reason for this is that Shakespeare's storms are never simply storms. The representation of the weather is never the only priority of the storm scenes; rather, the scenes are always concerned with human apprehension. Naturally, the title of the play is of key importance here also. Given that the first scene represents – and relies upon – a convincing presentation of a storm (even though afterwards the fiction will reveal the storm to have been derived from magic), *The Tempest*'s title is designed to misdirect the audience before the play begins: the tempest is not a 'real' one, *except* in the title and the opening scene. The audience are presented with the human apprehension of a storm; only later will they learn the extra-human force behind it.

What effect does the rendering of the storm in 1.1 have on the rest of the play? In 1.2, Miranda's lines, which open the scene, immediately raise the possibility that the storm itself was, anyway, an illusion. It is seldom acknowledged, however, that the lines simultaneously suggest that the storm is still taking place:

> If by your art, my dearest father, you have
> Put the wild waters in this roar, allay them.
> The sky, it seems, would pour down stinking pitch
> But that the sea, mounting to th' welkin's cheek,
> Dashes the fire out.

$$(1.2.1–5)$$

The second line of the speech, with its deictic 'this roar' and its imperative 'allay them' gives the impression, maintained throughout the passage, that the storm has not finished. This is the moment at which the provenance of the storm is revealed, but this revelation is not in retrospect: Miranda's lines allow the audience to experience the storm in the context of the supernatural, then, rather than prompting the audience to reimagine it retrospectively. The scene is the point in the play at which the aesthetic framework, hitherto concealed, starts to become acknowledged – a process that continues through to the metadrama of the masque in 4.1. There are no directions for stage effects in 1.2: the shift from the presentation of the storm as natural to magical is apparently dependent on the qualities of Miranda's language. The audience can experience the storm both as natural and supernatural while it is occurring. Importantly, the present tense and extended imagery of the passage relate its content to accounts of storms from other plays. In this regard, the description is consciously theatrical in the very way that, I have argued, the opening scene is not. Thus

Miranda's speech is related to the Mariner's in *The Winter's Tale*, 'The heavens that we have in hand are angry, / And frown upon's' (3.3.5–6) and Pericles' in *Pericles*, 'O, still / Thy deaf'ning, dreadful thunders; gently quench / Thy nimble sulphurous flashes! [. . .] the seaman's whistle / is a whisper in the ears of death / Unheard.' (3.1.4–10), or indeed, Caska's lines, quoted earlier, in *Julius Caesar*.[39] The extensive imagery of Miranda's speech locates it in this stylistic tradition of characters narrating storms as they occur, a tradition which is resisted in the opening scene of *The Tempest*. One particular image will have been especially familiar to a contemporary audience: the literary conceit of the sea touching the sky. A similar idea is used by William Strachey, whose *True Repertory* is a probable source for *The Tempest*: 'the Sea swelled above the Clouds, and gave battell unto Heaven. It could not be said to raine, the waters like whole Rivers did flood in the ayre.'[40] The image, however, is widespread; taking translations of Ovid as an example, we may see some variations on the theme in the following extracts:

> The surges mounting up aloft did seeme too mate the skye,
> And with theyr sprinckling for too wet the clowdes that hang
> on hye.[41]

> What boysterous billowes now (O wretch) amids the waves
> we spye,
> As I forthwith should have bene hev'de to touch the Azure
> skye.[42]

> Joves indignation and his wrath began to grow so hot.
> That for to quench the rage thereof, his Heaven suffisde not.
> His brother Neptune with his waves was faine to doe him
> ease.[43]

In including imagery in this vein, then, Miranda's speech is identifiably engaging in a literary tradition. This is exactly the type of allusion that the first scene of the play sought to avoid. The structure of Miranda's speech – the iambic pentameter, the florid description and the familiar, allusive metaphor – signals to the audience that they are watching an aesthetic construction. Just as Miranda intimates, then, that the storm is 'art', so art becomes acknowledged through its formal qualities. The opening scene withholds the poetic; the second scene revels in it.

Thunder and lightning in *The Tempest* are not restricted to the opening scene, however. There are two more scenes with storm effects in the play and in each of them the illusion of the first scene affects the way the audience is encouraged to respond. Because of the introductory storm, and its subsequent reimagining by Miranda (and later, of course, by Ariel), the sound of thunder in the play is questionable: its origin and hence its qualities, supernatural or other, are unclear.[44] Having witnessed a natural storm, which immediately becomes a supernatural storm, the audience is not in a position decisively to judge the next incidence of thunder:

> *Enter Caliban, with a burden of wood;*
> *a noise of thunder heard.*

All the infections that the sun sucks up
From bogs, fens, flats, on Prosper fall, and make him
By inchmeal a disease! His spirits hear me,
And yet I needs must curse.

(2.2.1–4)

Having established the possibility that thunder has a supernatural origin, the play consolidates the idea by directing the sound effects to be produced again. Thus the tension between natural and supernatural is created, and a hierarchical relationship between the two is brought about: the 'natural' in the play is subsumed by, and subject to the work of, the supernatural. However, Caliban's curses, like Lear's before him, are formed from 'his' – or, rather, Shakespeare's – understanding of early modern meteorology.[45] The sun, according to this set of theories, caused 'vapours' to rise towards it, much as we now understand moisture to be formed into clouds. If those vapours were from a noxious source, like a bog, then when they fell to earth as rain, they would spread their disease. This curse of Caliban's, then, requires a slight

acquaintance with the Jacobean understanding of the weather.[46]
The significance of the meteorological source of the later curse is
that it occurs following the sound of thunder. The weather in the
play has been exposed as magically derived rather than natural.
Caliban's curses rely on authentic natural processes: the sun drawing up vapours which eventually fall, a notion the Jacobean
audience believed. The curses, then, evoke the futility of Caliban's
position regarding authority: they are optimistic fantasies that
require a weather system outside the control of Prospero. Such a
weather system is precisely what is lacking at this moment. Caliban
acknowledges the 'spirits' making the thunder yet hopelessly
invokes a natural weather event. Nature is represented by the play
not only as subject to human control but as generating the reference points for the language through which its enslavement is
expressed. As with the opening scene, this use of sound effects
provides a backdrop for the representation for the human apprehension of a storm. The difference is that the audience now
understands the weather as supernatural and Caliban's curse is all
the more futile for it.

There is one more scene in *The Tempest* in which thunder is
staged, and, unlike the first two scenes, there are two stage directions for it:

> *Thunder and lightning. Enter Ariel, like a harpy, claps his
> wings upon the table, and with a quaint device the banquet
> vanishes.* (3.3.52sd)

> *He vanishes in thunder. Then, to soft music, enter the shapes
> again and dance with mocks and mows, and carry out the
> table.* (3.3.82sd)

Ariel's appearance and disappearance are part of a series of theatrical miniatures which convince both the onstage and offstage
audience that the scene is, as Sebastian puts it, 'a living drollery'
(21). It seems clear enough from these directions and from the
above discussion that, in the course of the play, the sound of thunder has shifted in meaning from one extreme to another: in the
first scene it represented a meticulously rendered natural storm,

but here it represents a commonplace theophany which revels in its theatrical tricks. Even with the basic effects of a noise of thunder, Shakespeare can achieve a bewildering array of variations in what they signify.

As I have argued, both in the open-air playhouses, and the indoor theatres, Shakespeare combines the effects of thunder and lightning with those of language, so that a storm can continue to resonate when the fireworks have faded and the cannonballs are still. We might, perhaps, describe Shakespeare's employment of storm effects as a conflation of the poetic with the practical: the language builds on, complicates and varies the effects. That means, though, that the Company of the Revels, on which this chapter opened, has made a bold, but perhaps ultimately reductive decision. In concentrating in *Two Merry Milke-Maids* on 'Good Words' alone, and dismissing stage effects altogether, the company may have thought it was being theatrically sophisticated. But, as this chapter has argued, they were abandoning the key resources, on which 'Good Words' had hitherto relied.

CHAPTER THREE

PERFORMING MATERIALITY: CURTAINS
ON THE EARLY MODERN STAGE
NATHALIE RIVERE DE CARLES

Arras, cloth, courtayne, canopy, curtain, hanging, traverse, valance and *veil*: these are words indiscriminately used in early modern plays to signal the actual or metaphoric presence of curtains. Whether a hanging is an ornament on a wall, a cloth of state, a bed-curtain or a partition between two spaces, this series of words initially evokes the intimacy and the aesthetics of domestic space, while also being part of early modern dramatic language. Despite the multiplicity of their names, shapes and functions, curtains characterise the general architecture of an area that they simultaneously limit and divide.[1] Wall hangings defined a place visually, aesthetically and socially. A plain curtain or traverse diverged from richly embroidered tapestries and from their plebeian equivalents, painted cloths. Hangings, then, did not tell a single story. Rather, they related a series of socio-political ambitions about their owners or their makers.

In early modern theatres, curtains did not play the same role as they do today, where their opening and closing signal the beginning and end of the play. Indeed, the lexical variety mirrors the different shapes, positioning and roles of stage hangings on the early modern stage. As we learn in this collection, early modern outdoor and indoor theatres were characterised by a thrust stage and a flexible tiring-house wall which featured a lower level with two doors sometimes framing a larger central opening (see Figure 1, p. 16). Meanwhile, the middle level was occupied by a gallery for seating actors, spectators or musicians, and an upper gallery. Curtains could be found all over the stage in early modern theatres.

They could adorn the railings of the galleries; they could be used to signify thresholds for the various openings in the tiring-house wall and they could also be part of the action, linked with movable props such as beds or a stately seats. Taking a great number of plays and their stage directions into consideration as well as the theatrical spaces in which they were performed, Alan Dessen and Leslie Thomson came up with a specific typology of curtains which can be enriched with David Carnegie's situational categories (he sees curtains as linked to extremely dynamic dramatic moments such as entrances, exits, comic concealment, spying scenes and discovery scenes).[2] However, it is also necessary to consider the material and textual perspectives of curtains in order to have a more complete idea of their function and performing effects:

- hiding the openings in the tiring-house wall enabling the discovery or concealment of a character. This hanging could be a plain curtain or an *arras*[3] i.e. a painted cloth which imitated the style of a tapestry, or an actual tapestry. When in front of the central opening in the tiring-house wall, the arras played the part of the medieval traverse used in booth-stage theatres
- attached to a four-poster bed.[4] Again the curtains could be either plain hangings or painted cloths
- in front of the central opening in the tiring-house wall. Arras, here, could also be used as a bed-curtain if a bed is dissimulated in the discovery space. This would enable a swift performance of a bed scene and a faster transition to a scene not requiring the bed as a prop
- as a cloth of state or backcloth to a royal throne
- on the railing of the balcony
- to reveal a painting or a statue

These concrete visual objects are either architectural elements (when the curtain is attached to the hard structure of the theatrical space, e.g. all the curtains that hide openings in the stage wall; the hangings in the galleries, etc.), or props (when freed from the hard structure and they draw nearer to the acting body), or performing objects (when they play the same part as the performing body). However, this short typology of curtains is not complete if we do not mention fictional hangings: curtains which only exist on the page and which do not always call for a visual embodiment on the stage. With 'fictional hangings' the playwright uses the visual shape of the theatre to enlighten his own text. The curtain, in this instance, is a purely rhetorical device meant to engage the spectator's imagination. The most famous example is to be found in Shakespeare's *The Rape of Lucrece* (1594) where the 'black stage for tragedies' (766) evokes the extinguished light of the heroine's chastity. However the use of the curtain as a purely textual metaphor is also a recurring device in early modern drama. For instance, Walter Montagu, in *The Shepherd's Paradise* (1633),[5] centres the conversation of Moramente and Genorio on the extended metaphor or conceit of the black traverse curtain, a pre-Renaissance dramatic term,[6] as evocative of the sad news borne by Genorio and of Moramente's sombre mood:

MORAMENTE

Dost thou bring news Genorio, that thou hadst rather thy clothes should tell than thou? What black traverse hast thou brought, to draw between me and my joys, which were ready to embrace thee.

GENORIO

I am happy Sir, to come to be imbraced by you in this infectious colour, which must fully and black you too.

MORAMENTE

Throw then Genorio those blacks over me, for nothing can appear so ugly unto me as this party-coloured doubt.

(Fol. 32a. 2068–74)

Curtains are simultaneously a material necessity of the setting and vehicles for creativity. They stand for a dramatic convention but cannot be considered as purveying a single visual code. Victor Bourgy stresses that the outer fixity of a prop is deceptive and that it can consequently be used to help build meaningful dramatic dynamics. He notices that 'major playwrights do not consider theatrical conventions as awkward, purely practical, interchangeable, or artificial, but as strategies, as flexible processes creating dramatic fluidity'.[7] As stage-hangings possess a significant mobility, they facilitate dynamic movement in other stage properties and actors. They can be understood as 'scenical contrivances',[8] which, as they can also be used all over the playing space, including on pieces of furniture, are not in fact confined to a single area of the early modern theatre architecture. In particular, curtains are associated with the stage-bed.[9]

The paradoxical mobility of these inanimate props is coupled with their dual function of hiding and revealing. Stage-hangings must be considered as significant objects enabling the spectator to 'see without what was within'.[10] They are instruments superimposing the Augustinian gaze of the mind to bodily eyesight,[11] thus associating abstraction with concreteness. However, the closer they get to the performing body, the more their materiality changes. They develop into new categories: hangings as surrogates (curtains replacing objects or characters), surrogated hangings (when the performing body acts as a curtain), and fictional hangings (curtains only existing in the text and not seen on the stage).

Andrew Sofer points to the multiplicity of stage properties in the early modern theatre and explains how they are imbued with inherent material characteristics but also how they reinvent themselves once put on stage.[12] Each prop has sometimes contradictory functions and meanings and so needs to be considered on a socio-cultural as well as a theatrical level. Hangings on the Elizabethan stage have both socio-historical and theatrical meaning as props. Indeed, early modern playwrights conjure up curtains physically and/or verbally as dramatic conventions as well as what Carlson calls 'ghostly tapestries':[13] tapestries that combine weaving and tale-telling, the tale they tell being made of a collection of transconscious cultural elements or ghosts. The curtains not only help to stage specific dramatic situations, they also carry with them a cultural, pictorial and human history. They are ghosts of the audience's collective past and present and are therefore symbols with a set of historical functions and meanings.

Curtains on the stage challenged the audience's vision, imagination and memory. They helped the actors and the spectators alike to expand the shape of the early modern stage and gave an added function to the performing body. This chapter aims at unveiling the dramatic and aesthetic role of textile props that have traditionally been seen as nothing other than ornamental fixtures. It will consider plays ranging from the Elizabethan to the Jacobean era, in order to show the continued use of stage-hangings and their increasingly active participation in the production of plays. Caught between their fixedness and the theatre's necessary mobility, curtains will emerge as the *loci* of a dramaturgic and aesthetic debate as well as the expression of spatial and temporal paradoxes. First, therefore, curtains will be considered as dramatic punctuation in a continuous performance. The static essence of the prop will, in such instances, be seen as an element of the rhythmic machinery of the play. However, as 'punctuating' is not limited to the initiation and limitation of the action, the use of curtains as a way of pausing the action and forcing the spectator to focus on their literal and symbolic impact – raising the question of aesthetic mobility – will also be explored. Finally, the discussion about the shape-shifting aspects of the curtains will lead to observations on their paradoxical dematerialisation and rematerialisation during the performance and their impact on the performing body.

STATIC PROPS AND THE CONTINUOUS ACT

The conventional nature of early modern stage-hangings is exemplified by the fact that they were used to identify a play's genre. Early modern spectators entered a venue and, particularly in outdoor theatres, were confronted with a stage space that suggested the type of play they were about to watch. As Tiffany Stern points out in her chapter in this volume, black curtains hiding the doors or the central opening and possibly black curtain valances hanging from the balcony indicated tragedy,[14] while a clown's head peeping through a curtain might indicate comedy.[15] Although such encoding might appear to illustrate the static nature of stage-hangings, it is important to consider the temporal as well as the generic function of the stage curtain. If the curtains define the atmosphere of the play and risk petrifying it into a single genre, contravening its structural hybridity, they also gesture towards what the action will be even before the start of the play. Temporally speaking, the curtains on stage before the play begins inveigle the audience into the action in advance of its starting. Shakespeare refers to the role of stage curtains as significant codes guiding the audience towards the genre of the play at the beginning of *Henry VI Part 1*: 'Hung be you heavens with black, yield day to night' (1.1.1). Thus, the play is identified as the story of the downfall of kings, a tragedy *de casibus*. However, the best example of the impact on the spectators of encoding curtains is to be found the induction of *A Warning for Fair Women* where the allegories of Comedy, History and Tragedy argue about the prevailing genre of the play which is finally exposed as a tragedy thanks to the colour code of the curtains: 'Look Comedy, I marked it not till now, / The stage is hung with black: and I perceive / The Auditors prepared for Tragedy' (Induction 74–6). The play, then, begins with its appearance rather than with its action, which confirms a paradox: the so-called fixed props are dynamic and have a role in sustaining action 'beyond' the play.

In his study of the use of what he calls the discovery space in the Globe theatre, Andrew Gurr notes: 'The players who are "discovered" in the Globe plays are almost all single figures who do not usually move, unless to step out on to the stage [. . .] This kind of static display is the clearest distinguishing feature of the discovery scenes.'[16] The act of drawing the curtains to reveal a solitary figure is a dramatic movement signalling a paradoxical event. Curtains could stage the partial or complete stasis of the character who is revealed, but they also induced his movements.

In the Prologue of Christopher Marlowe's *Doctor Faustus* (1592–93), the audience listens to the Chorus who situates the action and reveals Faustus' physical existence with 'And this the man that in his study sits' (Chor, 28). The use of '*this*' strengthens the impression that the Prologue is pointing at the tiring-house and one of its apertures as he speaks. The scene certainly ends with a revelation in the secondary space, identified by the introductory stage direction to 1.1: '*Faustus in his study*'. There is no mention of a curtain in the stage direction, but the necessity of revealing a character absent from the main stage before suggests that this play requires a curtained space. The curtain would, in such an instance, play the role of a visual landmark that signalled the start of the play. This scene exemplifies the active participation of the curtain property in the ongoing stage movement, for opening it does not mark a break in the dramatic rhythm but, rather, a way of organising the movements of the actors on the stage. The curtain allows the audience to focus on Faustus in his study and not on the retreating Prologue; it also marks the moment when the protagonist animates himself and enters the stage proper. The combination of the curtain's initial stasis and its secondary mobility acts as a dynamic pattern for Faustus' performing body.

As objects, curtains are static only until they are handled by an actor or blown by the wind. The movement of the curtains and also the expectation of this movement creates their dynamism. The spectator hopes that a discovery, signalled by the opening of the curtain, will be offered. The static nature of the prop is thus constantly challenged by the spectator's imagination and expectation. It tantalises audiences and is thus also the *locus* of dynamic tension. Moreover, the liminal status of curtains enables them to enact the perfect transition between different time slots in the play. As space-and-time devices, neither completely static nor mobile, curtains intensify the performance trajectory. They are material thresholds superimposing or separating different characters, places and times. The fixed nature of the prop is enslaved to the ineluctable movement of a theatre performance.

The paradoxical strategy of employing fixity to maintain stage mobility is used not just at the opening of a play, but throughout the performance of the text, as we can see in Shakespeare's and Fletcher's *Henry VIII* (1613). In 2.2 there is an instance of dynamic fluidity in the interplay between curtains as textual necessities and as stage properties:

CHAMBERLAIN

The king has sent me otherwhere. Besides, You'll find a
most unfit time to disturb him.
Health to your lordships.

NORFOLK

Thanks, my good Lord Chamberlain.

*Exit Lord Chamberlain and the King
draws the curtain and sits reading pensively.*

SUFFOLK

How sad he looks. Sure he is much afflicted.

KING HENRY

Who's there? Ha?

NORFOLK

Pray God he be not angry

KING HENRY

Who's there, I say? How dare you thrust yourselves
Into my private meditations?

(2.2.57–64)

Although certain editions rule out the presence of curtains at this
moment, the choice of Gary Taylor and Stanley Wells in their
edition of *The Complete Works*, and Gordon McMullan in his
Arden 3 edition to reintroduce the stage property signalled in the
Folio version of the play is justified by the split-stage effect created
in this scene.[17] Norfolk and Suffolk need to be positioned on stage
so as to observe Henry from afar while the King is made visible in
his study when the Chamberlain exits. The use of the discovery
space and the drawing of the curtains appears to be the dramaturgic device that most enables the performance of this scene. As the
play was performed first at the Globe, it is logical to think that the
actors would have used the flexibility of the stage's structure to
maintain their continuous act. As with Faustus, the character's
entrance is announced by the text before the actual movement of
the actor, for the various lords in waiting on the main stage broad-
cast a royal entrance is about to be made. None the less, from a

staging point of view, the exit of the Chamberlain as the King is revealed or 'enters', questions the Chamberlain's own description of the monarch. The drawing of the curtain establishes a significant connection between the Chamberlain's warning and the royal anger to follow. Henry's drawing of his own curtain strengthens the impression that the characters are intruding into the intimacy of the discovery space; in practical terms, it allows the entrance not to break the continuous act. The originality of such a staging resides in the fact that the curtain is drawn from inside the discovery space. Henry does not need to invade the main stage, for he seems to precede it, giving the impression that the royal meditation has been brutally disrupted.

The opening of the curtain provides a transition between the King's silent retreat and the turmoil of the court. The association of the visual convention of a discovery scene (the drawing of the curtain), and of the aural convention of impaired vision ('Who's there?') suggests that Shakespeare uses the curtains as signifiers of stasis and blindness so as to suggest the protagonist's inner strife. The subtle reversal of the conventional use of the discovery scene signifies the complexity of Henry's paradox. The curtain provokes the stage mobility of both character and performer; its stasis is now displaced on to characterisation. Henry, as a character, is troubled by his incapacity to gain clear insight, signalled by his repetition of the conventional 'Who's there?' The dislocation between the performing body and the character through the paradoxical use of both the textual dramatic convention and the curtains illustrates the character's instability.

Curtains are a stage materialisation of the script, but they are also a means to further the aesthetic impact of a scene. The 'discovery' behind the curtain can be seen as static because the positioning of the curtains gives it pictorial connotations. If curtains play a dynamic role in the exploration of stasis in discovery scenes, it is necessary to question their effects when they stop moving and are dematerialised.

CURTAINS AS PALIMPSESTS

Early modern drama uses curtains both as 'physical and abstract materials',[18] and as the combination of decor and a text. This dual nature of the curtain is obvious when considering its connection with the stage's flexibility. By framing entrances into the tiring-house, the curtains enable the main playing space to appear enlarged, but in themselves they represent a closed, fixed world, where time seems suspended. Drawing the arras reveals an image (a static picture) more than a scene (a moving picture). The ability of curtains to transform a segment of play into an 'icon', an idea inherited from painting, threatens the plasticity of the stage space. Conflating motion and stillness, curtains illustrate the paradoxical essence of stage properties and engage in a complex aesthetic relationship with time and space.

Curtains are recurrent in medieval and early modern visual culture. In pictures, they illustrate scenes of intimacy, prestige, religious and political heroism. And when a scene is brought to a standstill, the physical frame of the drawn curtains turns the stage into a three-dimensional tableau. Drawn curtains have the effect, then, of dissociating the action from vision; they focus the spectators' gaze on the action within the space of the curtains and on what is happening emotionally within the actor's body. Curtains are part of the performance as a whole (the primary action), but not of the specific or secondary action they enhance. Georges Banu underlines the way 'the curtain does not participate in the action it frames, but remains a marginal instrument'.[19] When deprived of mobility, curtains seem momentarily out of the dramatic narrative: they are suspended props. They single out a scene within the scene, and mark a pause in the action, so that the spectator can concentrate on an alternative show. The pictorial nature of the scene thus revealed is both a cause and a consequence of the stasis. This use of the curtains is, however, not confined to discovery scenes; it can apply to other dramatic situations such as scenes where playwrights combine tangible and intangible hangings. This creates a multi-level meta-tableau, inviting the spectator to analyse a moment through a single performing material.

Mobility in such scenes is two-fold: it is conveyed by a mobile character commenting on a static scene, and also by the paradoxical mobility created by the accumulation of different types of curtain-like props.

In 2.2 of *Cymbeline* (1610–11), Shakespeare makes a bold choice: he writes a static scene that is saturated with materials. The original opening stage direction in the Folio is economical with details, '*Enter Imogen in her bed, and a Lady*' but identifies 2.2 as a static scene brought centre stage with the bed as the inner stage. The scene would reach almost a complete standstill were it not for the restrained mobility of Iachimo's illicit intrusion. The beginning of the scene had shown a fairly mobile Imogen, talking and reading within the space of a bed which could have been ornamented with hangings.[20] Yet, progressively the spectacle of the bed ceases to change; Imogen falls asleep, and that is the moment when Iachimo comes out of the trunk and observes her as though she is a beautiful picture:

IACHIMO

[. . .]'tis her breathing that
Perfumes the chamber thus: the flame o'th' taper
Bows toward her, and would under-peep her lids,
To see th'enclosed lights, now canopied
Under these windows, white and azure lac'd
With blue of heaven's own tinct. But my design.
To note the chamber: I will write all down:
Such, and such pictures: there the window, such
Th'adornment of her bed; the arras, figures,
Why, such, and such; the content o'th' story.
Ah, but some natural notes about her body
Above ten thousand meaner moveables
Would testify, t'enrich mine inventory.
O sleep, thou ape of death, lie dull upon her,
And be her sense but as a monument,
Thus in a chapel lying.

(18–33)[21]

The scene is framed by actual and imaginary fabric, and becomes a static 'metapicture'. 'Th'adornment of her bed' may be interpreted as the curtains and the valances adorning a noble bed and 'the arras' could be an allusion either to bed-curtains made of or resembling tapestries, or to the arras or painted cloth hiding the central opening in the tiring-house.[22] The material performance of this scene can follow three possible patterns: no curtains or tapestry whatsoever and an entire reliance on the suggestive power of words; plain bed-curtains and a tapestry or painted cloth hung in front the central opening in the tiring-house wall which would be reinforced by Iachimo's words;[23] bed-curtains and valances made of tapestry with no fabric hanging in front of the central opening combined with the illustrative power of Iachimo's speech. Words intensify the material reality of the performance, but the effect of fabric on the scene changes quite radically from one staging to another. In the two latter scenarios combining bed-curtains and tapestry, the audience is faced with embedded stages reinforcing the stillness of Imogen's framed body. This hyperbolic presence of fabric around her almost transforms the performing body of Imogen into someone two-dimensional, a character in the arras described by Iachimo. Iachimo, meanwhile, is a figure who remains out of the frame of the tableau and points at the pictorial value of the scene. He is the one who tells the audience that the curtains, whether they are made of tapestry or not, are not innocent objects but erotic symbols of domesticity, intimacy and power. However, the complex meaning of such a plethora of materiality is not only confined to the socio-cultural symbolism of the fabric. Curtains are thresholds between the dramaturgy and the text. They represent a theatrical *paragone*[24] as they assume different shapes (bed-curtains and narrative tapestry), and are teamed with other complementary objects (books, movables, architectural elements, etc.). Indeed Iachimo's monologue (2.2.11–51) traces the aesthetic influences visible in the theatre, and turns Imogen into a body emblazoned by material objects, each representing a specific form of artistic expression (love poetry, architecture, interior design, sculpture, tapestry, writing). Imogen's static body on stage enables her to be re-created as a metacharacter: she is the celebrated beauty of Iachimo's awkward Petrarchan emblazoning (16–23), which turns her into the physical embodiment of a series of mythological characters adorning domestic objects, each of which is attached to a specific artistic medium.

Indeed she is first, through oblique references to Tarquin and to Cytherea (2.2), turned into a dubious Lucrece:[25]

IACHIMO
> Our Tarquin thus
> Did softly press the rushes, ere he waken'd
> The chastity he wounded. Cytherea,
> How bravely thou becom'st thy bed!
>
> (12–15)

Then she is compared with both Philomel[26] and a funeral image: she is assimilated with a 'monument, / Thus in a chapel lying' (2.2.32–3), and Iachimo specifies the content of the book she holds on her lap as though in prayer, 'She hath been reading late, / The tale of Tereus' (44–5).[27] Earlier in this speech when Iachimo says, 'I will write all down: / Such, and such pictures: there the window, such / Th'adornment of her bed; the arras, figures' (24–6) his use of the term 'figures' could allude to the figure in the arras, Cleopatra, flanked presumably by a paramour (2.4.69–74), or to a carving representing Diana (2.4.80–5), similarly flanked. His hesitation illustrates the role of the physical and the abstract body of the dramatic character as the possible *locus* for a conclusive paragone or artistic comparison. Indeed, Imogen, whose lips are ironically identified as 'Rubies unparagon'd' (2.2.17), is the *locus* of the resolution of the *paragone* in drama: the static performing body of the actor is the place of a *discordia concors* – a harmonious discord – between different art forms shaping theatre.

Thanks to the enclosure of Imogen's body within what are apparently drawn bed-curtains, Shakespeare offers the audience a multiple experience: through its own eyes, and through those of Iachimo, a surrogate viewer. The curtains frame a scene where the only form of mobility is through the limited movements of

Iachimo, and through the spectator's imagination, stimulated by objects both physical and abstract, or, as Carlson put it, 'memory-haunted material products'.[28] Every object Iachimo mentions brings with it a tale that is mythological or historical. Both myth and history, then, are ghostly entities that add to the meaning of the object and help to deepen the dramatic characterisation of the semi-active Iachimo, who is turned into a potential rapist through the references to Tarquin and Tereus, while Imogen is portrayed as a contradictory figure of lust (Venus), political bravery (Cleopatra) and endangered chastity (Lucrece and Philomel). The stasis is endowed with a form of thematic mobility that combines Shakespeare's play and the 'audience's collective and individual memories'.[29] Thus the stasis questions the impact of memory on the stage property. The textual tapestry woven by Iachimo in *Cymbeline* relies on an increase in timeless cultural references that offer the spectator a static experience of vision combined with a reinvention of the iconic figures that have been visible in the hangings. The images are now embodied in the actors and the scene could be interpreted as a three-dimensional expression of the arras evoked in the text. Considering the spectators' memories in terms of performance time is another way of exploring the paradoxical materiality of the early modern stage: inert objects are sometimes endowed with autonomous mobility in time.

CURTAINS AND THE PERFORMING BODY

Performance turns objects into props: it is only when an object is actively part of the performance that it gains a real theatrical value. At that moment 'we perceive [the props] as spontaneous subjects, equivalent to the figure of the actor'.[30] Though the spontaneity of the prop can be questioned – a static object needs an external force to motivate it – the moment when the prop and the actor come together can still be seen as the ultimate level of performance for an object on stage. This moment is, however, hard to define. Can a prop ever overtake or replace the actor, the palimpsest (overlaid text) becoming the inspiration for the actor's performance?

In order to pad out the space in lieu of an extra actor on stage, or to give an account of an offstage situation, curtains are sometimes used as material reminders of an absent body. Their role as stimuli for the spectators' immediate memory turns them into material actors in their own right. This gives them a certain level of symbolic autonomy, as they have two new interrelated functions: 'surrogation'[31] and a variant of this substituting strategy, 'remanence' or 'after-imagery'.[32]

'Surrogation' describes the moment when actor and prop are fused: for instance, when the skull becomes the sole visual expression of Yorick's body in *Hamlet* (1600–01). When the actor transfers human characteristics on to the object, the prop becomes more than a substitute; it becomes a performing object. The paradoxical association of the mobility of the actor's body and the stasis of the object climaxes in the interaction between prop and actor. When the actor largely disappears behind a curtain but leaves a hand or a leg to be seen or a voice to be heard, on the other hand, the effect produced on the spectator is that of 'remanence'. The actor's body, though incomplete or thoroughly invisible, is recalled in the spectator's mind through association with the prop. The concept of remanence explains how an image can remain partially present after it has disappeared. Though a fundamental concept to scholars writing about cinema, remenence is an equally useful way to describe staged drama: our retinas likewise retain the ghost image of some event already seen when we look at certain props. In the case of surrogation, the prop fully substitutes for the actor while, in the case of remanence, it reminds us of the actor's semi-invisible presence, functioning almost like a surface on which the actor's body can still be seen.

The curtain is defamiliarised and reinvented in the immediate memory as it comes to seem a materialisation of a spectral body. In Shakespeare, one example of this is used with the arras in *Hamlet*. The development of 3.4, 'the closet scene', reveals the way a stage-hanging is metamorphosed into a performing object that then itself becomes the memory of a performance. In this scene, the arras seems to stand for a threatening otherness, but also for the place of metamorphosis – a metamorphosis that will alter the concept of the object and the character's and actor's body. Ironically, Hamlet repeats 'What's the matter?' twice (3.4.7, 12), as though questioning the true nature of his material (made of matter) environment as well as his mother's purpose. The words focus the spectator's attention on the arras, behind which hides Polonius. The materiality of the stage-hanging is, in this instance, endowed with a double physicality: it is a reminder of the recently visible performing body of Polonius (1–6), and it is a surrogate for his skin: Hamlet will pierce both curtain and man with his dagger (23). The curtain, then, is both a metonymy for the actor playing Polonius, and for a part of his body: this dislocation of both actively participates in the destruction of the character and the intensification of the performance. The dramaturgic structuring of the scene emphasises the metamorphic process undergone by the arras. From lines 1 to 6, the curtain is used conventionally, then it is questioned, and finally it becomes a surrogate actor. Shakespeare's language reveals the simultaneity of the character's and of the arras' metamorphosis. When Polonius decides to hide behind the arras, he transforms it into a dangerous material reducing him to silence, 'I'll silence me even here' (4) in Q2 and F, while in Q1 he proleptically declares: 'I'll shroud myself here',[33] and turns it from an ornamental piece signalling an intimate domestic space into a symbol of death. In both cases the irony is preserved, yet Q1 has a greater impact as the arras is truly identified as deadly. The lethal proximity between Polonius' body and the curtain is symbolically asserted through the funerary image – 'shroud' – and increases the disquieting superimposition of the curtain and the performing body. This fusion of actor and prop through the medium of the curtain creates a synchronicity that is reinforced by the strange relationship of the curtain with the time of the murder and the time of the play. The arras does not only symbolise a present that is converted into an immediate past, it also represents the future. It represents the present before the murder takes place, the present during the murder, and the past afterwards, as it acts as a reminder of the murder that has happened. The linearity of time is abolished, the materiality of the tapestry is defamiliarised as Polonius' humanity is questioned by Hamlet's animal lexicon ('A rat', 22), and by his voice's absorption within the stage-hanging. The effect guarantees that Polonius is dehumanised as he moves from man to animal, from animal to symbolic object. None the less, the curtain is not simply a metonymic materialisation of the body; in its superimposition of immediate past, present and future (future, in that it is a material prolepsis announcing the short-term future of the action), it shows a dynamic depiction of the progress from life to death.

If curtains are used as surrogates for the actor's body, then actors' postures are equally sometimes surrogates for curtains: when the body is flattened and turned into an inert prop, it can become like a stage-hanging. Actors' bodies are enhanced by cloth but they can also be the raw material for cloths. In *Antonio's Revenge*, John Marston superimposes a tortured body on the black curtains used to create the 'black-visaged shows' (19–20) described as the decor of tragedies in the Prologue. The martyred body of Antonio absorbs the materiality of the curtains of tragedy, and is in turn exposed as, himself, a tragic stage-hanging:

ANTONIO

> See, look, the curtain stirs; shine nature's pride,
> Love's vital spirit, dear Antonio's bride!

>> *The curtain's drawn and the body of Feliche,*
>> *stabbed thick with wounds, appears hung up.*

> What villain bloods the window of my love?
> What slave hath hung yon gory ensign up,
> In flat defiance of humanity?
> Awake, thou fair unspotted purity,
> Death's at thy window! Awake, bright Mellida!
> Antonio calls.

(1.3.128–135)

This scene is particularly interesting for it is a disquieting rewriting of *Romeo and Juliet*'s balcony scene. Antonio is on the main stage looking up at the gallery where Mellida's window is situated. Just as in a love scene, he observes his place and awaits a sign of the beloved's presence. Yet Marston turns the expected display of beauty into a display of cruelty. The vertical division of the performing space – the distance between the horrible picture that is to be discovered (and that hangs above), and the placement of Antonio below – increases the framing effect of the scene. Instead of describing Mellida's beauty, Antonio is now compelled to describe the wounds of Feliche, an opponent to Mellida's tyrannical father in the previous play, *Antonio and Mellida* (1599), who helps the endangered couple. The words intensify the visual effect, as though Feliche's body itself is symbolically changed into a cloth, for once the actual curtain has been drawn, the body becomes an unnatural tapestry in its own right. Antonio suggests this using the words 'hung', 'ensign' (i.e. banner) and 'flat' to highlight the transformation of Feliche's body into an ornamental fabric as he is shown hanging from the gallery for the entire first act. As a result, Feliche becomes a curtain made of flesh, as is shown by the play's recurring references to the gory spectacle of his hanging body throughout the first act.[34] Marston's emblazoning of a tormented body leads to a flattening of the performing body, now materialised as a substitute stage-hanging. This pushes further a dramaturgic strategy that Christopher Marlowe had used in *2 Tamburlaine* (1590).[35] Marston here shows how stage-hangings could impact on the writing and performance effects of Elizabethan and Jacobean drama.

On the early modern stage, curtains progressively become paradoxical material markers. They enable the coexistence of traditional symbolism with novel stage activity and stage design. Some of the curtains' more complicated uses have survived even into modern performances. The problematic fixity of the prop was exploited by Steven Pimlott in his 2001 version of *Hamlet* for the Royal Shakespeare Company. Pimlott chose, for the scene of the murder of Polonius behind the arras, to add only few, but significant, properties to an otherwise bare stage. This choice raised questions as to where Polonius was to hide. What Pimlott did was to make the arras into a white screen, similar to a cinematic frame. Behind this screen could be seen the backlit shadow of Polonius. When Hamlet cried 'a rat', he tore the screen with his dagger: the inanimate prop was brutally animated by tearing as Polonius' hitherto animate human body fell into stillness. Thus, the stage prop still enables a significant though ambivalent depiction of stillness where the prop and the performing body swap places or are fused together creating the illusion of a life in death. Through the 'performing' curtain in this scene, Polonius is transformed into an object in a *vanitas* painting, a lesson about the transience of life learned and to be learned. Curtains, with their physical and abstract meanings, are not simply ornaments; they are instruments turning the playwright's language into performance.

PART TWO

TECHNOLOGIES OF THE BODY

PART TWO

TECHNIQUES OF THE BODY

CHAPTER FOUR

'*THEY EAT EACH OTHER'S ARMS*':
STAGE BLOOD AND BODY PARTS
LUCY MUNRO

One of the odder stage directions in early modern drama, the title of this essay is taken from *Claudius Tiberius Nero*, a tragedy which first appeared in print in 1607. The play focuses on the villainy of the Roman Emperor Tiberius, and in one of the many deaths that cluster in its climactic final stages, his two unfortunate nephews, Drusus and Nero, starve to death in a prison cell. Before they die, however, they attempt to feed each other with their own flesh; 'If thy hungry woolfe doe vexe thy soule', Drusus tells Nero, 'Feed on these cates, taste on this brawnie arme, / That will rejoyce to feede thy appetite', the exchange eventually climaxing in the direction '*They eate each others armes*'.[1] Although Drusus laments that they should be forced 'To be such loving Romane Canibals', the brothers are apparently unable to digest one another's flesh anyway; they die before the eyes of a third brother, Caligula.

Claudius Tiberius Nero has never been considered central to the early modern dramatic canon. Its authorship is unknown, and it may have been written for the academic rather than the commercial stage.[2] However, I begin with this traumatic moment because it brings together a set of key issues that underlie and form the basis of this chapter. First, it raises practical questions about how the body-part effect might have been brought about. It is possible that the dialogue was expected to do the bulk of the work, and that the actors were merely expected to nibble on each other's arms. But in the context of this notably sensationalist play, it is probable that something more complex and spectacular was envisaged, involving false limbs of the kind that appear in plays such as

Christopher Marlowe's *Dr Faustus* (?Strange's Men/Pembroke's Men, 1588–93), Robert Greene's *Orlando Furioso* (Queen's Men/Strange's Men, c.1591) or Robert Yarington's *Two Lamentable Tragedies* (?Admiral's Men, 1594–98), and/or the use of stage blood.[3] In this case, the effect would depend on the interplay between the brothers' gruesome speeches and the actors' dextrous handling of props.

Second, the use of stage blood and dismembered body parts has the potential to arouse a range of conflicting emotions, and to trouble seemingly hard-and-fast distinctions between prop and character, subject and object. The affective power of gory special effects has long been a contested area, particularly in relation to Shakespearean plays such as *Titus Andronicus*. As Katherine Rowe remarks, 'Read as grotesque and abstract, aesthetically engaging and distancing, dramatically pivotal and superfluous, the severed hands, heads, and tongue [of *Titus Andronicus*] have always had a profoundly equivocal status in the critical and theatrical reception of the play.'[4] The equivocal effect of staged body parts is also evident in *Claudius Tiberius Nero*, in which the moment at which the brothers attempt to consume one another's flesh has the capacity to provoke a range of conflicting emotions, including horror, incredulity and even amusement.

Moreover, the very theatricality of the use of the bloodied and fragmented body also raises important questions about its emotional impact and its effect on a spectator's understanding of the staged body's ontological status. Rowe's question about how dismembered body parts should be understood – 'As part of the world of stage properties or of character?' – is important not just for Shakespeare's plays but for the range of plays produced by his contemporaries and successors. As Margaret E. Owens remarks in her important study of dismemberment on the medieval and early modern stage, 'When a limb is amputated, the detached body part enters a disturbingly liminal state somewhere between subject and object status.'[5] In theatrical terms, it also blurs the distinctions between object and actor; Andrew Sofer asks, 'if any *thing* can become a prop, does this necessarily mean that *any*thing can become a prop? What of the human body itself?'[6] *Claudius Tiberius Nero*'s scene of cannibalism foregrounds this tendency: as the bodies of the brothers become potential sources of nourishment, the boundary between the eater and the eaten, between subject and object, is confused, and they become, in Julia Kristeva's term, 'abject', produced by and symbolic of a wider cultural and political crisis.[7]

These effects should also be viewed in relation to a third key issue: the way in which gory stage effects can also work on a spectator's intellect, invoking a range of broader thematic and symbolic contexts and associations. Drusus and Nero's cannibalism is not merely designed to shock, but to provide a horrifically spectacular example of both the control of the tyrant and the potential limits of that control. The brothers' fate is thematically and dramaturgically connected with the death of their mother, Agrippina, who in the preceding scene had choked on the food that she had been force-fed by Tiberius, whom she called 'Detested tyrant' shortly before her death (sig. M2r). The Roman setting is crucial; as David Carnegie writes, summarising the views of Clifford Ronan, 'in the Early Modern view, Romans had an almost physical appetite for human gore – an insatiable urge that variously demonizes them, wraps them in pathos, or makes caricatures of them'.[8] Plays such as *Claudius Tiberius Nero*, *Titus Andronicus*, Shakespeare's *Julius Caesar* (Chamberlain's Men, c.1599), and Webster and Heywood's *Appius and Virginia* (auspices uncertain, c.1625–26)[9] display this sanguineous tendency in different ways, but they share common concerns. When Drusus and Nero '*eate each others armes*', Brutus and the conspirators dip their hands in Caesar's blood, Lavinia enters '*her hands cut off and her tongue cut out, and ravished*' (2.3.0sd), or Virginius enters '*with a knife, that and his arms stript up to the elbowes all bloudy*' after his murder of his daughter Virginia,[10] stage blood and violence against the human body represent in vividly theatrical fashion both the exercise of tyranny and attempts to control or pre-empt it.

As a number of critics have explored, stage blood and severed limbs might have specific social and iconographical functions. One of the most famous examples can be found in *Titus Andronicus*, in which the hands lost by Lavinia and Titus are surrounded not only by a series of bleak jokes and puns – '''Tis well, Lavinia, that thou hast no hands, / For hands to do Rome service is but vain' (3.1.80–1); 'Lend me thy hand, and I will give thee mine' (3.1.188) – but also a sustained network of figurative associations. In Rowe's reading of *Titus Andronicus*, which draws on political theory and the emblem-book tradition, the hand is said to 'figure the martial, marital, and genealogical bonds so much at risk [. . .] In its vulnerability to loss and theft, its mobility onstage, the dead hand in Shakespeare's play paradoxically exemplifies the contingent and supplementary *condition* of agency.'[11] *Claudius Tiberius Nero* draws on these conventions, but the strongest iconographic tradition recalled is that of the pelican, which was famously said to feed its offspring on its own flesh. First appearing in the English emblem tradition in Geoffrey Witney's *A Choice of Emblems* (1586), the pelican and its self-sacrifice might represent divine love, dedication to one's country or parental devotion.[12] Each of these qualities is missing in *Claudius Tiberius Nero*, in which attempts at mutual protection or pelican-like self-sacrifice are characterised as deluded or futile; moreover, Drusus' description of himself and Nero as 'such loving Romane Canibals' also suggests the extent to which Rome as parent is consuming its children – an ironic reversal of the pelican motif.

The fourth, and final, issue *Claudius Tiberius Nero* raises is one of genre and tone. For obvious reasons, stage blood is often associated with tragedy – 'When the bad bleedes, then is the Tragedie good,' declares Vindice in Thomas Middleton's *The Revenger's Tragedy* (King's Men, c.1606), just after he and his brother have cut out the tongue of the depraved Duke.[13] *Claudius Tiberius Nero* is generally thought to be serious in its intention, if not always in its execution; as Anne Barton dryly remarks, 'Any intrusion of the comic spirit is entirely accidental'.[14] None the less, stage effects involving blood and body parts can often create an uncertainty of tone – it does not take much for *grand guignol* (a sensationalistic horror show) to tip into parody or even farce. The sequence in which Drusus and Nero '*eate each others armes*' might have provoked nervous or even wholehearted laughter from its early spectators, as it did at a staged reading of the play at Shakespeare's Globe in July 2006.[15] The ambiguity of tone occasioned by blood and body parts is not, however, always – or even usually – accidental; early modern playwrights were as alert as any twentieth- or twenty-first-century director of horror films to the disturbing effects that might be created through a combination of comedy and gore.

The remainder of this chapter explores the issues raised above in greater detail, attempting to put together a picture of the aesthetic, sensory and bodily impact of blood and dismembered body parts in the early modern playhouse. Surveying the use of stage blood and body parts in plays written between the 1560s and the 1640s, I focus in particular on the rare cases where specific effects and techniques are described in stage directions, arguing that the force of the early modern stage's use of blood and gore lies in its capacity for simultaneous naturalism and stylisation. Stage blood and dismembered body parts are rarely purely or simply naturalistic in their effect, despite W. W. Greg's dismissive comments on the 'crudely realistic methods of the Elizabethan stage'.[16] Instead, their impact lies not merely in the fact that blood and body parts are present on stage, but in the precise ways in which they are used.

The first section, 'Enter [. . .] bleeding', focuses on stage blood, tracing the evidence for its use and the problems that it might have caused early modern theatre companies, before turning to look in detail at two tragedies: Shakespeare's *Julius Caesar* and George Peele's *The Battle of Alcazar* (?Strange's Men, c.1588–89). Despite their differences in theme and technique, in these plays blood is both corporeal and symbolic, appealing to spectators' eyes, emotions and intelligence simultaneously. The second section, 'Enter "with a leg"', focuses on the fragmented body on the early modern stage. After plotting the ways in which different body parts appear in plays, I turn explicitly to the question of genre, looking at two tragicomic texts, Greene's *Orlando Furioso* and

Shakespeare's *Cymbeline* (King's Men, c.1609–11). The bulk of critical attention paid to gory special effects on the early modern stage has focused on tragedy and, to a lesser extent, the Elizabethan history play.[17] This is understandable, given the prominence of bloody effects in these plays; it has led, however, to the neglect of those plays in which stage blood and dismembered body parts are part of a wider negotiation of, and experimentation with, genre and tone. In an effort to redress this balance, I incorporate in both sections references to a number of plays which are not conventionally tragic; in looking in detail at *Orlando Furioso* and *Cymbeline* I argue that dismemberment can play a crucial role in the creation of a dramaturgy that is not wholly or uncomplicatedly comic or tragic.

'ENTER . . . BLEEDING'

Although often incomplete or missing, the stage directions of early modern plays – in both print and manuscript copies – present an intriguing picture of the use of stage blood and body parts.[18] More than sixty early modern plays include explicit references to blood in their stage directions, indicating that characters should enter 'bloody' or 'bleeding', 'smeared' or 'besmeared' with blood, or that they should carry 'bloody' swords, knives, handkerchiefs and other props. Characters might be wounded on stage and 'bleed', or they might 'bloody' themselves with the blood of others. These directions strongly suggest the use of stage blood, and it is probable that directions for characters to be 'wounded', 'hurt' or 'stabbed', which feature in more than 150 plays, also signal the use of stage blood.[19] In many other plays the action implicitly calls for blood even though none is mentioned in the stage directions. For example, in Shakespeare's *King Lear* (King's Men, 1605–06), Edmund pretends to have been injured at his brother Edgar's hands, commenting 'Some blood drawn on me would beget opinion / Of my more fierce endeavour' (2.1.34–5); there is no stage direction in either the quarto or folio text of the play, but the use of stage blood when Edmund wounds himself is suggested not only by this comment but also in his plea to Gloucester 'Look, sir, I bleed' (2.1.41). Dialogue here apparently first prepares an audience for the appearance of stage blood and then directs their attention towards it.

The vast majority of occasions on which stage blood is demanded involve actors entering the stage wearing bloodied clothes, carrying bloodied items, or with parts of their bodies smeared with blood: 'He draweth out a bloudie Napkin'; *'Enter Block bleeding, Gloster with him'*; *'Enter Butler bleeding'*; *'Her hands bloody with a knife'*; *'Enter Buffe woman, her head and face bleeding, and many women, as from a Prize'*.[20] Murder victims and ghosts are often required to display bleeding wounds, which indict their murderers and wordlessly declare their guilt. In Barnabe Barnes' *The Devil's Charter* (King's Men, 1607), a devil presents to Pope Alexander a vision of 'Gismond Viselli, *his wounds gaping and after him* Lucrece *undrest, holding a dagger fix't in his bleeding bosome'*, replaying the scene of Viselli's murder earlier in the play.[21] Similarly, allegorical figures such as Avarice, Homicide, Cruelty, Murder, Tragedy and Envy, and mythological figures such as Atë and Nemesis, appear smeared with blood, or carrying bloody props.[22] Prevalent in plays of the 1590s, this tradition is possibly recalled by Shakespeare in *Coriolanus* (King's Men, c.1609) when Martius appears on the battlefield *'bleeding, assaulted by the enemy'* (1.4.62sd) and is described by Cominius as looking 'as he were flay'd' (1.6.22).

Plays occasionally include information about the substances that were used to create these effects. Sheep's blood is specified in the 'plot' of George Peele's *The Battle of Alcazar*, apparently prepared for a revival by the Admiral's Men circa 1600–01, which requires '3·violls / of blood / & a sheeps / gather', 'raw / flesh' and 'Dead / mens heads / & bon<es> / banquett / blood'.[23] The fact that the reference to blood is followed by the reference to a 'sheeps / gather', or heart, liver and lungs, has suggested to theatre historians that real sheep's blood is required here.[24] This impression is reinforced by the apparent use of animal blood in conjuring tricks. For instance, in *The Discovery of Witchcraft* (1584), Reginald Scot describes a trick in which the juggler might appear to stab himself in the stomach by placing between a 'plate' and a 'false bellie' 'a gut or bladder of blood, which bloud must be of a calfe or of a sheepe; but in no wise of an oxe or a cow, for that will be too thicke'.[25]

There are, however, references to other red substances being used as blood in medieval and early modern plays. Stage directions in Thomas Preston's *Cambises* (auspices uncertain, c.1561) read 'strike him in divers places [. . .] A little bladder of Vineger prikt', as Cruelty gleefully declares, 'Even now I strike his body to wound: / Beholde now his blood springs out on the ground'.[26] Philip Butterworth points out a reference in the *Volume of Secrets of a Provençal Stage Director's Book*, dating to the late fifteenth or early sixteenth century, to 'vermilion', a bright scarlet pigment also used as a cosmetic;[27] vermilion is also mentioned in the payments made by Canterbury officials in 1528–9, apparently for a play on the subject of St Thomas.[28] In Kyd's *The Spanish Tragedy*, a stage direction suggests that Bel-Imperia's blood – in which she writes a letter to Hieronimo – is represented by 'Red incke' (E2r). Paint is specified in other medieval and early modern plays; in a sixteenth-century passion play performed at Lucerne, for instance, the actor playing Christ goes up to the mount for the third time, where 'the painter inside the mount is to splash him with the blood'.[29] The fact that paint might be used to represent blood perhaps suggests a metatheatrical edge to Shakespeare's use of the word 'paint' in relation to blood; for instance, when the French King in *Henry V* complains that 'Harry England [. . .] sweeps through our land / With pennons painted in the blood of Harfleur' (3.5.48–9) or when York in *3 Henry VI* describes his son, Edward, 'With purple falchion, painted to the hilt / In blood of those that had encounter'd him' (1.4.11–13).

As Jenny Tiramani, Director of Theatre Design at Shakespeare's Globe between 1996 and 2005, and Andrea Stevens, another contributor to this volume, have both argued, professional theatre companies would have seen a financial imperative in controlling the appearance of blood on their stages.[30] Clothing was expensive – especially the ornate costume often worn in tragedies focusing on affairs of state – and difficult to clean effectively, even with the use of substances such as soap, lye (a mixture of ashes and water) or urine.[31] Furthermore, all of the substances thought to have been used to represent blood on the stage – animal blood, vinegar, vermilion, ink, paint – were highly staining, making an already tough job even more challenging.

It is therefore perhaps unsurprising that a character normally enters with the blood already applied to an object, body part or item of clothing, and on the rare occasions when blood is required to be shed or otherwise manipulated on stage, considerable care is taken with it. In *The Fair Maid of Bristow* (King's Men, 1603–04) we find the explicit instruction: 'Heere he stabs his arme, and blodies Sentloes face, and pluckes out vallingers sword and blodies it, and laies it by him', and a similar direction is found in James Shirley's *The Politician* (Queen Henrietta Maria's Men, c.1639): '*Wounds him.* [. . .] *He bloodies himselfe with Sueno's blood, and falls down as dead*'.[32] A symbolic sequence in *A Warning for Fair Women* (Chamberlain's Men, c.1598), in which Tragedy dips the fingers of the future murderers in blood, none the less controls the risk of blood getting on expensive props or clothing by apparently having all of the characters exit immediately.[33]

Plays written by professional dramatists occasionally drop more concrete hints about the ways in which stage blood was managed on stage. Thomas Killigrew, active in the commercial theatre before and after the Civil War, twice specifies the use of a concealed sponge to produce a bloody effect. In *The Princess*, performed by the King's Men around 1637, and revived in 1661, we find the direction '*Bragadine shoots, Virgil puts his hand to his eye, with a bloody spunge and the blood runs down.*'[34] A similar direction appears in *Thomaso, or The Wanderer*, written around 1654, and projected for an all-female performance in 1664: 'Edwardo *strikes him, and they cuff in the Bed;* Edwardo *throws him down, there they cuff and struggle upon the floore, and are both bloody, occasion'd by little spunges ty'd of purpose to their middle fingers in the palmes of their hands.*'[35] Although the extant texts of both plays may incorporate Restoration stage practices, and *Thomaso* was apparently originally written as a closet drama – that is, a play aimed primarily at readers, which was almost certainly not staged – it is probable that sponges were also used before the Civil War. In *The Discovery of Witchcraft*, Scot describes a trick through which a conjurer might appear to stab himself:

> Take a bodkin so made, as the haft being hollowe, the blade thereof may slip thereinto as soone as you hold the point upward: and set the same to your forehead, and seeme to thrust it into your head, and so (with a little sponge in your hand) you may wring out bloud or wine, making the beholders thinke the bloud of the wine (whereof you may saie you have drunke verie much) runneth out of your forehead.
>
> (347)

Sponges could be used to deploy and to control blood, enabling an actor to draw additional attention to the 'wound' by clasping it with a hand.

On the rare occasions when blood flows freely, the plays concerned generally derive from the amateur rather than professional stage. When the title character in Thomas Goffe's *The Tragedy of Orestes* (Christ Church College, Oxford, c.1613–18) kills the little son of Clytemnestra and Aegisthus, stage directions and dialogue both suggest an atypically unrestrained use of blood. Orestes tells Aegisthus,

Yes, hee is thine, thy face, thy eyes, thy heart,
And would I knew where Nature had couchd most,
Of thy damnd blood, I thus would let it out,   *Stabs the child*.
And thus't should spirt in thy most loathed face.[36]

He later says of the child, 'Therefore this dies, this first shall have his due: / This mischiefe done, revenge shall prompt a new', and the stage direction indicates that he '*Stabs* [the child] *againe, that the blood spirts in* [Aegisthus'] *face. Turnes* [the child] *to* [Clytemnestra]'. The action, and the movement of the blood, is suggested by Aegisthus' response: 'O, the Gods blush, and heaven looks pale at this, / A fathers face besmear'd with his owne blood' (sig. G4v). Finally, Orestes '*Fills two cups with the childs blood:* [and] *gives it them* [i.e. Clytemnestra and Aegisthus]' (sig. H1r). The butchery of the child and the brutal treatment of his parents is obviously designed to shock, and to underline the extreme nature of Orestes' vengeance, and it is possible that the university stage – in which performances were one-offs and there was no need to recycle costumes – was able to be more gratuitous in its use of gory spectacle.

Even more freedom is displayed in T.B.'s *The Rebellion of Naples* (1649) which was apparently written as a closet play. The author apparently imagines blood spraying out from the decapitated Massenello, and provides the lurid stage direction, '*He thrusts out his head, and they cut off a false head made of a bladder fill'd with bloud.*'[37] T.B.'s imagination has apparently been fuelled by the gory effects of the professional and university stage; however, writing for the page rather than the stage, he did not have the practicalities of stained and ruined costumes to contend with. His stage direction suggests one way in which the effect might be achieved, but a professional company would probably have baulked at performing it in this way.

The material surveyed thus far sheds light, I suggest, on the treatment of stage blood in canonical plays such as *Julius Caesar*. In the aftermath of Caesar's assassination, Brutus tells his co-conspirators,

> Stoop, Romans, stoop,
> And let us bathe our hands in Caesar's blood
> Up to the elbows, and besmear our swords:
> Then walk we forth, even to the market-place,
> And waving our red weapons o'er our heads,
> Let's all cry, 'Peace, freedom, and liberty!
> (3.1.105–10)

When Mark Antony shakes hands with all of the conspirators in turn, the blood spreads to his hands. The play's language mimics and expands on this process; as Simona Corso summarises, the one

hundred mouths that Calphurnia imagines spitting blood from
Caesar's statue 'anticipate the thirty-three stabs on Caesar's body,
which become as many wounds, spilling blood just like Antony's
eyes spill their tears [. . .] the wounds are then transformed into
open but silent mouths with ruby lips, which command Antony to
speak on their behalf [. . .] Finally, after the funerary speech, the
silent mouths spill blood [. . .] but this time it is the blood of civil
war.'[38] Stage blood addresses the eye and, if animal blood was used,
the nose, while a consistently developed rhetoric of blood addresses
the ear; together, they create a multi-sensory impression of violence
and bloodshed. However, the spread of blood through the play's
language has perhaps encouraged critics to imagine it flowing too
freely in the assassination scene itself. The impact of the stage
blood is arguably more powerful if it is confined to the hands and
weapons of the assassins; *pace* Leo Kirschbaum, these are not
simply 'naturalistic stage effects' but effects that are simultaneously 'real' and symbolic.[39] The symbolic meaning is, however,
contested. While Brutus intends Caesar's blood to symbolise
'Peace, freedom, and liberty', it quickly gathers associations with
sacrifice, indiscriminate murder and the bloodshed that is to follow
as the state descends into civil war.

A still more heightened use of stage blood can be seen in one of
the most important sources for its use on the early modern stage:
Peele's *The Battle of Alcazar*. Although the play has often been
treated merely as evidence of 'realistic' stage practices, the interplay between verbal and visual elements in this play suggests that
its aesthetics are far more complex than Greg and others have been
prepared to admit. The tone is established in the dialogue of the
surviving playbook when, in the Presenter's first speech, Muly
Hamet is described as 'Blacke in his looke, and bloudie in his
deeds, / And in his shirt staind with a cloud of gore'.[40] However,
while the play's rhetorical style creates the expectation that bloody
stage effects will follow, Peele is remarkably adroit in his handling
of gore. Blood features heavily, but it is confined for the most part
to the Presenter's dumbshows, which often prefigure in stylised
form the events of later scenes. The Act 3 Prologue opens with the

lines 'Lo thus into a lake of bloud and gore, / The brave coura-
gious king of Portugall / Hath drencht himselfe' (D1r), and the
Plot suggests that a dumbshow – using the vials of blood and
sheep's gather mentioned above – will display the disembowelling
of King Sebastian, Stukely and Muly Hamet at the hands of the
Fates:

> *Enter Nemesis above* [. . .] *to her 3 · Furies bringin<g> in
> the Scales* [. . .] *to them <3_> div<e>lls* [. . .] *to them 3
> ghosts <:> w_* [. . .] *the Furies* [. . .] *<First Fech in
> Sebastian> & Carrie him out <againe, which done they>
> Fech in Stukeley <& Carrie him out, then> bring in the
> Moo<re & Carrie him out.*[41]

The impression that Sebastian, Stukeley and Muly Hamet are
doomed to a bloody death is reinforced by their appearance, with
the Duke of Avero, in a bloody banquet in the Act 4 Prologue,
where the Furies enter *'one wth blood to Dy<ppe li>ghts : <one>
<w>th Dead mens head<s > in dishes : an<o>ther <wt>h Dead mens
bon<es>'*. In the event, however, a spectator eagerly expecting
these characters to die bloodily on stage will be disappointed:
Sebastian and Muly Hamet actually die off stage, and only Stukeley,
who dies 'slaine with many a deadly stab' (F3v) at the hands of a
pair of Italian soldiers, is granted the luxury of a dying speech.

Like that of *Julius Caesar*, *The Battle of Alcazar*'s use of stage
blood is not the product of Elizabethan proto-naturalism. These
are not 'realistic' scenes, crude or otherwise; they display instead a
calculated use of gory spectacle in pursuit of very particular narrative ends, in which the future victims are objectified and made
abject, marked out as the victims of an arbitrary supernatural
force. Indeed, the function of these sequences is not unlike that of
the 'Penny Arcade Nightmares' in *Titus*, Julie Taymor's 1999 film
adaptation of *Titus Andronicus* – they are dream-like sequences
which rework, replay and project the events of the narrative in
fantastic form.[42] Peele's dumb shows are representations of the
dark heart of the play and its vision of tragedy, physical expressions of its blood-and-thunder rhetoric.

ENTER 'WITH A LEG'

A similar interplay between the corporeal and the symbolic is evident in the use of dismembered body parts on the early modern stage. Sources for our knowledge of these props include not only stage directions, but also a set of lists of the props and costumes belonging to the Admiral's Men in March 1598. These include, among other items, 'owld Mahemetes head', 'Faetones lymes', 'Argosse head', 'Kentes woden leags', 'Jerosses head', 'i frame for the heading in Black Jone', 'The Mores lymes, and Hercolles lymes' and 'iiii Turckes hedes'.[43] Like the sixty-plus surviving play-texts that mention such properties in their stage directions, these lists testify to the prominence of dismembered body parts on the early modern stage.

As the Admiral's Men's list of props suggests, heads most frequently appear, either newly severed or in the form of skulls. Newly severed heads are sometimes anonymous; for instance, the Roman's head presented by Caratach to his little nephew, Hengo, in John Fletcher's *Bonduca* (King's Men, 1611–14), or the dead man's head which the traitorous Edricus takes up on the battlefield and presents as that of his king in order to discourage the English troops in *Edmond Ironside* (auspices uncertain, c.1590). More often, however, the head is associated with a specific character, generally a victim of political violence, a rebel or a tyrant. The moment in *Macbeth* when Macduff appears '*with Macbeth's head*' (5.9.19sd) not only mirrors the appearance of the 'armed head' in the witches' lair (4.1.68sd), but also echoes the appearance of Lluellen's head in Peele's *Edward I* (Queen Elizabeth's Men, 1590–93), Jack Cade's head in *2 Henry VI* (?Pembroke's Men/ Strange's Men, c.1590–92), O'Neill's head in *Captain Thomas Stukeley* (Admiral's Men, 1596), Cromwell's head in *Thomas, Lord Cromwell* (Chamberlain's Men, c.1599–1602), and Queen Jane's head in *Sir Thomas Wyatt* (Worcester's Men, 1602). Memories of these ambitious, rebellious or victimised figures haunt the late Elizabethan and early Jacobean stage. Further, Macbeth's climactic decapitation itself set a pattern for later plays, as in the appearance of the renegade Duke of Sesse with the tyrant

Ferrand's head in John Fletcher and Philip Massinger's queasily tragicomic political tragedy *The Double Marriage* (King's Men, 1619–23). The overthrow of the tyrant is presented in starkly physical terms, his head symbolising both his bodily death and his removal as the 'head' of the realm.

Decapitations rarely take place on the stage, but examples survive in plays such as John Marston, William Barksted and Lewis Machin's *The Insatiate Countess* (Children of the Queen's Revels, 1610–13), Fletcher and Massinger's *Sir John Van Olden Barnavelt* (King's Men, 1619) and Dekker and Webster's *The Virgin Martyr* (Revels Company, 1620). As noted above, the 1598 Admiral's Men property list itemised a 'frame' that could be used for a beheading in a lost play called *Black Joan*, and the use of a false head in decapitation tricks is signalled in Scot's *Discovery of Witchcraft* and in the version of Marlowe's *Doctor Faustus* published in 1616, which was probably revised by Samuel Rowley and William Bird in November 1602.[44] Faustus enters 'with the false head', which is cut off by Benvolio, only for Faustus to rise again, telling him 'Nay keepe it: *Faustus* will have heads and hands.'[45] This moment of comic horror has the capacity to represent simultaneously the resurrection of a dead man, the use of satanically empowered magic, and the theatrical trick of a conjurer.

Skulls are often anonymous – as are the skulls which adorn the chambers of Hippolyto in Dekker and Middleton's *The Honest Whore* (Prince Henry's Men, 1604) and Jolenta in Webster's *The Devil's Law Case* (Queen Anna's Men, c.1610)[46] – but as often they are linked to named individuals. Yorick's skull in *Hamlet* (Chamberlain's Men, c.1599–1601) is followed onto the Globe's stage by Gloriana's skull in *The Revenger's Tragedy*, possibly 'played' by the same prop skull. While severed heads are usually presented in terms of their immediate theatrical impact and moral-political message, skulls are more often the object of contemplation and the focus of memory: they were standard in *memento mori* pictures. However, these memories may function in different ways and with different effects; where the memory of Yorick provokes Hamlet to contemplate mortality, the memory of his murdered lover in *The Revenger's Tragedy* is Vindice's spur to revenge.[47] The prop is, again, both physical and symbolic object, and its meanings can be manipulated in different dramatic contexts.

The next most common body part in early modern plays is the hand. Supernatural disembodied hands occasionally appear from the heavens, as in Greene and Lodge's *A Looking-Glass for London and England* (?Queen's Men, 1587–91) and Fletcher and Massinger's *The Prophetess* (King's Men, 1622), but hands abruptly severed from living bodies make more frequent appearances. In some plays hands are cut off as an expression of tyranny. Shakespeare's *Titus Andronicus* is the best-known example, but Greene's *Selimus* (Queen's Men, 1586–93) is almost as hand-orientated, featuring a climactic sequence in which Aga is blinded on Acomat's orders and then, when he declares 'both mine eyes be gone, / Yet are my hands left on to murther thee', his hands are severed. The sequence becomes even more grotesque as the sadistic Acomat tells Aga 'Here take thy hands: I know thou lov'st them wel' – a stage direction says 'Opens his bosome, and puts them in' – and Acomat asks Aga, 'Which hand is this? right? or left? canst thou tell?' and sends him back to present his hands to the Emperor Bajazet.[48] Hands often feature in this way, as macabre tokens: in Webster's *The Duchess of Malfi* (King's Men, 1612–14), Ferdinand presents the Duchess with a hand which he claims, falsely, to be that of her husband, Antonio, while in Thomas Middleton and William Rowley's *The Changeling* (Lady Elizabeth's Men, 1622) DeFlores presents Beatrice-Joanna with the severed finger of her fiancé, Alonzo de Piracquo. In a rare appearance of a severed limb in a play that is predominantly comic in tone, in Brome and Heywood's *The Late Lancashire Witches* (King's Men, 1634) the soldier cuts off the paw of a witch, Mistress Generous, when she is in the form of a cat, and it is later discovered that it has transformed back into a human hand. Here, as elsewhere, the detached body part carries wider dramatic, symbolic and generic associations.

Severed legs also appear periodically. In *Doctor Faustus*, the appalled horse-courser finds that Faustus' leg comes off in his hand ('Pull him by the legge, and pull it away'),[49] while *Two Lamentable Tragedies* includes an extended sequence featuring the severed legs and head of a murder victim. Noses are cut or cut off in *Edmond Ironside* (auspices uncertain, c.1590–1600) and *Edward I*, and an ear is removed in Marlowe's *The Massacre at Paris* (Strange's Men, 1593). Still more macabre, perhaps, are the plays featuring more intimate body parts: severed tongues, found in *The Spanish Tragedy*, *Titus Andronicus* and Marston's *Antonio's Revenge* (Children of Paul's, c.1599–1601), and hearts, which appear in Ford's *'Tis Pity She's a Whore* (Queen Henrietta Maria's Men, 1629–33), in which Giovanni enters with the heart of his sister and lover, Annabella, on his dagger; *Claudius Tiberius Nero*, in which Agrippina *'openeth the box with the heart of Germanicus'* (L3v); or Heywood's tragicomic classical epic *The Golden Age* (Queen Anna's Men, 1609–11), in which an animal's heart is substituted for that of the infant Jupiter. Some stage directions suggest the use of false eyes as props when characters are blinded; the most gruesome is the university tragedy *Andronicus* (c.1642–43), attributed to Thomas Fuller, which not only specifies that Spiculator *'binds'* Lapardas and *'bores out his eyes'* while *'the surgeon claps plaisters on them'*, but requires that Lapardas *'Holds his eyes in his hand.'*[50] As with the use of stage blood, amateur playwrights appear to outdo their professional counterparts in their use of gory special effects.

The plays discussed above present striking examples of the ways in which dismembered body parts might function on the early modern stage. Questions remain, however, about the tonal and aesthetic effects of such techniques, especially in plays which are not conventionally tragic in their form. Early modern theories of dramatic genre often focused on death as a key generic stress point; John Fletcher, for instance, comments that a tragicomedy 'is not so called in respect of wants deaths, which is inough to make it no tragedie, yet brings some neere it, which is inough to make it no comedie'.[51] If death was a key indication of a narrative's tragic trajectory, the dismembered body part could have a similar effect, in that its physical presence on the stage either reminded spectators of a death that had already taken place, or presaged the death or abjection of the individual who had been mutilated. A dismembered body part therefore had the capacity to disrupt, complicate or distort the narrative of a comedy or tragicomedy, symbolising tragic potential within a narrative which ultimately pulled in another direction. We can see these techniques in development in Elizabethan and Jacobean plays such as *Orlando Furioso* and *Cymbeline*, both of which fuse material deriving from non-dramatic romance with tragicomic narrative structures.

In *Orlando Furioso*, dismemberment plays a key role in the representation of Orlando's madness, provoked by the supposed infidelity of his beloved Angelica. In an intensely volatile sequence, Orlando is exposed to a grove full of carvings on trees and 'roundelays', supposedly written by Angelica's friend Medor but actually contrived by Sacrepant, Orlando's rival. This visual stimulus is accompanied by the insinuating comments of Sacrepant's servant, who is disguised as a shepherd. As the scene progresses, Orlando becomes increasingly unstable and incoherent, and eventually he attacks the 'shepherd', believing him to be Medor, and carries him off stage: 'He drawes him in by the leg'.[52] In Edward Alleyn's part for Orlando, Orlando comments before he drags the shepherd away, 'Ile tear him pecemeale in despight of these';[53] in the version published in quarto, his violent intentions are less clearly presented.

Orlando's page, Orgalio, calls to the Duke of Aquitaine for help and, in doing so, keeps the audience informed about Orlando's offstage actions, crying that 'the Count Orlando is run mad, and taking of a shepheard by the heeles, rends him as one would teare a Larke. See where he comes with a leg on his necke' (D4v). Orlando then enters 'with a leg', which he proceeds to use as a prop in a maddened impersonation of Hercules:

> Villaine, provide me straight a Lions skin,
> Thou seest I now am mightie Hercules:
> Looke wheres my massie club upon my necke.
> I must to hell, to seeke for Medor and Angelica,
> Or else I dye.
> You that are the rest, get you quickly away,

> Provide ye horses all of burnisht gold,
> Saddles of corke because Ile have them light,
> For Charlemaine the Great is up in armes.
> And Arthur with a crue of Britons comes
> To seeke for Medor and Angelica.[54]

A further stage direction then says, 'So he beateth them all in before him' (sig. D4v). This sequence sets a pattern for the depiction of Orlando's madness, which is marked by random acts of violence against those who he encounters; the rending of the shepherd limb from limb is merely the first, and most extreme, example. However, it is not Orlando's violence per se which indicates his insanity; prior to his discovery of the tokens in the wood, he is shown fighting enthusiastically in the cause of his father-in-law, and when he is cured he returns to battle immediately. Rather, it is the uncontrolled use of violence which is presented as a sign of madness, and of the potential for the story to develop into a full-blown tragedy. Although the play apparently ends happily, with the promise of Orlando and Angelica's marriage, Orlando's appearance with the leg, which recalls the madness of the hero in Seneca's *Hercules Furens*, is both an emblem of and a synecdoche[55] for the play's tragic potential.

Orlando Furioso and other late Elizabethan romance narratives set a pattern for the use of violence within mixed-mode plays, and in their Jacobean descendants stage blood and dismemberment similarly become the focus of tonal and generic anxiety. Included among the 1623 Folio's tragedies, *Cymbeline* is notably unstable in generic terms. Not only does Shakespeare incorporate the familiar tragic motif of the bloody handkerchief, presented to Posthumus by Pisanio as a sign of the supposed murder of Imogen, he also treats the body of the would-be rapist Cloten with both comic disrespect and gruesome irony.

Cloten dies off stage, and when his head is brought on stage by his murderer, Imogen's long-lost brother Guiderius, it becomes the butt of a series of jokes. Characterising Cloten as 'a Fool, an empty purse', Guiderius comments,

> not Hercules
> Could have knock'd out his brains, for he had none:
> Yet I not doing this, the fool had borne
> My head, as I do his.
>
> (4.2.114–17)

He then throws the head down the stream, telling Belarius and Arviragus, 'I have sent Cloten's clotpoll down the stream, / In embassy to his mother; his body's hostage / For his return' (4.2.184–6). Although Guiderius is reluctant to take Cloten's death seriously, the body is eventually laid to rest next to the apparently dead Imogen, who, when she wakes, mistakes it for Posthumus, whose clothes Cloten is wearing:

> A headless man? The garments of Posthumus?
> I know the shape of's leg: this is his hand:
> His foot Mercurial: his martial thigh:
> The brawns of Hercules: but his Jovial face –
> Murder in heaven? How? 'Tis gone.
>
> (4.2.308–12)

The treatment of the prop body is in some ways conventional in its combination of physical object and oral narration. However, the technique is relatively rare outside tragedy, and the aesthetic impact is perhaps greater as a result of its generic incongruity. Imogen's blazon of the parts of Posthumus' body, and her readiness to take the clothes for the man, gives the prop body a momentary theatrical life in that identity, even though an audience is aware that the 'body' should not be associated with Posthumus but with Cloten.[56] The effect perhaps becomes still more ironic if Posthumus and Cloten were doubled by the same actor, a casting strategy which the extant text makes possible and which has been used to good effect in recent productions of *Cymbeline*.[57] In addition, Imogen's mistaken identification creates a disjunction between the character's intense emotional experience and that of a watching and listening spectator, but it is debatable whether the pain of her lament is 'mitigated by the complex irony of her misunderstanding the circumstances', as Martin Butler argues, or is in some peculiar way intensified by it.[58] In *Orlando Furioso* and *Cymbeline*, therefore, a bloodied prop leg and a bloodied prop body become the focus of generic and tonal uncertainty, and in each play the bloodied prop marks a moment at which the narrative of the play has the capacity to veer headlong into tragedy.

CONCLUSION

In addition to surveying the evidence available for the use of stage blood and body parts on the early modern stage, this chapter has sought to emphasise the range of stage technologies and effects that were available to dramatists and the companies with whom they worked. In particular, I have highlighted the presence of blood and dismemberment in genres in which the use of these elements is often overlooked, and I have also paid close attention to the different forms in which they might appear within tragedy. Gory special effects function in complex ways; dramatists create a wide range of visual and visual/aural effects, and the conventions established depend on various generic, aesthetic and tonal considerations. What such a survey demonstrates, however, is that the use of stage blood and body parts on the early modern stage is rarely realistic or naturalistic in any uncomplicated manner; as my examination of *Julius Caesar* and *The Battle of Alcazar* has suggested, this is as true for tragedy as it is for comic or mixed-mode plays. Instead, elements of what we might now think of as naturalism and stylisation are presented in varying combinations – the result being that the symbolic potential of blood or limb is always to the fore, but that we are also simultaneously aware of its association with the raw physicality of the bleeding or damaged body.

CHAPTER FIVE

COSMETIC TRANSFORMATIONS
ANDREA STEVENS

> If we want to understand the perceptual dynamics of
> Shakespeare's theater, we must turn our attention to the
> physical stuff against which, out of which, through which,
> between which the dramatized events took place.[1]

When a troupe of travelling actors arrives at Elsinore, Hamlet asks
to hear a speech about the slaughter of princes. It begins, so
Hamlet reminds them, with Pyrrhus:

> The rugged Pyrrhus – he whose sable arms,
> Black as his purpose, did the night resemble
> When he lay couched in the ominous horse,
> Hath now his black and grim complexion smeared
> With heraldry more dismal, head to foot.
> Now is he total guise, horridly tricked
> With blood of fathers, mothers, daughters, sons,
> Baked and imparched in coagulate gore,
> Rifted in earth and fire.
>
> (7.340–50)

The power of this speech resides in the picture it creates of a trans-
figured body. After a false start with a less visually precise simile
('Pyrrhus, like th'Hyrcanian beast'), Hamlet delivers what sounds
like a stage direction: red, black and grim as night, Pyrrhus stalks
the streets of Troy covered head to foot in the blood of his enemies.
The implication is clear. To become a successful revenger is not
merely to act – a vexed question throughout *Hamlet* – but also to
look the part, in Pyrrhus' case to appear to Priam, like the murderers in *Macbeth*, 'steep'd in the colours of [his] trade' (2.3.113).

The passage cited above comes from the 1603 Q1 *Hamlet*. In the 1623 printing of the play, Pyrrhus, no less striking, is described as 'roasted in wrath and fire', 'o'ersized with coagulate gore, / with eyes like carbuncles' (2.2.458–60). In this version, too, the heraldic term for 'red', 'gules', replaces the more theatrical 'guise' or costume, the lexical shift (whatever its origins) transforming blood into the formal heraldry of armour. Larger than life, Pyrrhus thus achieves the literal and symbolic 'thick skin' that the critic Klaus Theweleit associates with the fascist fantasy of the male body become 'steel-hard' and impregnable.[2]

Pyrrhus does not, of course, actually appear on stage in *Hamlet*, although we might well note the passage's 'Marlovian ring' and ask whether this moment invokes Shakespeare's own memory of a performance of Christopher Marlowe's *Tamburlaine*, since the titular hero's personal iconography relies heavily on black and red colour symbolism.[3] Hamlet's description does, however, have a metadramatic dimension in that it invites us to imagine bodily effluvia and otherwise 'natural' materials (blood, sweat, dirt) as a theatrical 'guise' that none the less actually transforms the body beneath, if we consider this blood and blackness as 'baked' on to Pyrrhus' body like a second skin. And if Pyrrhus had indeed appeared on stage coloured as black and red as the text suggests, he would have done so via a process of cosmetic transformation – in other words, he would have been a 'painted tyrant' in truth (1623 text, 2.2.476).

That process is the subject of this chapter, which takes up one of the early modern stage's more ubiquitous and often unruly pros-thetics: stage paint. Throughout the late medieval and early modern periods and in an array of dramatic circumstances, theat-rical paint created a range of visual effects beyond the representation of femininity in an all-male theatre, including blood, racial difference, beauty, ugliness, health and deformity. Indeed, early modern defenders and detractors of the stage alike imagined paint as embodying the essence of theatricality. In his *Apology for Actors* (1612), for example, Thomas Heywood suggests the word 'tragedy' derives from the Greek for 'a kinde of painting', implicating the roots of theatre in such cosmetic transformations, and John Webster describes the close association between paint and player as axiomatic: '[a player] is much affected to painting, and tis a question whether that makes him an excellent Plaier, or his playing an exquisite painter' (if, as it has been suggested, this 'character sketch' by John Webster refers to Richard Burbage, chief actor of Shakespeare's company and also a painter of portraits, the slippage between cosmetics and the fine arts might be deliberate).[4] For the anti-theatricalist Phillip Stubbes, paint helped players forge the protean identities he found so alarming: 'beware, therefore, you masking players, you painted sepulchres, you doble-dealing ambodexters'.[5]

For the purpose of this chapter, I use 'paint' as an umbrella term for the theatrical materials applied directly to the player's body, often sharing a similar physical constitution, and behaving similarly in performance.[6] This definition therefore encompasses cosmetics as well as more 'industrial' paints, and it should be noted that in the early modern theatre, the same substances were often used to paint scenery and props as well as bodies – and thus we should not think of early modern theatrical paint as necessarily producing what we would view as a naturalistic effect.[7] In what follows, I examine three plays that feature scenes showing paint being applied to or washed from a player's body in full view of the audience: first, the use of stage blood as a disguising mask in the anonymous play *Look About You* (1599); next, the use of emblematic colours to signify 'beauty' and 'ugliness' in Thomas Heywood's comedy *Love's Mistress, or the Queen's Masque* (1634); and finally, the use of blackface, also as a disguise device, in William Berkeley's tragicomedy *The Lost Lady* (1637). Ephemeral by definition, paint is more difficult to remove than other identity tokens or costumes; because of this, performances must be timed to accommodate its application and removal. These three examples therefore allow me to address the way paint affects the practicalities of staging, fails to conform to prevailing definitions of stage properties or prosthetics, and engages with and exhibits the body in performance.

As Erika Lin observes, however, 'not all moments in early modern plays are created equal'.[8] In each of these case studies, paint is no mere accessory to dramatic illusion; it is the medium for a dramatic transformation and a material that itself receives metadramatic attention within the fiction. Recognising how plays self-consciously address this aspect of their own stagecraft clarifies the early modern theatre's inventions of interiority. Repeatedly, dramatists use paint to focus questions about what lies 'within' or behind a character's disguise or adorned surface. Like the entrance doors or stage hangings whose movements help create impressions of unseen interior spaces (places like '*further within*'), paint, when applied to or removed from a body, fosters effects of depth, gestures towards 'hidden' passions, and constructs and dismantles identities, and I shall be arguing below that the actor's own physiology or corporeality is a 'potentiality' within the play that is activated when players are painted or stripped of paint in view of the audience, or when players metadramatically comment upon what it feels like to inhabit their painted bodies.[9]

'A MASK OF BLOOD'

I begin with Alice Rayner's discussion of the backstage life of stage props to demonstrate the ways in which paint frustrates standard accounts of theatrical objects:

Especially when they are simply sitting backstage or in the prop room prior to their uses in a performance, bereft of both text and performance, prop objects can seem suspended between both worldly and fictional uses. Stored in a prop room, the objects constitute both an archive of past productions and a promise of possible ones. A prop room holds objects out of context, neither fully in the world nor yet onstage, in representation [. . .] Once put into a stage space, an object is destined to travel. Traveling, it is subjected to the power and authority of users (performers) as well as 'sender and receiver,' with their often competing or contradictory investments of

'content' within the object [. . .] A particularly haunting
image on a prop table, however, is the outline that graphically marks the place where a prop belongs.[10]

Although Rayner has in mind the collection of props assembled
for a production of Suzan-Lori Parks' *The America Play* (1994),
her analysis applies to the stage objects that commonly circulate
within early modern drama: crowns, swords, chairs, skulls, handkerchiefs. Performed by the Lord Admiral's Men, the play *Look
About You* (1599) contains, however, one 'object', a saucer of blood,
that squares less well with the account Rayner provides. [11] The plot
of this 'aggressively theatrical' comedy of multiple disguises is not
driven by literary concerns, but rather by the desire to give free
and giddy rein to its lead actors' histrionic skills.[12] The trickster
Skinke, for example, goes through nine changes of identity, and in
one sequence makes inspired use of supposed animal blood. In the
scene below, Skinke enters disguised as Prince John (he's wearing
the Prince's hat, cloak, and sword), discards those tokens, changes
clothes with a servant boy, and then bloodies his face:

SKINKE

> What Pyg, or Goose, or Capon have you kill'd,
> Within your Kitchin new?

DRAWER

> A pyg new stickt.

SKINKE

> Fetch me a sawcer of the bloud, quicke run;

Exit.

> [. . .] Lend me thy Aprone, runne and fetch a pot from
> the next roome.
> [. . .] O brave boy, excellent bloud: up, take my cloake
> And my hat to thy share, when I come from Kent, ile pay
> Thee like a King.

(1547–64)

The ruse works. The real Prince John and those pursuing Skinke
mistake him for an abused servant, and he escapes arrest: 'Hange

your selves, this darkenes shall convay me out of doors / Ile swim the Thames, but Ile attaine Black-heath' (1587–88). Elsewhere in *Look About You* beards are hastily attached, clothes are changed, gaits are altered, and voices disguised.[13] To wash the face of blood within a compressed time frame, however, is an altogether more difficult feat to manage: Skinke receives the saucer of blood probably on 'O brave boy', bloodies himself between that moment and the entrance of the real Sir John four lines later, exits, and later returns 'like a Hermit' 250 lines later; in other words, the actor needs far more time off stage to remove the blood, than time on stage to apply it (Skinke's boast that he'll 'swim to Blackheath' even calls attention to this process of cleansing). This feat of actorly virtuosity can also be viewed as a comic revision of a familiar theatrical convention; for example, in the play *A Warning for Fair Women* – also anonymous and performed in 1599 – the emblematic figure of Tragedy enters 'with a bowle of bloud in her hand [. . .] Murther settes downe her blood, and rubbes their hands' (see also 3.1 in *Julius Caesar*, when the conspirators bathe their hands and weapons in Caesar's blood).[14]

An analogous moment in which blood eradicates identity can also be found in the first act of *Coriolanus* (1609), when Caius Martius returns from battle so 'masked' and 'mantled' in blood that Cominius only recognises him from his voice:

> *Enter MARTIUS, bloody.*

COMINIUS

> Who's yonder
> That does appear as he were flayed? O gods!
> He has the stamp of Martius, and I have
> Before-time seen him thus.

MARTIUS

> Come I too late?

COMINIUS

> The shepherd knows not thunder from a tabor
> More than I know the sound of Martius' tongue
> From every meaner man.

MARTIUS

Come I too late?

COMINIUS

Ay, if you come not in the blood of others

But mantled in your own.

(1.6.21–9)

Martius later metadramatically acknowledges his blood as a 'painting' that conceals his blushes from view and that must be removed off stage: 'I will go wash; / And when my face is fair, you shall perceive / Whether I blush or no' (1.6.68; 1.9.67–9). In pointed contrast to his comfort with his public visibility in Act 1, in Act 2 Martius argues that simply to appear in the marketplace in the ceremonial gown of humility is a 'part' he would 'blush in acting, and might well / Be taken from the people' (2.2.144–5). What John Ripley calls Martius' 'sanguinary appearance' conceals those blushes that would otherwise betray the soldier's involuntary and therefore authentic response to the idea of public exposure: shame at being seen to court, seen to crave, public approval. To be sure, Martius' embrace of his blood as a disguising costume is worth noting, given the predominant view of this character's animus against acting.[15]

Although this moment from *Look About You* has sometimes been cited as proof that pig's blood was used in the early modern theatre (alongside animal viscera such as the '3 violls of blood & a sheeps gather' mentioned in the 'plot' of the *The Battle of Alcazar*), I take at his word Martius in *Coriolanus*, and argue that when the early modern stage required the *body* of the actor to be bloody, red paint was used, as was clearly the case when reusable props such as swords and handkerchiefs needed to be bloodied.[16] Simple and capable of producing sophisticated effects, water-soluble paint was, after all, one of the primary methods for transforming bodies on the stage; other red fluids such as red vinegar or red wine could perhaps be used to represent pools of blood, but they would be insufficiently adhesive for application to the skin. Moreover, entries in *Records of Early English Drama* reveal that paint was also widely used to create blood effects in late medieval drama. To cite a few representative examples from York, the Painters' guild helped mount the pageant of the *Crucifixion* in the annual Corpus Christi play by supplying the pigments necessary to indicate Christ's wounds, and the York Mercers' property inventory of 1433 (of items used to stage the pageant of the *Last Judgment*) lists a leather coat painted with the red marks of Jesus' wounds.[17] Evidence from outside England offers further instances of the labour of painters. The Admont play of the Passion, for example, deploys red paint at the Flagellation, the crowning of Christ with thorns, and the Deposition: 'a servant brings whips and rods dipped in red paint. When they strike Christ's body it becomes bloody'; 'They press the crown onto his head together with a small sponge dipped in red paint'; 'The servants go along and break the thieves' legs with a club wound round with sponges dipped in red paint'.[18]

In *Look About You*, the suggestion that the paint is in fact 'real' blood is not so much an admission of actual stage practice, then, but a fiction that emphasises Skinke's extraordinary resourceful-ness: this consummate trickster can make a disguise out of anything. And although the audience knows no animal has just been butchered backstage, the spectacle is still comically grotesque – 'Skinke' and the actor playing him share the same skin, and the idea of animal blood applied directly to the face draws the actor's own corporeality into the fiction. To borrow a phrase from Bert O. States, 'something indisputably real leaks out of the illusion', although in this case something real leaks *into* the illusion that no doubt elicits from the audience a pleasurable frisson of disgust.[19] For Anthony Dawson, the audience's awareness of the actor himself as distinct from the character he impersonates, 'while potentially present throughout the performance, could of course be activated at certain moments as part of an effort to achieve a specifically self-reflexive effect'.[20] The convention of cross-gender disguise is the most frequently discussed, and best theorised, example of such an activation; engaging the audience's awareness of the actor's own physiology, a gesture such as Skinke's applica-tion of 'blood' to his skin in view of the audience is clearly another.[21]

If paint adorns stage subjects like Skinke, it is itself an object. On the one hand, the prevailing definitions of 'prop' including Natasha Korda and Jonathan Gil Harris' account of the prop as any 'moveable physical object of the stage' and Andrew Sofer's definition of the prop as any 'discrete, material, inanimate object that is visibly manipulated by an actor in the course of a performance' obviously accommodate Skinke's 'sawcer'.[22] On the other hand, if we press more forcefully on the constitution and behaviour of the 'blood' itself, we run into problems above all with the word *discrete* in that, from both a conceptual and a practical point of view, paint is difficult to disentangle from the body of the actor; Stubbes' accusation that the actor is a 'painted sepulchre' is especially suggestive not for its hostility to the morality of acting, but to its more literal evocation of a body buried under layers of adhesive paint. Skinke's stage blood therefore fails to demonstrate the easy detachability that is the primary characteristic of the prosthetic. Furthermore, the stage life or 'mobility' of paint within a performance is primarily confined to the duration of its attachment to the player's body. In other words, there is no 'elsewhere' for paint after it has been used, no place to travel.[23]

Finally, this inventive use of blood as a mask has additional consequences beyond its theatrical appeal, witty reversal of expectations about genre, and impact upon the timing of a live performance. Drama scholars have tended to discuss stage blood as an element of realism. The consensus on medieval drama, for example, is that graphic realism encouraged what 'pale abstraction' could not: sympathy with the suffering of Jesus and his martyred saints.[24] Likewise, critics have also regarded the stage blood that flows in post-Reformation drama as one of the few reliably 'realistic' elements erupting within an otherwise non-illusionistic space.[25] This particular usage, however, upends this view of stage blood's capacity somehow to express transcendent truths; in the case of Skinke, cosmetic blood disguises, rather than emanates from and therefore verifies, a body becomes 'real' by the violence done to it, and, in so functioning, perhaps troubles our view of stage blood as a sign, or indeed as *the* pre-eminent sign,

of 'realism'. This scene of Skinke's disguising would also potentially evoke for audiences a number of other masking practices
rarely thought of in relation to spectacles of bloodshed, even comic
ones. Just like the 'mummers' who used soot, ashes, dirt and other
ad hoc ingredients to obscure their faces during occasions of carni-
val and misrule, Skinke improvises with the materials at hand to
obscure his face, the location that Sarah Carpenter and Meg
Twycross call 'the center of communication of the self'.[26] To return
to Rayner's evocative description of offstage props above, we might
well consider the painted body as itself constituting an 'archive of
past performances', and see the 'ghosted' traces of other cultural
and dramatic practices haunting this disguise scene; accustomed
as we are to tracing the intertextual relationships among plays, we
ought to bear in mind as well the potential *intermaterial* echoes,
allusions, and correspondences inscribed on the very bodies of
painted actors.[27]

'A BOX OF BEAUTY'

My next example comes from Thomas Heywood's comedy *Love's
Mistress, or the Queen's Masque* (1634).[28] Performed by Queen
Henrietta's Men and commissioned by Henrietta Maria herself
for Charles I's birthday, Heywood's play was, according to the
quarto title page, 'three times presented before their two Excellent
Majesties, within the space of eight dayes; In the presence of
sundry Forraigne Ambassadors'. The first occasion was before a
private courtly audience at an invited dress rehearsal at Christopher
Beeston's indoor playhouse, the Phoenix (formerly the Cockpit);
the next two performances were at court at Henrietta Maria's own
performance venue, Somerset House, and included fixed scenery
designed by the celebrated architect and stage designer, Inigo
Jones. In a note 'to the Reader', Heywood praises Jones for 'his
excellent inventions [that] gave such an extraordinary lustre, upon
every occasion changing the stage, to the admiration of all the
spectators' (20–3). Raymond Shady speculates that when the play
returned to the public stage 'some of the scenery and machinery'

probably went with it.[29] Exploiting the physical, visual and aural resources of the stage to the fullest, the play joins masque and anti-masque-like elements to a host of spectacular effects, including musical interludes, dance numbers, dumbshows, feigned storms, magic banquets and multiple costume changes.

The comedy dramatises Apuleius' version of the myth of Cupid and Psyche. Apuleius himself appears in a sub-plot as a choric figure who interrupts the action laboriously to unpack its neo-Platonic allegory to his testy interlocutor, Midas; there is also a third level of action featuring a rustic Clown. Each level of the plot represents feminine beauty as a commodity to be coveted and strictly policed. Those who possess it – who are themselves beautiful or, more important still, are able to make or to mar beauty in others – are the most powerful. This becomes most evident in the play's fifth act, which prominently features a misdirected 'box of beauty' (a cousin to the hypermobile 'love juice' from *A Midsummer Night's Dream*) and its dark double, a 'box of ugly painting', containing black paint.

The play thus opposes the iconic reds and whites of English beauty to a form of blackness that, while not explicitly racialised, nevertheless invokes a complex performance history, from the use of blackface to turn white players into Moors in popular plays such as *Othello*, to the use of symbolic blackness in the older Tudor interludes and morality plays, to the use of blackface in late medieval drama on the faces of devils and doomed souls.[30] Given that this is a court-sponsored production, however, the most relevant performance context for *Love's Mistress* is a courtly one: by choosing this box of beauty device, Heywood cites Ben Jonson's twin masques of *Blackness* (1605) and *Beauty* (1608), but also a much more recent court entertainment: Walter Montagu's *The Shepherds Paradise* (1634), a pastoral romance performed by the Queen and her ladies at Somerset House just the year before. In *Blackness*, Queen Anna and her ladies performed as the 'daughters of Niger' who, after learning that foreign poets have slandered their African beauty, journey to Britannia in order to wash themselves white (this transformation is not shown in the 1605 masque, but instead deferred to the companion *Masque of Beauty* three years later).[31] *The Shepherds Paradise* also features a woman who temporarily masquerades as a Moor, although in this case she is, in fact, shown restored to whiteness at the play's conclusion. All of these plays therefore raise questions about the compatibility of blackness and beauty – although the court masques performed by aristocratic women, rather than professional men, offer more nuanced answers to this question than does Heywood. Tracing the journey of these boxes reveals the centrality of paint to the play's materialisation of 'ugliness' – and, in a play performed by professional male actors, its materialisation of 'femininity' and 'beauty'.

The first few scenes establish the play's anxiety over any beauty that exists outside the proper spheres of authority: Venus, interpreting the mortal Psyche's beauty as a usurpation of her own power, orders her son to make Psyche 'dote / on some ill-shapen drudge, some ugly fool' (1.3.70–1). Cupid instead defies his mother's orders by marrying Psyche, although, as in the myth, he interacts with his human wife only under the cover of darkness. When Psyche disobeys her husband's prohibition never to look upon his face, Cupid orders 'Boreas' to destroy the paradise in which they live and 'blast' Psyche's beauty:

> Lay waste and barren this faire flow'ry grove,
> And make this paradise a den of snakes.
> For I will have it uglier then hell,
> And none but ghastly screech-owls here shall dwell.
> Breathe winter's storms upon the blushing cheeks
> Of beauteous Psyche; with thy boisterous breath,
> Rend off her silks, and clothe her in torn rags;
> Hang on her loathed locks base deformity,
> And bear her to her father; leave her there,
> Barren of comfort, great with child of fear.
>
> (3.1.66–75)

Exiting 'with a great storme', Psyche re-enters in another 'blustering' storm approximately 140 lines later with disordered hair, torn clothing, and a face disfigured by the addition of black spots:

PSYCHE

> Where art thou Psyche, how art thou deformed?
> What air affords thee breath? What men be these?
> Where shall I hide me? Let no human eye
> Behold me thus disfigured, and ashamed.
> My Father, Brothers, and my Sisters too,
> That wrought my fall, what shall poor Psyche do?
> [. . .]

ASTIOCHE

> Spurn her away,
> 'Tis some infectious strumpet, and her breath
> Will blast our cheeks; her sight is worse than death.
>
> (3.2.140–52)

Apuleius confirms for the audience that 'Till Psyche be made fair, and angel-white / She's not to stand in Cupid's glorious sight' (3.3.50–1).

By 1634, besmirching the face with black paint was a common method for signalling ugliness and moral corruption on the stage.[32] For example, in a probable source for *Love's Mistress*, Robert Wilson's *Three Ladies of London* (1581), the figure of 'Usury' brings on stage a 'paynted boxe of incke' out of which 'Lucre' paints the face of 'Conscience':

> *Here let Lucar open the boxe and dip her finger in it,*
> *and spotte Conscience face, saying as followeth.*

Hould here my sweete, and them over to see if any want,
The more I doe behold this face, the more my minde doth
    vaunt:
This face is of favor, these cheekes are reddy and white,
These lips are cherry red, and full of deepe delight.
Quicke rowling eyes, her temples hygh, and forhead white as
    snowe,
Her eye-browes seemely set in frame, with dimpled chinne
    below:
O how beautie hath adorned thee with every seemely hew,
In limmes, in lookes, with all the rest, proportion keeping
    dew:

Sure I have not seene a finer soule in every kinde of part,
I can not choose but kisse thee with my lippes that love thee
   with my heart.

(1173–82)

In turn, this visual shorthand of blackness and spotting evokes pre-Reformation morality plays such as *Wisdom Who is Christ*, in which Anima or the 'soul' progresses from innocence, through a period of defacement (appearing on stage 'in þe most horrybull wyse, fowlere þan a fende'), and finally again to beauty.[33] We likewise can see Psyche's temporary blackness as the visible evidence of her human trespass against the immortal Cupid. Psyche's own family rejects her as 'infectious', a charge that invokes what Farah Karim-Cooper has called the 'devastating effects' of early modern cosmetics that included poisonous ingredients such as mercury; as Karim-Cooper, Tanya Pollard and others have shown, anti-cosmetic literature consistently depicted the painted woman as a dangerous source of physical and moral contamination.[34] Together with the spiritual degradation the wearing of cosmetics was thought to imply, the real-world risks posed by cosmetics with hazardous ingredients reinforce the dramatic fiction of Psyche as diseased. Further complicating this presentation of Psyche's body is the fact that when Psyche returns defaced, she also returns visibly pregnant (carrying a 'rich burthen' in her 'wretched wombe'); this appears to be a potentially comic, if not slyly cheeky, reference to the 1605 *The Masque of Blackness*, in which Queen Anna famously danced as a 'daughter of Niger' while six months pregnant (3.2.252).

An angry Venus continues to torment Psyche by charging her with a number of impossible tasks culminating in an order to fetch her a 'box of beauty' from out of hell:

> Hie to Proserpina, the black-browed Queen.
> I'll send thee on my embassy to Hell;
> Tell her that sickness, with her ashy hand,
> Hath swept away the beauty from my cheeks,
> And I desire her send me some of hers.

> Fetch me a box of beauty then from Hell.
> That's thy last labour, urge not a reply;
> Do my command and live, refuse, and die.
>   (4.1.183–90)

If black paint exemplifies and possibly hastens Psyche's bodily disintegration, Proserpina's paints promise to preserve and revivify the female body, a view of the remedial power of cosmetics that can also be found in period defences of the application of cosmetics, albeit under the right conditions: when authorised by a male expert such as a physician.[35] For example, in his pro-cosmetic tract titled *Artificiall embellishments* (1665), Thomas Jeamson proposes that 'The Body, that weak and moving mansion of mortality, is exposed to the treacherous underminings of so many Sicknesses and Distempers, that its own frailty seems petitioner for some artificial Enamel, which might be a fixation to Natures inconstancy' – enamel here meaning a hardening and perfecting addition to the body's surface.[36]

Psyche duly retrieves the box from Proserpine, who cautions her 'not to look into't / As thou respect'st thy safety'; again, this toys with the view of cosmetics as dangerous, though the taunt must also reflect back to Psyche's sin: looking at Cupid (5.2.98–9). The Clown, however, tries to intercept the box in order to make his homely lover, Amaryllis, more beautiful. In a complicated eavesdropping scene in which Psyche is watched by both Clown and Cupid – Cupid sees Clown and Psyche, Clown sees Psyche, Psyche sees neither – Psyche succumbs once again to temptation:

Enter Cupid.

Many a long look have my watchful eyes
Sent out to meet with Psyche. Here she comes,

Enter Psyche.

And in her hand the box. Cupid, stand close,
And overhear the sum of her discourse.

Enter Clown.

CLOWN

This is she, I know her by her martyred face; Venus did
well to send her for beauty, for poor soul she hath need
on't. I have dogged her, to see if I could find her at any
advantage, to steal away her box. I have already got love
from Cupid; I have got Poetry from Apollo, and if I could
now get beauty from Psyche, Phaon the fair ferry man
was never so famous in Sicilia, as I, Corydon, shall be in
Arcadia.

PSYCHE

You traitorous thoughts, no more assault me thus.
My lovely Cupid charged me not to see
What Proserpine sent Venus in this box.
The like command did Hell's Queen lay on me.
Oh heaven, yet I shall die except I do't.

CUPID

Ay, Psyche, what, still in your longing vein?

CLOWN

That's it. Nay I shall know't, if I see't again.

PSYCHE

It's beauty Psyche, and celestial,
And thou art ugly; this will make thee shine,
And change this earthly form to shape divine;
Open it boldly – but I shall offend,
Why say I do, 'tis but the breach of duty,
And who'll not venture to get heavenly beauty,
Rich beauty, ever fresh, never decaying,
Which lies entombed in this heavenly shrine.
Nor in this bold attempt think me profane,
Striving thus spotted, to be free from stain.

She opens the boxe and fals asleep.

CLOWN

Nay I thought I should take you napping,
And thou shalt go with me; for 'tis my duty,
My mistress being a blowse, to find her beauty.

Cupid charms him asleep.

CUPID

> To make thee lovely in thy mistress' eyes,
> Make use of that, and boast of thy rich prize.

Cupid layes a counterfeit Boxe by him.

(5.2.1–34)

Luckily for Psyche, Cupid takes pity on her: 'But, foolish girl! Alas, why blame I thee, / When all thy sex is guilty of like pride, / And ever was?' (5.2.35–7). Her offstage transformation evidently authorised by Jove himself, Psyche reappears restored to beauty 5.3.55: 'Her leprosy, through labour, is made clear / And beauteous in your eye she'll now appear' (5.3.53–4; see 68–72 for Cupid's explanation that she 'quaffed' from a 'cup of Immortality' and was then 'made fair'). The play therefore concludes with the familiar progression from disorder to order, blackness to whiteness and 'beauty', common to the Stuart court masque.

If Pysche's dramatic changes of face and clothing take place in lengthy intervals spent off stage, the Clown plot directly dramatises the action of defacement in view of the audience.[37] Thinking he is making himself an object of polymorphous, glowing appeal – and switching from prose to iambic couplets to commemorate this upgrade of status and appearance – the Clown decides to apply the paints first to his own face, and instead deforms himself with paints from the 'ugly' box, to predictably comic effect:

CLOWN

> Rejoice all mortals that wear smocks, for I have found rich beauty's box. I was before but a man made, but I am now a very made man [. . .] But come as many as will, and as fast as can, by their favours, my Amaryllis shall be first served. And yet not first neither: am I in possession myself? and shall not I be the white boy of Arcadia? Adonis is dead, and shall not I be Venus' sweetheart?

The boxe is full of ugly Painting.

> Come box of beauty, and for white and red.
> Put down Jove's Page, the smooth-faced Ganymed.
> Daub on, daub on, as thick as thou canst lay on,
> Till thou exceed the ferryman called Phaon.
> Cupid compared with me, shall be a toy,
> And look but like the sign of the black boy.
> My face shall shine just as my hand disposes:
> In one cheek I'll plant lilies, in t'other roses.
>
> (5.2.55–78)

In 'daubing' on these magic cosmetics, Clown believes he is transforming himself into an ambiguously gendered 'master-mistress' such as that immortalised in Shakespeare's Sonnet 20. To be sure, the Clown also seeks to emulate the archetypal fashionable courtier or 'gay man' John Donne satirically describes as 'so *glistering*, and so *painted* in many *colours* that he is hardly discerned from one of the *pictures* in the *Arras* hanging'.[38] Rather than acquiring social capital and upward mobility through beauty, however, Clown becomes instead a blackened devil or comic monster (thus some fifty years after the suppression of the mystery cycles, the association of blackness with devils and doomed souls remains firmly planted in the cultural imagination):

3rd SWAIN

Oh monstrous Corydon! How cam'st thou thus changd?

CLOWN

Changed? I hope so! I have not travelled thus far for nothing. Speak you mortals, doth not my brow relent? Shines not my nose? Springs not here a lily, there a rose?

2nd SWAIN

A rose, a lily? A blue-bottle and a canker-flower! What is that upon thy face?

CLOWN

Beauty, boys, beauty.

2nd SWAIN

Beauty dost call it! I prithee from whence came it?

CLOWN

Marry, from Hell.

2nd SWAIN

> From Hell, I believe it, for it hath made thee look like a
> devil already.

$$(5.2.89\text{--}100)$$

Unlike Psyche, however, the Clown is never shown restored to his
normal face.

Sponsored by the Queen herself and acted by the troop that
bore her name, the play's performance history confirms that it was
very well received at court. Because it revisits the self-same themes
of blackness, beauty and feminine transformation that played out
just the year before in *Shepherds Paradise* (again, a play performed
by aristocratic women rather than by professional male actors), I
suggest it contributes to what Sophie Tomlinson dubs a 'poetics of
female performance' attached to Henrietta Maria's court – albeit a
somewhat cheeky or complexly satiric contribution, given its
comic or almost burlesque tone. The message of *Love's Mistress* is
a conservative one that does not, in the end, celebrate unauthor-
ised acts of self-fashioning, especially feminine ones.[39] This
argument might seem counter-intuitive (why would a play sponsored by the Queen satirise or parody any aspect of her courtly
iconography?), but *Love's Mistress* offers at the very least an ambivalent attitude towards feminine theatricality and unlicensed
role-play, an ambivalence that can also be found in other ostensibly
pro-Henrietta Maria plays of the period, most notably James
Shirley's *The Bird in a Cage* (1633).[40] To treat these issues more
fully is beyond the scope of this chapter, but it is always important
to note richly suggestive intermaterial, in addition to thematic and
verbal, echoes among plays.

'A MAID AS MOOR'

The two examples above show how paint was used to materialise a
range of bodily states not always thought of as similarly constituted: bloodiness against health, beauty against deformity,
blackness against whiteness. I have also argued that the presentation of face- and body-painting scenes allowed dramatists to invoke

the potentially injurious or, alternatively, remedial effects of theatrical paints upon the skin, and by so doing, engaged the audience's awareness of the physiology of the player in much the same way that the convention of cross-dress disguise often strategically drew attention to the 'real' body of the boy actor. My final claim is that the early modern period's well-documented concern with the relationship of interiority to outward show makes paint, in the late sixteenth and seventeenth centuries, an especially effective material through which to dramatise anxieties about false outer appearances. Among other evidence, the popularity of treatises that elaborated techniques for self-concealment and for the scrutiny of others indicates that early modern subjects were increasingly concerned with the body's transparency or opacity, and that these conditions of transparency or opacity had important consequences for social relationships. Performed by the King's Men at the Blackfriars theatre and also performed at court, William Berkeley's tragicomedy *The Lost Lady* (1637) stages a plot that responds directly to this anxiety over potential gaps between 'inward disposition' and 'outward show'.[41]

The play opens with the tragic tale of the lady Milesia, 'barbarously murthered' by her uncle after he discovers her love affair with Lysicles, an enemy of her family. Milesia's ashes are buried in a tomb which Lysicles visits 'nightly' (16; 233). Unknown to everyone including the audience, Milesia is alive and present on stage disguised as the Moor, Acanthe. Although she has adopted blackface to escape her uncle's custody, she retains the blackface disguise after she hears a rumour that Lysicles is to marry someone else. Like the 'Egyptian charmer' who supplied Desdemona's handkerchief to Othello's mother and who 'could almost read / the thoughts of people', Milesia/Acanthe has a reputation for being able to read minds (3.4.58–60):

Her father was of Greece, a wealthy Merchant
And his busines enforceing him to leave his Countrey
He marryed a Ladie of that place where he liv'd,
Who excellent in the mistery of Divination hath

> Left that knowledge to her only daughter, enrich with
> Thousand other modest virtues.

(637–42)

The very opacity of Milesia/Acanthe's black makeup makes visible her ability to remain herself undiscoverable, impenetrable. This evokes what we might call a 'counter-discourse' attached to blackness in the early modern period that diverges from Heywood's invocation of the colour's negative emblematic and religious associations: even as blackness is devalued it sometimes is praised, as, for example, in lyric poems that celebrate black complexions for their supposed constancy and resistance to cosmetics.[42] In contrast, the reds and whites of feminine beauty can easily be faked, as Mote reminds Armado in *Love's Labour's Lost*: 'most maculate thoughts, master, are masked under / such colours' (1.2.88–9). Thus Berowne in *Love's Labour* praises Rosaline's 'black' beauty that needs no 'painted rhetoric'(4.3.235), and Niger in *The Masque of Blackness* likewise celebrates his daughters' 'fixed' and 'faithful' complexions (120; 125).

The contradiction should be evident: the notion that black skin resists artifice, and therefore signifies in positive moral terms, jostles uncomfortably against the idea of black skin as an impenetrable screen that might be masking just about any 'maculate' thought at all. In similar terms, Milesia/Acanthe is called 'as secret / as the night she resembles', and her guise of paint affords her the mobility necessary to allay her anxiety about male fidelity (1475–6; in an altogether different context, Skinke's mask of paint performs similarly in that it, too, allows him the liberty to work his will).

The play does not, however, embrace female theatricality, but instead comes to punish it as transgressive – and here, we might well locate a connection between this 1637 tragicomedy and *Love's Mistress* beyond the deployment of some iteration of blackface. In Act 4, Milesia/Acanthe dons a veil and appears to Lysicles as the ghost of Milesia in order to harangue Lysicles for his lack of fidelity in love (the veil therefore allows her temporarily to double back to her white identity). After Lysicles has resolved her doubts about

his love for Milesia, the ghost informs him that Acanthe is respon-
sible for Milesia's death: 'all that I ever did shee's conscious of /
and jealous of your love unto Hermione [. . .] this Moor is the
cause that I do walke in shade' (1869–70; 1886). Only the play's
sudden shift in attitude towards female theatricality and the necessity of artifice explains the self-accusation. That is, once her doubt
about Lysicles' constancy is satisfied, Milesia/Acanthe comes to
despise herself for her own lack of faith, and consequently impli-
cates her persona of Acanthe as punishment for what she now
views as her duplicitous theatricality. Lyscicles responds to this
confession more warmly than she perhaps intended. Vowing to
avenge his lost love, Lysicles arranges for Acanthe to be poisoned;
although the blackface itself is not the medium of the poison's
delivery, the play invites us to see death by poison as the inevitable
outcome of Milesia's choice of disguise.

The fifth act therefore opens with 'the Moore' writhing in pain
on a thrust-out bed, ready to die rather than to admit to her true
identity, and loudly berating herself for her 'jealousy' (the stage
direction reads '*Enter Lysicles finds the Moore tortured*'). Providing
a tantalising insight into the management of stage effects involving
paint, a direction preceding this scene notes '*Bed ready water &
Towell*', and in a powerful *coup de théâtre* revelation, Acanthe's
disguise is breached when a sympathetic attendant moistens her
face with water:

IRENE

> Bring some water here, she does but swoone:
> So chafe her Temples, – Oh Heavens! what prodigy
> Is here! her blacknesse falls away: My Lord, looke on
> This Miracle, doth not Heaven instruct us in pitty
> Of her wrongs, that the opinions which prejudice
> Her vertue, should thus be wash't away with the
> Blacke clouds that hide her purer forme?

HERMIONE

> Heaven hath some further ends in this
> Than we can pierce: More water, she returns to life,
> And all the blacknesse of her face is gone.

IRENE

> Pallas, Apollo, what may this portend? My Lord,
> Have you not seene a face like this?

LYSICLES

> Yes, and horrour ceazeth me: 'Tis the Idea
> Of my Milesia. Impenetrable powers,
> Deliver us in Thunder your intents,
> And exposition of this Metamorphosis.

(2233–49)

The material source of Acanthe's blackness is never explained within the play's fiction: as befits the genre of tragicomedy, this revelation of identity is perhaps meant to be a seen as a miraculous resurrection akin to the awakening of Hermione's painted statue in *The Winter's Tale*, and not simply as a costume change (that said, audiences would clearly be able to understand the device in terms of other court and popular plays of racial disguise from the 1630s). Milesia/Acanthe declares she is 'by miracle preserv'd', confirms her identity, and 'asks pardon' of the 'constant' Lysicles. At this juncture of the play, however, only part of the blackface disguise has been washed off (the actor returns completely white some 150 lines later). Lysicles therefore uses his poetic rhetoric to augment this scene of revelation, describing Milesia as

> white as Lillies, as the snowe
> that falls upon Pernassus, if the red were heere
> as I have seen't enthron'd, the riseing day
> would get new excellence by being compard to her
> Argos nor Ciprus, Egipt never saw
> A beauty like to this.

(2303–08)

Because Milesia/Acanthe is for the moment both Moor and white heroine Lysicles compliments colours she is not yet displaying: '*if* the red were here'. The passage captures a moment of transition from blackness to beauty. Describing a face poised on the threshold of a flush, Lysicles insists upon the blush's authentic evanescence, its groundedness in the body and in his own corroborating language rather than its origins in cosmetic artifice.

But of course the actor playing Milesia is not a white woman, but a white boy. Given that gender on the stage, like racial difference, is materialised out of stage paints, we must consider, then, what audiences actually see when a male actor playing a female part is washed white, so to speak – that is, the removal of one layer of black makeup must also involve the temporary displacement of the reds and whites of stage femininity, since presumably the face that is revealed under the paint is the bare face of the actor.[43] Far from dismantling the illusion of stage gender, however, the sudden revelation of the 'Maid' under the guise of 'Moor' distracts attention from the fact that the maid is a tricked-out boy whose red-and-white, when next we see 'her', will be similarly materially produced: as a boy's body is washed white, audiences see one system of cosmetic significations yield to another, the triumphantly restored and reinvigorated red and white of artificial stage femininity presented, by contrast to the temporary black 'guise', as real, natural and authentic. In this play, the sudden reversion to Milesia/Acanthe's apparently 'essential' underlying whiteness dispels worries about female duplicity and theatricality; in other words, this particular whitewashing ritual naturalises the prostheticised body of the boy actor.

CONCLUSION

Painted in emblematic and culturally significant colours, the decorated body of the actor is an important aspect of the visual field of early modern theatre. Early modern dramatists consistently turned to theatrical paint to signify a variety of effects, embracing the very risks the technology introduced of aborted transformations, of theatrical unpredictability, and also of worrisome physiological change. To use paint on a performer is inevitably to enlist the audience's awareness of the body of the player; it is precisely the uncertainty surrounding the 'real' complications that accompany staged scenarios of body painting, I argue, that give this method of representation its signifying power.

CHAPTER SIX

COSTUME, DISGUISE AND SELF-DISPLAY
BRIDGET ESCOLME

JULETTA

> I am any thing,
> An old woman, that tells fortunes.
> [. . .] And frights good people,
> And sends them to Segovia for their fortunes:
> I am strange airs, and excellent sweet voices.
> I am any thing, to do her good, believe me;
> She now recovered, and her wishes crown'd
> I am Juletta again, pray Sir forgive me.
>   (John Fletcher, *The Pilgrim*, 5.6.111–17)

By 1621, when Fletcher's *The Pilgrim* was first performed by the King's Men at the Blackfriars playhouse, disguise was such a familiar theatrical device in the early modern theatre that the play could plausibly base plot twist upon plot twist on a plethora of changing disguises. *The Pilgrim*'s heroine, Alinda, spends the play fleeing, in disguise herself, from her furious father who wants her to marry against her liking. In the speech above, her serving woman and friend describes the Ariel-like ways in which she has used disguise to aid Alinda in her flight. The play pushes the device to its limit: Alinda disguises herself as a deranged boy and, along with Juletta, as an old woman and as a shepherdess. Disguise sets the plot in motion in 1.2, when Pedro, the man whom Alinda loves, arrives at her home disguised as a pilgrim: Alinda comes close to seeing through his disguise. Pedro tells his love that he is unhappy because he has 'lost [him]self' (1.2.165), a phrase she half-recognises from the engraving on a piece of jewellery he once gave her. Once he has left, Juletta is told to fetch the jewellery, as Alinda realises she has failed to recognise her love:

ALINDA

Take this Key, and fetch me
The marygold-Jewel that lies in my little Cabinet;
I think 'tis that; what eyes had I to miss him?

(1.2.176–8)

By this point in the history of stage disguise, it is possible to ask the question, how could anyone fail to recognise someone they have known so well? Alinda's excuse to herself is one of reasonable plausibility: Pedro's troubled time as a travelling Pilgrim has changed him and he is older and paler – 'he had no beard then, and / As I remember well, he was more ruddy' (1.2.180). But in the majority of cases in early modern drama to this point, no one, however familiar with a disguised character, is in danger of exposing him or her. Moreover, when all is finally revealed, no one feels the need to give a realistic account of why they were fooled. Most disguises in the early modern theatres simply work.[1]

After the Restoration, disguise ceased to be the hugely popular device it was before the closing of the theatres. Peter Hyland points out, in the most significant study of the phenomenon published to date, that in the modern theatre disguise is largely used in parody.[2] *The Pilgrim*'s use of multiple disguises can be read as a later, extravagant flowering of the device. In this chapter on disguise, power and self-display, I discuss the implications of this ubiquitous early modern stage convention for our understanding of costume/clothing and explore its relationship to dramatic identity in the theatre. A theatre audience willing to accept that one might don another's set of clothes and instantly be taken for that other, is an audience that has different expectations about theatrical representation from a modern one, and a different understanding of the way clothing confers identity. Here, I am going to discuss three plays that feature rulers who dress up. Two are the best known of that contested genre the 'disguised ruler play',[3] John Marston's *The Malcontent* (1602–04) and Shakespeare's *Measure for Measure*

(1604); the third features the seeming theatrical opposite of disguise, a ruler who dresses up with the primary motivation of self-display: Cleopatra in Shakespeare's *Antony and Cleopatra* (1606–07).

The theatrical technologies of costume and disguise are most productively considered in the context of clothing in early modern culture more broadly. After all, 'costume' is something of a misnomer for what early modern actors wore on stage, as their clothing was always 'real': items made by tailors, items bought by or passed on to the playing companies, or the actors' own clothes. In this way they differed from the stage costume of modern production, made for theatrical convenience or to fit a particular design aesthetic. What early modern audiences saw on stage was the clothing worn by themselves, their neighbours or their social 'betters'. But I am going to suggest that in early modern performance, these clothes were put into theatrical quotation marks in such as way as to emphasise the playfulness and fragility of identity itself, and that this must have been particularly exciting for audiences watching actors dressing up as heads of state. Stage kings, queens and dukes hold positions of absolute power but are rendered fascinatingly vulnerable on stage, in the moment of putting on and taking off new identities with new sets of clothes.

REPLAYING EARLY MODERN DISGUISE

Two examples from modern Shakespeare productions illustrate the ways in which the convention of disguise must be relearned by the spectator today. The first is a remark made by a woman watching *King Lear* at the Young Vic in 1981.[4] I recall simple grey, black and white costumes, the sleeping Lear and a pale-cloaked Cordelia seemingly illuminated by their costumes' whiteness against a dark set. I don't remember much of a transformation for Kent when he disguised himself as Caius. He perhaps donned a cloak with a hood. The simple, unmemorable disguise clearly mattered a great deal to a woman sitting behind me, however: she provoked a ripple of laughter by remarking loudly of Kent/Caius' costume, 'Not a very good disguise, is it?' The expectations produced by a history of scenic illusion and cinema had presumably made the simple donning of one or two new items of costume an implausible way for the exiled Kent to conceal his identity from a master who knew him so well. This moment demonstrates, obviously, that there are certain early modern theatrical conventions of costume and disguise that an audience simply has to accept in order to engage with the dramatic narrative. The limited evidence available to us regarding what early modern actors would have worn on stage suggests that the donning of a Friar's cowl or a serving man's garb indicated a complete transformation that was instantly plausible to early modern audiences, when accompanied with appropriate changes in accent and gestural language. Play-texts suggest that disguise costumes were easy to remove for sudden moments of revelation: in *Measure for Measure*, Lucio pulls Duke Vincentio's Friar's cowl from him in seconds to reveal the latter's true identity and his own doom; Antonio in Thomas Middleton and William Rowley's *The Changeling*, disguised as a fool in the hopes of cuck-olding the madhouse keeper, suddenly reveals himself to Isabella seconds after her husband's assistant Lollio has exited, with the words ''Tis opportuneful now, sweet lady! Nay, Cast no amazing eye upon this change' (3.3.131). When women disguise themselves as men, necessitating something more than a swiftly removable garment, and when time does not allow for a complete change at a point of revelation, an onstage change can, of course, be avoided by the playwright altogether. At the end of *Twelfth Night*, much has been made of Orsino's deferring Viola's change into her 'women's weeds' - but, as Peter Hyland has pointed out, while 'critical speculation about Shakespeare's use of Viola's plight to make a point about the blurring of gender distinctions is interest-ing', the potential homoerotic frisson of this moment is likely to have been an effect of Shakespeare's solution to the 'intractable technical problem of getting the boy playing Viola into a dress in the time left at the end of the play'.[5]

My second modern example is from a recent Royal Shakespeare Company *Measure for Measure*, in which comic capital was made of Duke Vincentio's encounter with Escalus (Geoffrey Beevers) while Duke Vincentio (Ray Coulthard) is disguised as the Friar (3.2).[6] It was decided by the company that of all the characters with whom the Duke-as-Friar has intimate conversation, Escalus is the one who knows him best and who is therefore most likely to recognise him. In this version of the scene, then, the Duke shifted and turned away from Escalus, who looked somewhat bemused to find that on repeated occasions he was unable to address the Friar face to face as they conversed. This moment, though deftly performed and very funny, is one that Shakespeare is unlikely to have recognised. Once the Duke has his Friar's garb on and has learned how 'formally in person [to] bear like a true friar' (1.2.47–8), he is able to move freely about his kingdom without being exposed, even by Angelo, who may have had as many opportunities to view him up close as Escalus. In this RSC production, we are asked to assume that intimacy and friendship will endanger the disguise and therefore, perhaps, that Angelo, Isabella, Claudio, Juliet, Mariana, the Provost and (significantly, given his pretensions to intimacy with the Duke) Lucio have only seen him on progresses or other occasions of state when the Duke has had, under duress as he tells Escalus, to 'stage' himself to the 'eyes' of the people (1.1.67–8). The body of the Duke as generally beheld by the likes of Lucio is the body that supports the head of state on public display, rather than the individual who tells his courtier that he does not very much enjoy such displays. But for an audience in 1604, even intimates are not expected to penetrate the disguise convention. Moreover, in a social and theatrical culture in which it is not assumed, as perhaps it is in current Western culture, that everyone has a truer, more intimate self hidden beneath clothing and office, an Escalus can have familiar daily intercourse with a Vincentio and still see him solely as Duke. It seems impractical to suggest that the Duke spent a whole scene on the open stage at the Globe with his face entirely covered by a cowl, blocking his expressions from much of the audience (see Figure 3). I suspect that, rather, a simple Friar's garb with a cowl that exposes the face plus the correct Friar-like vocal range and gestural vocabulary produced

Figure 3 Mark Rylance as Duke Vincentio in disguise (as friar), in
Measure for Measure, at Shakespeare's Globe, photograph by John Tramper.
With kind permission of The Globe Theatre

a figure that no one except the audience would recognise as anything but a Friar.

A third example from recent production does not directly involve disguise but offers a way in to examining how clothing might have been read in the early modern theatre. It is from the Royal Shakespeare Company's production of *Antony and Cleopatra*, also performed in the Swan, in 2005–06.[7] In the first scene, Harriet Walter as Cleopatra entered in a sharply bobbed dark wig that recalled iconic film and stage Cleopatras past. Once the teasing of Antony over the Roman messenger was done with, Walter pulled off this wig with something of a sigh of relief, as if pleased to be momentarily relinquishing the burden of having to play Cleopatra. This is, of course, a modern interpretation. The boy player Cleopatra could never have rested from his wig-wearing role or his carefully constructed illusion of femininity would have been spoiled (though Mark Rylance, in the Globe's 1999 all-male production, did remove his wig to reveal Rylance's own hair, shorn off in clumps and mixed with stage blood, suggesting 'the frenzy of self-mutilation hinted at by Plutarch',[8] and creating a striking contrast with Cleopatra's self-reconstruction through headdress and costume before her death). The removal of Walters' wig did highlight, however, both the theatrical construction and self-fashioning strategies of Cleopatra, who, on the early modern stage, is at once a boy dressed up, a notoriously flighty construction of the female and an agent in her own drama. As we will see, the trope of disguise hovers around this play in ways that illuminate this endlessly replayed player queen's acts of self-fashioning. Cleopatra's uses of clothing put into productive theatrical quotation marks the versions of clothing, disguise, leadership and masculinity at play in dramas where men, particularly leaders, disguise themselves.

CLOTHING CULTURE AND THE
TECHNOLOGIES OF DISGUISE

Andrew Gurr's extensive work on the playing company the Admiral's Men in *Shakespeare's Opposites*, suggests that the large number of plays featuring characters in disguise in this period can be accounted for by the acquisition, by the playing companies, of permanent venues for their work. Though Peter Hyland points out that Gurr's argument cannot account for the popularity of disguise on the early modern stage more broadly, Hyland, too, writes that 'it was the acquisition of permanent playing places that allowed for the broad fixing of the structure of acting companies and the flourishing of players with specialist skills, and also for the development of large and varied wardrobes'.[9] For Gurr, once the Admiral's Men have got a 'wholly novel security of tenure' at the Rose in 1594, the challenge for the company is to entertain their regular audiences with as varied a repertoire as possible, using actors with whom those audiences soon become very familiar; many of these actors needed to double roles.[10] Gurr argues that 'one immediate effect of [. . .] how familiar the recurrent members of the Rose's audiences became as they recognized the double identities of the different characters on stage was in the variety of clothing the players needed to wear', and, as he reminds us, clothing and props were the most expensive outlay of the playing companies, more expensive than the fees paid to writers for the delivery of the plays themselves.[11] Gurr fascinatingly links these theatre pragmatics to the development of the Admirals' dramatic repertoire, which, he demonstrates, exploits the disguise device more often and more brilliantly than Shakespeare's company, which does not acquire a permanent venue until 1599.[12] For an audience who expected to be entertained by familiar actors, constantly changing roles, what better dramatic device to employ than disguise? 'Their customers were getting used to seeing the players change their dress daily. Now they could exploit that expectation with new games.'[13] The fact that the disguise that fools the characters in a dramatic plot does not fool the audience, gives that audience a delightful sense of superiority. In this reading, the play whose plot centres on disguise is an effect of performance indeed, and Gurr rightly argues that its playful metatheatricality is essential to its success.

Gurr's account of disguise as an effect of playing in a permanent theatre is a testimony to the way in which developments in theatre technology produce meaning. But as Dave Postles points out in his article '"Flatcaps", Fashioning and Civility in Early Modern England', clothing works as metaphor for and construction of identity not only in the early modern theatre but in early modern culture more generally. Postles traces the history of the ubiquitous sixteenth-century flat-cap to its eventual fate as symbol of poverty and dull-wittedness after the rise and rise of high-domed, feathered hats among the fashionable. He offers examples of the use of 'flat-cap' as a metonymic insult not only in the drama but in accounts of legal disputes.[14] The much-cited re-enactments of sumptuary legislation in the sixteenth and early seventeenth century (many of which were eventually repealed by James),[15] testify to the fact that, despite Lucio's declaration in *Measure for Measure* that 'cucullus non facit monachum' ['the cowl does not make the monk'] (5.1.261), the notion that one might buy and then perform social class through clothing was productive of both theatrical pleasure and cultural anxiety in early modern England.

THE DESTIN'D LIVERY

Clothing in early modern culture is not only used by individuals seeking to make statements about their social selves. The judiciary used clothing, as well as legislating against certain of its uses, as an element in highly theatrical shame punishments, and the controlling of misbehaviour and labelling of the wrongdoer is echoed sartorially in the drama. Shakespeare's audience, as late as the first performances of *Measure for Measure*, would have been familiar with highly visual, enforced performances of shame. Martin Ingram's fascinating essay 'Shame and Pain: Themes and Variations in Tudor Punishments' describes both ecclesiastical and secular shame punishments in which the guilty parties have to perform public penance dressed in white sheets (a practice that continued after the Reformation but without the Catholic candles and tapers); they were then paraded, partially naked, for their crimes of immorality. He describes elaborate 'charivaresque folk punishments', in which convicted criminals had to ride backwards through city streets wearing symbols of their crimes.[16] Communities of onlookers were attracted, by the use of ringing basins and performing minstrels, to witness the display of bawds with shaved heads[17] and harlots carrying white rods and wearing striped hoods.[18] Swiss tourist Thomas Platter's diary of 1599 describes the public removal of clothing as part of the standard punishment of prostitutes, 'great swarms' of whom haunted London's 'taverns and playhouses': 'The woman is taken to Bridewell, the King's palace, situated near the river, where the executioner scourges her naked before the populace'.[19] These were the kinds of theatrical punishments which, though being overtaken by public whipping during James I's reign, were still being recorded into the seventeenth century.

This visual labelling of criminality is to be found overtly staged in the 1578 source play for *Measure for Measure*, George Whetstone's *Promos and Cassandra*. In this play, no bed trick is devised so that a substitute heroine can save the Isabella prototype's honour; instead, the heroine Cassandra herself is persuaded, after her interview with her imprisoned brother, to come to the Deputy Promos' court 'Cloth'd like a page (suspect for to prevent)' (I *Promos and Cassandra* 3.2.460; II *Promos* 3.7.467sd), where she is to sacrifice her virginity for her brother's life. Interestingly, Ingram cites sixteenth-century records in which 'common strumpets' were punished for dressing as men (which they did to disguise their trade) by being paraded wearing men's bonnets rather than respectable women's kerchiefs on their shorn hair.[20]

In *Promos and Cassandra*, once Cassandra has given her virginity for her brother's life, she is betrayed by the Deputy, who, as in *Measure*, orders that her brother be put to death anyway. Her next entrance is 'in black' (1 *Promos* 5.6.479sd). Polina, the *Promos* equivalent of Shakespeare's pregnant Juliet, wears 'a blue gown' (1 *Promos* 5.3.475sd) as a woman condemned for unchastity, and then, when she believes her lover to be dead and is going to visit his tomb, 'a blue gown, shadowed with a black Sarcenet' (2 *Promos* 1.1.480sd). Blue signifies the publicly known loss of chastity: it is the colour Polina must wear as a punishment for sex before marriage; it is the garment with which *Promos and Cassandra*'s Lamia the courtesan is threatened as punishment for plying her trade. The black trim is, of course, for mourning. George Whetstone was not a writer for the early public theatre and his play was probably never performed, though the stage directions about who should be ready to come on next and what settings and properties might be needed for performance, suggest that he was certainly imagining his play in the theatre. This black-for-mourning, blue-for-shame code does not emerge in texts of *Measure for Measure*, but Juliet is paraded through Vienna to be 'shown to the world' along with her lover Claudio (1.2.114sd).[21] The notion of women's clothing proclaiming their social status and selfhood – and the two being inextricably linked sartorially – is also echoed in the later play where Angelo maintains that women's destiny is to service men: if Isabella is a real woman, she will not actually need to dress as a page, but must put on the 'destined livery' (2.4.138) and have sex with him.

A particularly suggestive point made by Ingram is that theatrical punishments involving dress or undress were resonant for the communities that watched them, because such punishments exposed those who had disguised their criminal activities from the upright citizen. He suggests that what linked the kinds of crimes punished in this way – sedition, theft, deception and sexual offences – 'was a sense of false dealing, the inverse of what was expected of the "honest" citizen',[22] so that the culprits' exposure through clothing or its removal would have seemed particularly appropriate. Condemned culprits of crimes of deceit were stripped of their disguises and revealed, naked, or dressed in clothes that signified what they 'really' were. In *Measure for Measure*, sexual misdemeanour is similarly exposed in the parading of Claudio, who feels the shame of being shown to the world. In this Dukedom, so full of barely disguised vice, the fact that the puritanical Angelo is attracted to Isabella is unsurprising, much though it startles the Deputy himself. Isabella represents a physical and moral beauty that appears to Angelo pure and undisguised, in comparison to the beauty performed through other women's deceptive sartorial adornments. The 'black masks' that 'Proclaim an enshield beauty ten times louder / Than beauty could displayed' (2.4.78–81) cannot attract him like this open and presumably plainly dressed young novice. The medieval and early modern judiciary used clothing to proclaim the criminal previously hidden within the community and many of the crimes punished by shameful sartorial display are crimes of female sexuality – unsurprising, given the role that the visual supposedly plays in the machinations of the strumpet or prostitute in tempting the upright to sin. Angelo falls for Isabella because she is not, like the female temptress of misogynist and legal discourse, in disguise.

I am going to return now to a dramatic disguise motif which, superficially, could not be more different from that of the disguised/exposed, strumpet of the dramatic and legal imagination: the disguised head of state in the dramas of the early seventeenth century. These rulers choose disguise for reasons ultimately beneficial to their state and subjects. But however supposedly upright, well-meaning or justified the disguised ruler in the early modern drama might be, disguise is still deception and is always vulnerable to removal and premature revelation. This is not because other characters are in danger of penetrating a disguise when it is 'on', but because the very fragility and unreliability of identity is marked by its construction through clothing. If, as the frequent re-enactment of sumptuary legislation suggests, anyone with money might dress above his or her station, if a prostitute could tempt and deceive with clothes – and if the law could proclaim what she 'really' was by re-dressing her – how could one ever be sure of who or what one was encountering in social life? How could one be sure of one's neighbours, one's leaders, oneself? While I am not suggesting that clothing is a constant source of anxiety to every early modern citizen, I do want to argue that stage clothing, particularly disguise, might not only be a source of theatrical pleasure, as Gurr suggests (see above p. 125) but was also a source of a range of social anxieties. In the next section, I am going to consider the effects of the fragile power and shifting vulnerability produced when a figure of absolute power – a head of state – chooses to disguise himself in the drama.

THE COWL MAKES THE MONK: LEADERS DRESSING UP

Disguise in the early modern drama ostensibly confers power or protection on the wearer. Crooks use disguise to hide their criminal actions; lovers use it to gain access to their beloveds; vulnerable figures in strange lands are safer in disguise; banished servants or usurped kings use disguise to move freely about their native lands. The disguised rulers I will examine next, however, complicate the rule that disguise gets you what you want or protects you from what you don't. In Marston's *The Malcontent*, the ostensibly less powerful figure of outsider played by the Duke Altofronto both gives him theatrical power and problematises the power he wields in the world of the play. In Shakespeare's *Measure for Measure*, disguise gives Duke Vincentio an ultimate, dramaturgical power: as a humble Friar he completely controls the plot, whereas as a Duke he was unable to control his kingdom. But as we will see, disguise renders Duke Vincentio psychologically vulnerable and therefore the potential object of comedy. In these plays, the early modern theatre audience is given the opportunity to hear disguised heads of state muse on the vulnerability of power and so to see them as other than all-powerful.

THE MALCONTENT

Altofronto's dukedom has been usurped at the beginning of *The Malcontent* and although, as we shall see, there is one scene in which his disguise may be momentarily at risk of exposure, the device seems to offer an impenetrable psychological resilience and

complete safety from persecution in this time of crisis. The effect
of impenetrability is strengthened by a dramaturgical move that
Peter Hyland marks as unprecedented:[23] the audience is not party
to Altofronto's decision to disguise himself in the first scenes of
the play and sees him not as a disguised Duke but as the Malcontent,
Malevolve. His role as Malcontent/antic ensures that he is physically and psychologically protected by the licence given to bitter
fools, a role he plays exceptionally well; indeed, a number of
commentators have remarked that it is difficult to differentiate
between Altofronto himself and the Malcontent he plays. Even his
'true' name, which means 'other face', suggests that he *is* his
disguise. Altofronto seems to enjoy as good a rant as his alter ego,
despite the stage direction that he 'shifteth his speech' (1.4.43sd)
when he readopts his disguise for the benefit of the fickle courtier
Bilioso. He makes a great Malcontent - and he makes a great Duke
when, in the last scene, he winds up the plot with startling rapidity
and metatheatrical finality, achieving with a speech of nine lines
what it takes *Measure for Measure*'s Duke Vincentio the best part of
an act to accomplish: justice and forgiveness for all, his own restoration and a thankyou and goodbye to the audience to boot.
Significantly, though, the Malcontent role that protects Altofronto
and finally allows him to regain his Dukedom, permits him an
unfettered critique of his state - and of the state of leadership in
general.

The frontispiece to Q3 of *The Malcontent* announces that the
play has been

Augmented by Marston.
With the Additions played by the Kings Majesties servants.
Written by John Webster.

The play was first performed by the Children of Chapel/Queens
Revels at the Blackfriars, and the additional Q3 induction clearly
suggests that it was then acquired by the King's Men. In the
Induction, King's Men actors, playing themselves, discuss the play
and its additions with the character of a young gallant, who wants
to sit on the stage as he is permitted to do 'at the private house'

(Induction 2). Whereas this induction and the scenes featuring the Fool, Passarello, are thought to be by Webster, the passages of the play particularly pertinent to my argument here are both from the Q3 augmentations now assumed to be by Marston. The debate around the status of the Marston augmentations was reopened by Charles Cathcart in 2006; his close reading of the play for echoes of *Hamlet* suggests that Marston may have been commissioned to write the extra passages for the King's Men's performances at the Globe, rather than lengthening the play for the Children, though he otherwise had no history of writing for the adult companies. Cathcart's argument is of interest here, as it would mean that a passage in which Altofronto reveals his disguise directly to the audience in soliloquy, and another in which he problematises leadership and visual display, might have been written for performance at the Globe rather than the indoor playhouse.

In Altofronto/Malevole's speech after the usurping Duke Pietro's exit of 1.3, Altofronto shifts to soliloquy (1.3.153–70). It is here in the Q3 text that the Malcontent reveals his disguise to the audience, whereas in the Q1 and 2 versions, it is in conversation with his faithful friend Celso that Altofronto first reveals his true identity. In the Q3 augmentation, the Duke points to his disguise, suggesting he may be removing the hat, cloak or beard of which it comprises. The revelation opens with a comically bathetic 'Well', rhythmically reminiscent of the 'Why' of Hamlet's self-deprecating commentary on his own attempt at the performance of revenge hero – 'Why, what an ass am I! This is most brave' (2.2.584). It is as if he is done with performance and reverted to himself again:

> Well, this disguise doth yet afford me that
> Which kings do seldom hear or great men use –
> Free speech; and though my state's usurped,
> Yet this affected strain gives me a tongue
> As fetterless as is an emperor's.
>
> (159–63)

In the Q1/Q2 Children's versions, there is no indication that Altofronto reveals himself visually as another, yet Celso, when he enters for 1.4, straight after Altofronto/Malevole's rant to Pietro, seems to recognise him immediately. It is clear that Celso is the only one Altofronto has confided in, though there is some comic mileage to be had in the Q1/Q2 version from the fact that Celso walks on stage and addresses 'My honoured lord' as though he has completely forgotten that the said lord is meant to be in disguise; Altofronto has to silence him with 'Peace, speak low – peace!' (1.4.2).

The other passage of interest here is a thirteen-line extension of another of Altofronto/Malevole's speeches, part of the play's dénouement, in which Altofronto scorns to kill Mendoza, the usurper of usurpers, undefended. In this augmentation, Altofronto critiques the common crowd's reception of leadership, in a lecture on the superficiality of the people's love:

> Oh, they that are as great as be their sins,
> Let them remember that th'inconstant people
> Love many princes merely for their faces
> And outward shows, and they do covet more
> To have a sight of these than of their virtues.
>
> (5.1.138–42)

To see a prince's face is not to know his virtues, and Altofronto/Malevole here mourns the fact that faces and outward shows are all 'the people' want. Leaders are, in fact, 'as great as be their sins' and should remember the superficial, visual construct that is political power. What these two passages add to the play is an emphasis on leadership as a problem for leaders, bound up with a sense that the identity of the leader is partially visually constructed. In the 1.3 augmentation, Altofronto/Malevole reveals himself to the audience as disguised, then comments on the unwonted freedom of speech, the 'tongue / As fetterless as an emperor's', which the disguise gives him (1.3.162–3). It is ironic that he uses this emperor simile here: after all, he is proclaiming that, as head of state, he cannot speak his own mind. In the 5.6 augmentation, he marks the limitations of the ruler's public presence to superficial visual display.

Fascinatingly, these moments in *The Malcontent* where Altofronto/Malevole explicitly reveals his disguise and problematises the role of leader are in the augmentations to the play, which may only have been performed by the King's Men at their open-air Globe. What makes for profitable speculation here is whether or not the meanings produced by disguise are differently inflected in the indoor and outdoor playhouses. The public amphitheatre may produce different theatrical effects and thematic meanings for disguise. In a larger, outdoor theatre, with its multiple qualities of publicness, the sense of a ruler always being on display as ruler – as opposed to being recognisable for his private virtues – is perhaps all the greater. Potentially, the conditions of performance that the two types of playhouses might produce enabled a varied complex of effects when it came to theatrical disguise.

MEASURE FOR MEASURE

Soon after the King's Men's acquisition of *The Malcontent*, Shakespeare wrote his own disguised ruler play, *Measure for Measure*. Much has been made of the convention as an early Jacobean dramatic obsession, reflecting interest and anxiety around the ascension of a new and seemingly somewhat introverted king (see below, n.3). Here, though, I want to concentrate on the effects of disguise in performance: *Measure for Measure* once again uses the popular and exciting performance convention of disguise in its portrayal and discussion of leadership, this time creating a Duke whose disguise seems to render him more, rather than less, vulnerable, despite the control of the plot it allows him.

In dressing up as a Friar, Duke Vincentio enters into a very different relationship with his subjects from that of the leader who must appear before them in public. He describes himself as a father of his people and admits to the Friar who provides him with his disguise that he cannot bear to be thought an overly strict one (1.3.23–31, 34–9); he then dresses up as a religious 'father', who brings souls to inner sanctity, rather than a ruler who inflicts punishment on the body. However, though it enables him to escape

Lucio's public displays of leadership, Duke Vincentio's Friar disguise renders him psychologically vulnerable before the theatre audience, when he is obliged to listen to insulting misrepresentations of Lucio. He is unable simply to dismiss Lucio's slander as gossip and later seeks reassurance from Escalus about his own reputation (3.3.230–1). Lucio is the only condemned figure not to be pardoned in the final scene of recognition and reconciliation; he is to be whipped, as well as hanged, presumably publicly.

Duke Vincentio not only admits he has been a less than perfect leader; he does not, at first, make a particularly good father confessor. Though his speech to Claudio before the young man's imminent execution is virtuosic and temporarily persuades Claudio of the paltry meaninglessness of social life, the Duke/Friar's first effort at the role involves blurting out to the pregnant Juliet that her lover is to die the next morning, reducing her not to religious humility but sinful despair. Whereas for Altofronto, the Malcontent role seems to come naturally, Shakespeare's disguised leader must learn his Friar part.

Though these are in many ways very different disguised Dukes, in both cases the disguise device produces a rich admixture of new freedoms and vulnerabilities for the rulers in question. The acid-tongued Malcontent role protects Altofronto and gives him the freedom of bitter commentary. The stage-shy Vincentio's disguise gives him the power of redemption as he prepares young souls for death, then prolongs the plot as he tests Isabella's forgiving grace to what should surely be its limits. Malevole may be briefly in danger of being recognised as Altofronto, when he is obliged to quieten his friend Celso, but his disguise and the strength of the persona that goes with it seem otherwise impermeable. Vincentio never appears to be in danger of recognition until his disguise is physically pulled from him, at which point his power is instantly restored. However, his reluctance to restore moral order to his Dukedom and his psychological vulnerability to Lucio's mis-recognition of his qualities make him an altogether frailer leader, until he wrests control of the plot and draws it out to the complicated dénouement of the last scene. Even that dénouement itself, the ultimate demonstration of judicial and dramaturgical power, involves his proposal to Isabella and her famously ambivalent silence.

ANTONY AND CLEOPATRA: OVERT DISGUISES

I move lastly to a play around which the disguise trope hovers but in which there is no disguise plot, to explore the ways in which a consideration of disguise and power on the early modern stage might productively illuminate a discussion of a different kind of onstage dressing up and playacting. Shakespeare's Cleopatra is, inevitably, partially constructed in a misogynistic discourse in which all women are disguisers and deceivers, dressing up and constantly changing. She is the fickle female *par excellence*. However, where our disguised male rulers demonstrate the theatricality of power, partially escaping it, partially exposing its fragility, Cleopatra understands that she *is*, inescapably, her displayed, clothed self.

Cleopatra is a character prone to playacting and dressing up rather than literally to disguising herself. However, in Thomas North's translation of *Plutarch's Lives* (1579), Shakespeare's source for the play, her pastime of 'wander[ing] through the streets and not[ing] / The qualities of people' (1.1.53–4) involves a familiar disguised ruler device, in which the ruler disguises him/herself to mix with the people – in order to discover their misdemeanours.[24] In Plutarch, this is very much Antony's idea of fun, though Cleopatra joins him. He is willing to make himself the butt of jokes and the victim of blows in the process, though it is difficult to decide whether the 'mocks' he gets for fighting with common men are due to being accompanied by a woman or whether the woman, Cleopatra, is laughing at him herself:

> And sometime also, when he would go up and down the city disguised like a slave in the night, and would peer into poor men's windows and their shops, and scold and brawl with them within the house: Cleopatra would be also in a chambermaid's array, and amble up and down

the streets with him, so that oftentimes Antonius bare away both mocks and blows.[25]

In Shakespeare's play, it is the consummate player Queen who 'desire[s]' this entertainment: Antony diverts her from the Roman messengers in 1.1 by alluding to disguise as a favourite pastime of hers.

Shakespeare's Antony is a man divided between soldierly duty and the pleasures of Cleopatra's court and bed; in the Roman world, Caesar's much-cited speech mourning Antony's old, manly habits of eating bark and drinking horse urine when on his tours of duty (1.5.66, 62) epitomises, for the Romans, Antony's 'true', lost identity. However, in Plutarch, he is manly, soldierly, singularly scruffy and, simultaneously, a somewhat debauched lover of the theatre and playful disguise. Leadership and theatricality are not mutually exclusive in Plutarch as they are for Shakespeare's Caesar. Plutarch links Antony's masculinity and concomitantly unorthodox choice of dress with his decadent sociability in this passage:

For when he would openly shew himself abroad before many people, he would always wear his cassock girt down low upon his hips, with a great sword hanging by his side, and upon that, some ill-favoured cloak. Furthermore, things that seem intolerable in other men, as to boast commonly, to jest with one or other, to drink like a good fellow with everybody, to sit with the soldiers when they dine, and to eat and drink with them soldier like: it is incredible what wonderful love it won him amongst them.[26]

Plutarch's Antony refuses the performance of leadership through clothing; though unorthodox, his careless dress is part of the persona that wins the love of those he leads. However, Plutarch also remarks upon Antony's love of playacting in his account of the Roman warrior's attempts to cheer the 'sour' Fulvia by playing 'her many pretty youthful parts to make her merry'.[27] He records

Antony's fondness for watching and socialising with performers, and how it won him the disapproval of the noblemen of Rome:

> In his house they did nothing but feast, dance, and mask: and him self passed away the time in hearing of foolish plays, or in marrying these players, tumblers, jesters and such sort of people.[28]

Shakespeare's Cleopatra famously understands the power of personal playacting and public display. While, according to Plutarch, both Antony and Cleopatra are fond of disguise and theatricals, according to Shakespeare, it is Cleopatra who pulls Antony in to a world of display, cross-dressing (2.5.20–3) and decadent playfulness. What we have in Shakespeare's Cleopatra is a queen whom readers of Plutarch might have known as a disguised ruler but who, on stage, consciously plays with dress to display, rather than to hide, what she is. Cleopatra's feigned fainting fit, where she calls for Charmian to cut her lace (1.3.71), is a clear reference to the Jacobean dress that the boy player would have been wearing to play this role; *Antony and Cleopatra* is famously the play in which the boy under the dress is most blatantly referenced. Cleopatra dreads the moment when 'some squeaking Cleopatra will boy [her] greatness / I'th'posture of a whore' (5.2.220–1), in Caesar's parade of triumph. Cleopatra's barge pageant, as related by Enobarbus, demonstrates that she understands that power is constructed visually; this power would be doubly removed from her in Caesar's penal parade, in which she will be both displayed and performed as herself. She would rather die in 'a ditch in Egypt' (5.2.57) than be displayed like the punished prostitutes her paying audiences might have been familiar with. When it comes to the death that defies Caesar, she, of course, demands to be shown 'like a queen' in her 'best attires' (5.2.27–8), choosing her own end, her own clothes, her own final signification.

Of our three dressed-up rulers, the male figures both evade and critique problems of leadership and identity, recalling and interrogating early modern evocations of the theory of the King's Two

Bodies, according to which the ruler has a 'body natural' and a 'body politic', the first being his mortal frame, the second the abstract construct of 'policy and government'.[29] In royal regalia and on public display, the ruler figure on stage might represent the Body Politic, the abstraction of leadership; in disguise he potentially demonstrates the fragility of that body and the flawed nature of the private man. Cleopatra's bodies private and politic are, on the other hand, truly indivisible. Her leadership is inflected with her private passions; her private self enacts the theatrical Queen. Vincentio and Altofronto demonstrate the vulnerabilities of leadership through the disguise motif; Cleopatra overtly performs vulnerability, thus rendering herself less vulnerable.

Early modern audiences, for whom showing one's self in and through clothes is an important quotidian and theatrical reality, might well have understood Cleopatra's decision to choose her last act of dressing up – in death – as an alternative to Caesar's parade of shame. Yet Cleopatra is also, of course, a destructive force in Shakespeare's play. In a fit of temper she threatens to 'unpeople Egypt' if letters from her are not conveyed to Antony every day (1.5.77–8) and her flights in the face of battle must cause the death of many. Her performance of fainting is comical and has the court rushing to her side, but in playing dead she precipitate's Antony's actual suicide. Our disguised male rulers are forced or feel obliged to dress up as other people but finally, in *Measure for Measure* and *The Malcontent*, disguise brings recuperative closure and the restoration of authority. Deliberately chosen, overt playacting such as Cleopatra's is both delightful and anxiety-provoking, filtered through a history rooted in the misogynistic fear of women's quotidian disguises, their deception and self-adornment; it is provocative of anti-theatrical anxiety as well as theatrical pleasure. When Juletta from the opening quotation says that she is 'Juletta again', she is renouncing her role as multi-disguiser, because her mistress's desires have been fulfilled; the disguises were, in fact, all part of her true identity as good servant, and now she safely reflects that role in her dress. When Cleopatra says 'and I'll be Cleopatra' (3.13.184–6), recalling the moment when she first was so, her birthday, no such subjective stability is promised. Cleopatra always seems to be disguised as herself.

For early modern culture, clothing produces the inextricable constructs of self and social status, and for the early modern theatre, quick changes for doubled roles and disguises produce different stage figures in an instant. Dressing up is an essential part of the temporary change of identity that is acting, so that although actors in minor parts wore their own clothes on the early modern English stage, much anti-theatrical anxiety was produced by actors dressing up as noblemen and as women. You are also what you wear in early modern culture more generally, hence the repeated re-enactment of sumptuary laws during the period and the continued use of dress as part of shaming punishments. In the figure of Cleopatra, the notion that the human body in clothing can be 'anything' provides a source both of cultural pleasure and social anxiety. Disguise in early modern performance demonstrates the virtuosic abilities of the performer on the one hand, and the fragility of social performance on the other.

CHAPTER SEVEN

CHARACTER ACTING
PAUL MENZER

Everything we know about Shakespeare and his age is precon-
ceived by print. This 'knowledge' extends even to cultural
expressions that might seem to evade ink, paper and moveable
type, such as acting. This is strange since among the few things
that we can say with certainty about early modern theatre is that
actors fashioned performance from handwritten – not printed –
materials. Yet even when we do not mistake the *materials* available
to actors we casually employ print-derived metaphors such as
'typecasting' to consider the personnel practices of the early
modern stage. It seems safe to conclude with W. B. Worthen that
'print – the printing process, the forms and shapes of printed
books – has long troped our understanding of a lush variety of
cultural production' including 'our understanding of stage
performance'.[1] As Worthen implies – and the current chapter
argues – the master tropes of print potentially occlude rather than
clarify our thinking about early modern acting, since print privileges qualities quite alien to performance: standardisation,
reproducibility and, above all, uniformity.

Nevertheless, for much of the twentieth century, scholarly work
on Shakespearean acting has understood performance in precisely
these terms. Generalising about an industry standard of acting, a
scholar will write that 'an evolution towards a representational
style of acting can conveniently be adduced from a chronological
study of Shakespeare's plays'.[2] (Adducing an acting 'style' from a
play is a bit like inferring a chef's style from his menu, but let that
pass.) We should be cautious, however, in assuming a common
approach by early modern actors across the profession. This was,

after all, an age without drama academies where players might receive uniform training. In trying to determine a generic acting approach, scholars assume a default acting 'style' that, oddly, threatens to turn all actors into the same actor.

This idea of stylistic sameness finds its analogue in scholarly work that seeks predictable casting patterns predicated upon 'type'. Of an individual actor such as Robert Benfield (who joined the King's Men in 1615), a scholar can write that, '[t]he business of Robert Benfield is also well established. He always takes dignified parts, such as kings, senators, and old men, regularly ranking third or fourth in number of lines taken'.[3] Indeed, since the work of T. W. Baldwin in the 1920s, we have been urged to believe that actors pursued dramatically consistent 'lines' – another print metaphor – that depended above all on a consistency of histrionic approach. In 1992, T. J. King refreshed Baldwin's work in his *Casting Shakespeare's Plays: London Actors and Their Roles, 1590– 1642*.[4] King is less prescriptive than Baldwin, but still relies on print to shape his thinking since he identifies principal players by the number of lines they speak. In sum, the search for consistency and predictability characterises much of the work on actors and acting in the period. Actors 'evolved' towards a uniform style, and at the individual level the body is as predictable as a piece of type, producing the required character within the theatrical machinery's generation of performance.

It may be objected that there is no alternative way to think about casting, for instance – that is, actors themselves conform to character 'types', that is just 'what actors do'. Some crude counter-examples might, however, include those few moments in Shakespeare where the size of the performer is detailed in the dialogue. There's the thin (the lean and hungry Cassius; the bull's pizzle Hal); the fat (the tun of bombast Falstaff); the long (painted maypole Helena) and the short (that minimus of knot grass Hermia). Or even Rosalind and Celia in *As You Like It*, who are alternatively and then simultaneously taller than one another according to the Folio text. Today, producers of these plays have to bend their casting around typographical characters, shaping one kind of body to another. Originally, it is almost certain that these textual characters took shape from the physiques of the actors designated to perform these roles. Rosalind is not tall because the text says so, the text says so because Rosalind is tall – at least the boy playing her was. Here it is the body of the performer that left an impression in print, not the other way around. If we begin with the bodies of the actors rather than with bodies of type, we may be able to think anew about playing in the period.

After all, repertory playing requires if not relies upon versatility. Consider the dexterity an actor like Richard Burbage commanded since, as John Astington recently noted, 'When we imagine Burbage's playing as Hamlet, Lear, or Macbeth, we should also think of him, say, as Malvolio, adapting his physique, face, and voice to the frosty confines of that role'.[5] Indeed, it was often for their 'Protean' abilities that the period's leading players were celebrated. Not only is this a useful caveat against any notions of a monolithic early modern acting style, but also a reminder that, for the individual, variation was essential. When it comes to the technology of the actor's body, idiosyncrasy might be among the most important functions a player could command.

In summary, we need not imagine that acting tends towards conformity simply because print does so. This chapter, therefore, attempts to counter the master tropes of print with a hermeneutics of the handmade, an idea that privileges not regularity and standardisation but idiosyncrasy and quirkiness. Materially and metaphorically the handmade 'characters' of early modern English drama – in all senses of the word 'character' – may have evaded conformity, strayed from the line, and, above all, resisted standardisation. Ultimately, this chapter argues that typography has led us into typology, into analyses of acting 'style' beholden to a medium that performance frequently evades: print.

Of course, it is hard to resist print when we are so indebted to it (as these very words attest). For us, imagining a world without print is like imagining the exterior of a room that we can never leave. This exploration of acting without print raises an immediate methodological problem, since any answer inevitably relies upon the medium it tries to circumvent. To read print for evidence of handwriting's primacy is like asking a witness to testify against himself. The four linked excursions into the playing culture of early modern England that will make up this chapter each, therefore, tack towards a new understanding of acting by estranging us from the familiarity of printed drama – by getting 'outside' print in order to think anew about the acting effects generated by the imperfect technology of the human body. Whether challenging the priority of writing and printing in the theatre, examining unusual representations of spoken dialogue, thinking about the effects of handwriting and rolls upon performers and performances, what links these excursions is a commitment to performance that dislodges print by thinking through, with and about handmade characters (both written and performed). Ultimately, the aim of this chapter is to audition an idiosyncratic idea of 'character acting' and to reframe critical work on the period's performance culture.

Such a reframing has implications not just for acting but for the way we imagine early modern plays in performance altogether. Positing an across-the-boards uniformity of style and/or imagining actors to be locked into a single line turns the early modern theatre industry into a sort of drama machine, churning out smoothly consistent self-similar plays day after soggy day. When we think about 'technologies of the body', however, we need to remember that 'technology' does not mean only those things invented after we were born. Part of the shimmer of modern technology is, of course, its predictable consistency, the promise that, be it your iPhone or my supercollider, our technology works the same way every time we switch it on (would that it did). But while 'technology' etymologically promises a 'systemisation' of arts and crafts, each body is a unique piece of machinery, limited by its ever-changing physique but capable of great customisation, variation and versatility. To think about acting in terms more idiosyncratic than uniform is to reanimate early modern drama in its infinite variety. It is to think about early modern drama as an art both hostage to but beneficiary of the quirkiness of its human producers.

HAND TO MOUTH

As noted above, what we know of early modern acting, we know through early modern writing. While a robust bibliographic industry has worked quite hard to ensure the survival of early modern texts, a certain convocation of politic worms has eaten most of the archives of early modern actors. We therefore have to privilege print when we evaluate acting in eras that pre-date audio-visual recording technologies. While print inevitably dominates (and dictates) our conception of early modern acting, however, we should be cautious about extending our print-centric conception to early modern actors. To begin with, we might ask if the period's actors conceived of spoken dialogue as taking place in print or handwriting, or, for that matter, if they conceived of spoken dialogue as primarily occurring in *writing* at all. After all, Hamlet's request that the clowns 'speak no more than is set down for them' (3.2.37) suggests a culture of extemporisation that enfranchised dramatic speech from writing altogether. This question about the relationship between speech and writing is meant to flirt with the possibility that early moderns primarily imagined the material source of sounded speech to be either handwritten characters on scrolled-up strips of paper (as opposed to printed characters bound up in books) *or* as speech that was only later transcribed (if at all). That is, just possibly for these actors, all writing was transcription and began as speech (either by playwright or player). At stake in this question and its answer(s) might be some purchase on the approach that actors took towards 'characterisation', some sense of their methods of sounding upon the stage, and the relationship that an actor's voice bore to the hand(s) that gave his speech a material form.

It is a commonplace that stage players – then and now – work at the intersection of writing and speech, at the point where the one becomes the other, the much-discussed transaction between literacy and orality. The familiar scholarly jingle 'from page to stage' prioritises writing in the theatre, however, with speech always the secondary form. In these terms, spoken dialogue is conceived of as bracketed between forms of inscription (preceded by written script on one side, and succeeded by type on the other), which renders the performed speech itself as either belated writing or incipient print. This familiar teleology assumes that all articulation tends towards print, the triumphant rationale of all inscription.

The assumption that print is the desired end of all writing may, however, be a thoroughly modern idea, since the early modern period sometimes prioritises speech, sometimes praises the durability of writing, but always implies a cycle of articulation that troubles any simple sequence running from hand to mouth to print. Early modern stage players worked at the intersection of writing and speech all right, but the relationship between the two was reciprocal rather than sequential. Indeed, in some accounts of the period, communication starts with an act of *ur*-utterance, an original vocalisation that precedes (and transcends) any subsequent act of articulation. Schoolmaster Richard Mulcaster outlined, in the *The First Part of the Elementarie* (1582), a myth of origins for grammar that reads writing as a 'fining of the naturall tung'. 'Fining' – or, in our terms, 'refining' – for Mulcaster is a discipline, in which the native wildness of the natural tongue is made to conform to the rules of writing. Jonathan Goldberg gives this original myth extensive treatment in *Writing Matter*, where he explains the grammatical and ideological implications of 'fining'.[6] For my purposes, Mulcaster's emphasis upon the tongue's precedence situates writing as, paradoxically, always subsequent to speech even when it enables it, as in the playhouse. Mulcaster stresses that the point of grammar is to 'reduce our English tung to som certain rule, for writing and reading, for words and speaking'.[7] In Mulcaster's terms, we are our own scribes, our hands being the servants of the master tongue, where all articulation begins.

Robert Robinson's *The Art of Pronunciation* (1617) endorses Mulcaster's formulation and offers a sublime description of the collaboration between eyes, ears, hand and voice. Robinson praises writing but describes it as a means of charactering (i.e. putting into characters or written script) the voice, setting up a chicken-and-egg idea of communication. For Robinson, as with Mulcaster, articulated thought – either spoken or inked – originates as voice:

> God [. . .] hath given us a voice to expresse the minde unto the eare, so hee hath given us hands to frame letters or markes for the voice to expresse the minde unto the eyes. So that the eyes and eares are as it were the receivers of message sent unto the heart, the hands and voice as deliverers of message sent from the heart: And though the voice be a more lively kind of speech, yet in respect it is but onely a sleight accident made of so light a substance as the ayre, it is no sooner uttered but it is dissolved, every simple sound doth expel and extinguish the sound going before it, so that the eare can have but one touch of the ayre beating upon it to declare the speech unto the mind: but the hand though it give a dumbe and more dull kind of speech, yet it gives a more durable. A letter is a grosser substance, and therefore is of more continuance then a sound: what is once written still continueth though the hand ceaseth. If the eyes have not satisfied the mind at one view, they may looke on it againe, yea till they have satisfied it's [sic] desire: And by this meanes of noting and charactring of the voice, all things worthy of memory are defended from the injury of forgetfulnesse.[8]

The eloquent sergeants of the articulate heart, the hands and voice express a 'message' that, in Robinson's terms, seems to start as speech. The hand gives a 'dumbe . . . kind of speech', and letters function primarily to note 'the voice', scrambling a simple sequence of hand-to-mouth (or page-to-stage). In any event, Robinson's formulation conceives of the relationship between writing and speaking purely in terms of *hand-lettered* articulation, leaving out print entirely (even while he protects his ideas from the injury of forgetfulness by printing them in the pages of a book).

Robinson's description of reproduction and transience, remembering and forgetting, should remind us that just because actors engaged in memorisation (converting characters into character) they were not engaged in memorialisation, not paying belated homage to an act of writing. Dramatic speech, while enabled by ink, is not merely incipient print nor a subsidiary of inscription. Arguably, memorised speech began *as* a voice, a 'lively kind of speech', before being given dumb but durable expression by the writing hand, which in turn might prompt the player's memorial ability to re-utter writing as sound. As is well known, early modern educators encouraged school children to sound words aloud while reading *and* writing, as John Brinsley instructed in *Ludus Literarius*, where he advises teachers to 'utter each word leasurely and treatably; pronouncing every part of it, so as every one may write both as fast as you speake, and also faire and true together'.[9] Glossing Heminge's and Condell's frontispiece puffery of Shakespeare – that 'what he thought, he uttered with that easiness that wee have scarce received from him a blot in his papers' – Leah Marcus conjectured that Shakespeare had a habit of speaking 'the speeches aloud to himself or to others as he wrote them down'.[10] Whether this be the case or not, it is possible that some actors may have spoken their lines aloud while memorising them and/or memorisation may have been a purely aural experience, their exemplars not textual at all but the voice of another actor if a player could not read. Spoken dialogue may, for some actors, have circumvented writing entirely.

Robinson's approach to speech and writing helpfully previews the most important terms of this chapter: part of the player's task is to engage in a circular system of writing and speaking, a system that may *include* but does not *require* print or, conceptually, require writing at all. What is most important, for my purposes here, is that within the system that Robinson describes, writing never has the final word – and may not have had the first one – and that players might depend on but not require the writing they needed to remember. Indeed, though a linguistic coincidence allows us to speak of the 'body' of a piece of type and the 'body' of an actor, the two bodies do not perform the same functions. The bodies of actors do far more than simply reproduce writing, which is a critical, but just one critical, accessory to performance, which employs more kinds of communicative technologies than just writing (including but not limited to bodies, costumes, properties, architecture, sound and speech). While my project is to challenge the master metaphors of print with those of the writing hand, we should nevertheless be cautious lest we simply trade one master for another: both print and handwriting share a metaphorical preoccupation with inscription. In sum, simply because early modern drama is, for us, a thoroughly textualised affair, does not mean it was so for its original creators, purveyors and audiences.

FORMS AND SHAPES

Worthen's suggestion that the 'forms and shapes of printed books' have troped our understanding of performance, even acting, might suggest that we have no alternative. However, there are other material traces of past performance – other 'forms and shapes' – that can help us challenge book-bound, print-privileged notions. For instance, the period's graphic depictions of speaking characters offer a way of thinking about spoken dialogue that alienates us from our usual access to the spoken word and helps establish new lexicons for thinking about acting.

Woodcuts and engravings in the period that wish to show subjects talking invariably depict strips unfurling from speakers' mouths like New Year's Eve party blowers. The convention seems to derive from the scrolls – called 'banderoles' by art historians – held by prophets in medieval art; it is found across a wide range of illustrations in dramatic and non-dramatic texts in the period.[11] If not a common feature of title pages in the period – R. A. Foakes counts roughly seven or eight 'speaking scrolls' in the period's printed drama[12] – representations of speech are none the less strikingly consistent (as consistent as the modern cartoonist's 'speech bubble' or 'word balloons', which communicate our own ideas about speech). As Holger Schott Syme points out, the scrolls do not just stand in for dialogue but 'insist on the particularity of writing and the material form', since these banderoles bend, interact with other objects, cast shadows, are handled and – unlike 'speech balloons' – obey gravity.[13] It is no coincidence that 'speaking scrolls' precisely resemble the rolls actors received in the period, suggesting that, if the spoken word on the early modern stage *did* have a conceptual written source, it was both materially and metaphorically hand-worked characters incised upon unfurling scrolls. We can then contrast this graphic convention with printed dialogue to alienate our thinking about *spoken* dialogue and, potentially, resituate our work on acting without or at least to one side of print.

In these illustrations, a partly unfurled pennant of text awaits further unwinding, suggesting a flow of language unbroken by the end-stopped lines of printed dialogue and uninterrupted by the 'lines' of other speakers. Unlike books, these scrolls (considered in more detail below) do not contain 'dialogue' since each scroll contains only the words that a single dramatic character is meant to utter. The letters of the words etched on each scroll are hand-engraved, not printed, into the wooden or metallic surface from which the impression was initially taken. The products of a hand-held moving stylus, these title-page 'characters' generally precede books composed of slugs, ingots of lead with raised letters stamped on one end. Therefore, title pages produce a spectacle of speech on the verge of typography, as illustrators attempt to make the viewer virtually *hear* their characters.

The stylus and the slug hieroglyphically represent not just two methods of inscription, but also contrasting ideas about acting. Broadly speaking, the stylus 'performs' where the slug is 'pre-formed'. Print reifies its own belatedness, that is, where a woodcut performs in the present tense. Summarising the period's conception of writing's sensitivity to time and presence, Bruce Smith notes that, for the early moderns, 'writing operates in three time frames at once: it remembers the past, it captures the process of thought in the present, and it opens out into the future. Printing – or at least the *act* of printing – has always the quality of *past*ness about it'.[14] The 'forms and shapes' of woodcuts might, therefore, challenge a print-privileged notion that actors body forth something that already exists, to *re*-present a pre-existing typographical phenomenon rather than to create something anew. The engraving hand, like the writing hand, has the *present*ness of performance about it, a quality of what we call 'in the moment'-ness to which print bears but a second-level relationship.

Occasionally, a title page's hand-engraved letters (re)produce verbatim the printed letters of the play's title, offering a stark contrast between the scriptive and the typographic. The title page to John Cooke's *Greene's Tu Quoque, or the Cittie Gallant* (1614; Figure 4) provides a provocative example, not least because the name of the play is an idiomatic phrase *spoken* in the play. On the title page, an exorbitantly cod-pieced gallant (presumably modelled on the Queen's Men's clown, Thomas Greene) utters a crescent of script, which reads, 'To quoque. To you sir', in contrast to the same (but not the same) 'Tu quoque' printed above him – a spectacular contrast of two related but separate ways of character-ising the voice: the scroll attempts to make us *virtually hear* Thomas Greene's catchphrase; by contrast, the typographic title organises the material that follows, it is the name of all the printed matter to come. Thus the title page collaborates between the protocols of performance and print. Again, the stylus produces what Greene *says*; the slug what the play *is* textually. In other words, the stylus individualises Greene's performance, while the slug collects disparate printed events (dialogue, running heads, speech prefixes, signatures, stage directions etc.) into an entity we call the printed play. Print conforms where the hand individualises.

The title page to the 1615 quarto of Thomas Kyd's *The Spanish Tragedy* (c.1587) provides a further example, since the 'characters' of Hieronimo, Bel Imperia and Lorenzo depicted as scrolling letters appear later in the quarto in a format more familiar to us: horizontally stacked lines of print broken after five stresses (if verse) and justified left into a rationalised typographical grid (Figures 5 and 6). The disparity between Hieronimo's curved characters, 'Alas it is my son Horatio' depicted on the title page and his printed line 'Alasse it is *Horatio* my sweete Sonne:' on the recto of signature D2, emblematises the question this section is

Figure 4 Title-page detail from John Cooke's *Greene's Tu Quoque*, or *the Cittie Gallant* (1614). The Bodleian Library, University of Oxford, 4°T.36 (4) Art

attempting to answer: if we depend upon textual residue for access to the early modern actor – as we must – what can we conjecture about acting by dislodging print's privilege and examining other 'forms and shapes'?

Figure 5 Detail from the title page of *The Spanish Tragedy* (1615).
Title page of Q7 with the woodcut showing scenes 2.4 and 2.5
(© The British Library Board, C.117.6.36)

Firstly, the most 'graphic' contrast in this pair of images lies in the shape of the respective speeches: the crescent versus the line. In fact, in instance after instance, illustrations of speech in the period represent speech as curvy, perhaps to differentiate 'speech' from

The Spanish Tragedie.

Hor. O ſtay awhile, and I will die with thee,
So ſhalt thou yeeld, and yet haue conquered mee.
Bel. Who's there, *Pedringano?* We are betrayde.
  Enter Lorenzo, Balthazar, Serberine, Pedringano diſguiſed.
Lor. My Lord, away with her.   *Take her aſide.*
O ſir, forbeare; your valour is already tride.
Quickly diſpatch my maiſters.   *They hang him in the Arbour.*
Hor. What, will yee murder mee?
Lor. I thus, & thus: theſe are the fruits of loue. *They ſtab him:*
Bel. O ſaue his life, and let me die for him :
O ſaue him Brother, ſaue him *Balthazar* :
I loued *Horatio,* but hee loued not mee.
Bal. But *Balthazar* loues *Belimperia.*
Lor. Although his life were ambitious proud,
Yet is he at the higheſt, now he is dead.
Bel. Murder, murder : helpe *Hieronimo,* helpe.
Lor. Come, ſtop her mouth : away with her.   *Exeunt.*
  Enter Hieronimo in his Shirt.
Hiero. What out-cry cals me from my naked Bed,
And chils my throbbing heart with trembling feare,
Which neuer danger yet could daunt before?
Who cals *Hieronimo?* ſpeake, heere I am.
I did not ſlumber, therefore t'was no Dreame.
No, no; it was ſome Woman cride for helpe,
And heere within the Garden did ſhe cry,
And in this Garden muſt I reſcue her.
But ſtay, What murderous ſpectacle is this?
A man hang'd vp, and all the Murderers gone;
And in my Bower, to lay the guilt on mee?
This place was made for Pleaſure, not for Death,
                           He cuts him downe.
Thoſe Garments that he weares, I oft haue ſeene:
Alaſſe, it is *Horatio* my ſweete Sonne :
O no, but he that who whilome was my Sonne.
Oh, was it thou that call'dſt mee from my Bed;
Oh ſpeake, if any ſparke of life remaine :
I am thy Father; Who hath ſlaine my Sonne?
What ſauage Monſter, not of humane kind,
          D 2   Heere

Figure 6 Text detail from *The Spanish Tragedy* (1615), D2r.
(© The British Library Board, C.117.6.36)

printed dialogue. The artist has made no attempt to (re)produce
level lines of dialogue (Lorenzo's 'line' comes close, though it runs
on the bias). The artist emphasises each character's idiosyncrasy at
the expense of typographical regularity. *The Spanish Tragedy* 'by

the book' is an organised sequence of parallel lines (as is, for T. W. Baldwin, an actor's career); on the printed page, every character 'sounds the same' since typography tends towards conformity. But banderoles bend towards individuality. To speak casually, as we do, of 'Hieronimo's lines' or 'Hamlet's lines' performs conceptual (if not ideological) work, shaping the way we think about acting, as though the parallel lines of printed dialogue suggest a conformity of histrionic approach to which all players, perhaps, 'evolve'. In any event, it makes no more sense than to speak of 'Hieronimo's lines' than of 'Hieronimo's curves'.

Secondly, speech-like text in illustrations is frequently unpunctuated, contrasting with what is at least some light pointing in many early modern manuscripts. In the detail above, Hieronimo's words appear to be full-stopped, but the illustrator makes no attempt to reproduce the fastidious punctuation of Bel Imperia and Lorenzo's 'lines' as printed on sig. D2r. Of course, one is not meant to *sound* punctuation (if anything, they indicate silence or inflection), while most written characters in playbooks (both print and manuscript) attempt to guide vocalisation. (Punctuation terms were, originally, rhetorical terms, that were guides to vocal articulation; increasingly, punctuation came to represent grammar visually.[15]) Other title page illustrations frequently dispense with punctuation altogether since they attempt to reproduce the sound of speech rather than its syntactical sense; as Syme points out, the banderoles 'represent the live voice as well as a documentary record' of it.[16] For all of our attention to it, punctuation, in performance, has no substance, makes no sound, and may have been literally immaterial to performers and audiences in the period. While the punctuation of early modern printed playbooks has led some to develop typographically driven ideas about acting, these largely unpunctuated 'speaking scrolls' cast further scepticism upon the idea.[17]

Thirdly, there are semantic discrepancies between the *Spanish Tragedy*'s title page and its printed forms that might disrupt our print-driven notion of word-perfect performance and even question whether print or illustration provides a better 'documentary' record of performance. With the *Spanish Tragedy*, the illustrator has excerpted and conflated his characters. He is on-book but, if we anachronistically privilege the print form of dialogue as an executive record of the script and/or performance, out of his text. Syme notes of this title page that the banderoles 'stand [. . .] for an originary text (in this case, Kyd's), which they render faithfully, or as faithfully as an actor might', but of course we do not *have* Kyd's originary text; we only have, in this instance, a 1615 quarto, which is easy – perhaps too easy – to mistake for the 'originary text'. [18] Similarly, R. A. Foakes notes of *The Roaring Girl*'s 1611 title-page comment, 'My case is alter'd, I must worke for my living', that the sentence 'is not from the text of the play'.[19] He furthermore notes of Greene's 'Tu quoque. To you sir' that the character 'never uses these exact words', presumably meaning that the words do not appear in this precise form in the printed text, which implicitly stands in for evidence of a performance.[20] Again, this is to privilege the printed play-text over the title-page illustration (which is then, in an approach so familiar as to seem anodyne, not considered the 'text of the play').

It is fascinating to speculate what the illustrator's 'copy text' might have been in, for instance, the case of *The Spanish Tragedy*: his own memory of this oft-performed play? A prompt copy? Kyd's holograph? Or was he simply working from or to the stationer's specifications, in which case, how did the stationer arrive at his text? In terms of acting, the illustration here and elsewhere might trouble our notion that printed texts provide us with an accurate account of the dialogue actually spoken on the early modern stage. It might further suggest to us an approach more focused on 'remembering' than 'memorising', in Laurie Maguire's useful distinction.[21] Specifically, the question might be, which is it more likely that Edward Alleyn said on stage: the iambically perfect 'Alas it is my son Horatio' or the lyrically spiky 'Alasse it is *Horatio* my sweete Sonne:'? As 'authentic' witnesses to early modern performance, printed texts have no more authority than the illustrations here. Either both forms are 'authentic' or neither is. Finally, recalling Robinson's diagnosis of the relationship between voice and text, writing in these woodcuts begins as voice – scrolls issue from the mouth not the hand – blurring the question of which has priority (a question nowhere more alive than in the playhouse). However, while Hieronimo's speech unfurls from his mouth – voice producing writing as in Robinson's scenario – the speaking scrolls of Bel Imperia and Lorenzo complicate the matter, since their scrolls unfurl *into* their mouths if, as we must, we read their dialogue left to right. Furthermore, the composition violates the print protocol by which the order of uttering is arranged from the top to the tail of the page; in the illustration, Lorenzo speaks 'over' Bel Imperia, though 'after' her if we read left to right. Similarly, the title pages of the non-dramatic texts *An Honest Ghost* (1658) and *An Age for Apes* (1658) also feature written scrolls in which the reading sequence moves from bottom-to-top. The artist's compositional instinct collides with Western left-to-right, top-to-bottom reading practice, so that in the case of Bel Imperia and Lorenzo, the artist is literally putting words into the characters' mouths, which we have always assumed to be the playwright's job. At the same time, if one reads the *image* left-to-right, it violates the temporal sequence of the events in the play; image and text collide where they ought to collude, and this particular collision/collusion of speech and writing appears as well on the title pages of Middleton's *Game at Chess* and *The Witch of Edmonton* and elsewhere. All graphically demonstrate the conflicting conventions of playwrights, players, printers and illustrators and should remind us that print conventions are not the only ones to which acting conforms.

Broadly speaking, these collisions result from conflicting protocols of print and proximity. For the illustrator includes what is, in print, only obliquely signalled through speech prefixes: bodies. In print, the speech prefixes are all the same size, all the same font, whereas in performance – or as here, in illustration – bodies can appear starkly different. On sig. D2r '*Bel.*' and '*Lor.*' achieve a consistency of setting (both names are shortened to three letters, set in the same font, capitalised and punctuated with a full stop), while on the title page, their bodies are as different as black and white. Neither are illustrative bodies neatly arrayed in a tidily stacked column justified left (as on a printed page), just as bodies in performance jostle for precedence, blurring priority, speaking over one another, and competing for attention even when not speaking. The 'bodies' of individual typefaces aspire to a degree of conformity and consistency that the infinitely quirky human form can simply never achieve. Above all, these illustrations remind us that speech comes from the bodies of actors, not from bodies of type. What then might we conclude about acting if we consider the craft through these illustrations rather than through printed texts? First, early modern actors may have imagined speech not in the rigid geometry of stacked lines but in the unfurling curlicues of the scrolled-up rolls from which they worked. Their performances may have, analogously, 'curved' off the standard line that dominates *printed* drama and our conception of its onstage realisation, producing, for instance, verse speaking more metrically free than printed texts suggest. Furthermore, while printed lines might encourage a 'one at a time' speaking style (each line begins after the previous one has decorously drawn to a close) the fluttering pennants of title-page talk crowd each other, signalling to us, perhaps, that the early modern performance style was a lot less polite than the printed page suggests. In addition, the illustrated actors who perform on the period's title pages dominate their 'text', tethering it to their bodies and reminding us of physical presence in a way that printed speech prefixes simply fail to do. It is possible, ultimately, to argue that our very idea that actors 'speak verse' at all or observe 'line endings' whatsoever is purely a product of print culture.[22] Curvy, lightly pointed, semantically promiscuous, spatially idiosyncratic, physically embodied, these illustrations of speech-like text above all confound modern notions that confuse the homogenisation of print with a homogenisation of acting style.

HAND AFFECTS

The ink that prompted speech on the early modern stage flowed from the nibs of hand-held quills, and this section therefore asks how 'character acting' instigated by handwritten parts might differ from that facilitated by print. For the fact is that early modern actors memorised words from *handwritten* parts, and while those parts may have been a remove or more away from the play's author, each part bore the mark of the hand that transcribed it and that gave it its peculiar character. An actor found in the twisted graphemes of his part a bespoke character, one that potentially promoted performances so idiosyncratic as to render the idea of an ubiquitous early modern acting 'style' absurd.

* * *

Shakespeare was a terrible writer – at least on the evidence of 'Hand D' in *The Book of Sir Thomas More*, the section of the manuscript play that scholars believe to be written by Shakespeare himself. For in the period, a cardinal virtue of a writer lay in legibility, as well as stylistic facility. Actors of the time will have spent some of their private preparation focusing on more than just semantic comprehension. For before an actor could absorb what John Astington describes as 'the entire development and emotional contour of a role contained within a written part', he had to be able to read it.[23] An actor may have been at least initially as concerned with the scriptive contours of the writer's hand as his part's 'emotional contours'. So while, today, an actor's preparation might start with semantics, in the early modern period it began with something more basic: apprehension. A potentially inscrutable scribal hand may have demanded a variety of interpretation (or of interpenetration) from performers unfamiliar to us today. For, as Paul C. Gutjahr and Megan Benton suggest, an 'ethic of typographic invisibility' means that '[f]or most readers [today, the] formal, intermediate presence of print is so familiar and conventional that it is [. . .] unseen and unpondered; we see only text on the page'.[24] Scribal copy may have been more insistently visible, particularly when it resisted rather than enabled understanding. It would be overly deterministic to conclude that idiosyncratic characters produced idiosyncratic character, but the 'intermediate presence' of handwritten script may have played an overtly mediating function in actor preparation. How many slips twixt quill and lips took place between pen and performance?

On the other hand, since scribal copy was the playhouse norm (and an actor's many parts may all have appeared in the familiar hand of a company book keeper), handwriting may have been as invisible to the early modern actor as the font in which this book appears. However, as Tiffany Stern has recently observed, Edward Alleyn's extant part from *Orlando Furioso* contains 'gaps and spaces' where the scribe has obviously struggled to interpret illegibilities in *his* handwritten copy.[25] (If we wish to know 'who really wrote' the words actors uttered on the early modern stages, the answer is those scribes who copied the parts of a play, and whose hand(s) an actor had, at least initially, to decipher.) The scribe's lacunae were handed on to Edward Alleyn, who inherited the scribe's frustration in a version of the children's game where whispers are passed around a group to see how many misunderstandings accrue with every transaction. The period's handwritten parts required actors not just to interpret but – in some cases – to decipher, and this level and degree of contact influenced performance then as surely as the 'forms and shapes' of print influence performance now.

To begin with, actors usually derive 'character' today from linguistic codes that are themselves sourced in automated reproduction (hence our many, many print-derived terms for performance, including 'lines', 'type', 'casting', 'stereotype', 'word perfect', and 'off book'. Print metaphors leached early into the ground water of performance, however, including the 'casting' of actors in parts. Consider the title of Richard Brathwait's 1631 collection that, while non-dramatic, employs familiar terminology: *The Whimzies: or, a New Cast of Characters*). Furthermore, Shakespeare in performance is, today, underwritten by a publishing industry that produces and reproduces his work in reams of reiterative texts. Textual reproduction is so easy, so effortless, so relatively inexpensive that the modern Shakespearean actor faces a bewildering selection of available texts from which to choose. Whatever text an actor ends up with, his access is, above all, non-exclusive.

By contrast, the scribal production of parts minimised the proliferation of dramatic scripts in the interest of, presumably, time and money. When it came to the distribution of dialogue, companies in the period seemed to be trying to determine how little they could get away with, and still get away with it. When an early modern actor received his squat baton of scrolled scrawl, it was, exclusively, *his*. One of the starkest differences between the Shakespearean actor today and in the past can, then, be expressed as the contrast between textual multiplicity and scriptural singularity. Whereas the Shakespearean actor today chooses a text (or, more likely, has it chosen for him or her) from a vast array of options, the popular Admiral's Men's player Edward Alleyn possessed the *only* part for the title role in *Orlando Furioso*. For the early modern player, character was not an open book; it was furled within his closed roll, an occult account passed from the playwright's hand to his own (through, albeit, at least one other set of hands). This proprietary relationship between a player and his part may have encouraged an equally exclusive performance. The audience for Alleyn's Orlando would not (because it *could* not) verify the fidelity of Alleyn's words to the text, nor evaluate his performance in textual terms at all. Being 'perfect' in his part was a self-enforced affair. An early modern actor created a character from out of a range of characters inscribed for him in something like a private communication.

Actors therefore possessed unique if not bespoke texts. Whether playwrights wrote with particular actors in mind (a luxury Shakespeare and other 'attached playwrights' could have enjoyed) is a matter of conjecture, but if writers did not 'customise' each part for each player, players will anyway have customised parts for themselves. To the extent to which Alleyn's part is exemplary (a caveat applicable to much work of this kind, though Alleyn's part is far from the only one in the period), his willingness to alter his part suggests a permissiveness promoted, we might guess, by his proprietary relationship to it. While Alleyn's source for his changes is unclear – his 'copy' may well have been his own creativity – what *does* seem evident is that something about the material form of the handwritten scroll invited alteration and, in some cases, such as when it was illegible or gap-filled, demanded it. Performers today imperil the integrity of their characters if they alter the 'characters' printed on the mass-produced edition from which they are working. Perhaps the fact that an early modern actor was writing upon a written (as opposed to printed) document – engaging his hand with another's in a similarly inscriptive act – encouraged this form of personalisation, whereas the authority of a printed text (authorised by its own multiplicity) militates against alteration. An actor like Alleyn could correspond with (and to) his part quite literally and literarily. And so he did; some of the corrections to Orlando – the attempts to fill in the gaps – are in Alleyn's own hand.

Writing may seem the province of playwrights, not players. At the same time, the culture of handwriting may have invited players to produce new copy themselves, to supplement their original copies in a manner that favoured not fixity but fluidity, the reciprocal flux of mouth-to-hand-to-mouth between writing and speech imagined by Robinson. An actor's ability to write back on to a part, and, to some degree, 'author' his own part, may have encouraged something more quirky, more personalised than the assembly-line standardisation implied by notions of 'typecasting' or a related sense that repertory actors might pursue a single 'line' of characters.

We might just as easily see performances as being as idiosyncratic as the hands that scripted them (though, and there's the rub, only as *legibly idiosyncratic* as the hands that scripted them). In this regard, actors are not 'typecast' but 'pre*scribed*' by hand and in hand. And while a 'prescribed' character might also imply fixity, the emphasis upon 'scribal' practice should remind us of the individual labour behind the unique contours of its creator's own 'characters'. This is to make a claim distinct from that about a 'typecast' actor, with its figurative emphasis upon regularity, reproducibility and similarity; it is instead to promote the idea that acting is as individualised as the hand(s) that produced the matter they converted into speech.

Thus far, the work here has concentrated upon a roll's singularity in order to point up its difference from a printed play. A printed play is made up of a cast of characters. Each 'c' or 'u' or 't' aspires to the condition of sameness (and fails of course). By contrast, every written character is created anew each time the scribal hand pushes his inked quill across the page. At the same time, it is fair to say that when a part reached a player, it was already a copy at one or more removes from the playwright's hand. Again, to be a 'good writer' in the period meant not to be creative but reproductive, not a stylistically original producer of text but a conformist to pre-scripted originals. As Jonathan Goldberg puts it, 'In the manuals and pedagogic texts, to write means to copy the exemplary texts and alphabets [. . .] Duplication is the aim, reinscriptions [. . .] found the human and the habitual in this entirely secondary activity'.[26] Writing by hand could not evade the regime of copying upon which, after all, legibility depends; a truly unique hand would be truly illegible. Throughout the seventeenth century, handwriting was aspiring to but failing to achieve the condition of typographic consistency.

Metaphorically at least, handwriting may ultimately offer us a better model for thinking about early modern acting than print. For generating 'new copy' by hand, where the goal was both to transcribe the exemplar and make visible the expertise of one's own hand, is a paradoxical goal familiar to the performer, who labours to produce a character both new *and* legible to attract attention not just to the product but the producer. To put this baldly, printed books efface the labour that produced them; handwritten copy makes evident its creation. Analogously, actors aspire not to 'typographic invisibility' but ostentatious legibility. If we trope acting with print we may end up effacing the actor's peculiar person, making him or her a mere slug in the service of the author's intent. Attention to the dominance of handwriting and of the handmade on the early modern stage can make visible the vanished bodies of the men and boys who gave first flesh to the period's plays and while 'personating' others impersonated themselves.

MATTER MATTERS

If you have read this far, you have turned several pages of this book, holding at least momentarily in your memory the catch word of a recto while you move to its verso, perhaps wetting an index finger as you move from page to page while this argument 'unfolds'. At the same time, I reminded you earlier that an idea had been 'noted above' and then mentioned some matter 'below'. Your effortless ability to negotiate physically the pages of this book while navigating the idea that this piece of writing occupies a roll (as it appears to do in the on-screen composition in which I am engaged) relies on the coincidence of two different textual physiques: the book and the roll.

The prepositional language of the roll – 'below', 'above', 'before', 'after' – can alert us to the ways that differing textual physiques require different kinds of use that may imply different approaches to performance. Parts were made of strips of paper that were then joined top-to-tail and rolled around a wooden baton, requiring motion. A 'roll' takes its name from the action it demands in its use. You 'read' a book, but you 'roll' a roll. Books have as many moving parts as they have pages and may be so numbered; rolls have but one moving part – it – and force the reader to encounter a swath of materials to reach a particular place. The material encounter of actors with the physical requirements of a roll literally shaped their preparation and performance, as they converted the motion of the roll into the motion of their bodies across the stage.

While early modern actors certainly may have owned, read, purchased or traded in printed or handwritten playbooks (as we know Edward Alleyn did), their access to performance material was, invariably, through a hand-lettered roll. Actors possessed, in these terms, a seamed but linked unfurling of characters, and might be encouraged by their material to imagine their character not unfolding or changing – as in a book – but rather unrolling, unravelling, dwindling even as the future of their role shrinks in their hands while the past continues to swell. Our modern insistence that characters 'change', that they demonstrate some dynamic behavioural divergence within a fiction potentially privileges a book-bound notion of turning the page on the past, or, even closer to home in early modern terms, 'turning over a new leaf'. The contrast between the turning leaves of a book and the unfurling roll has a range of material implications since they facilitate different approaches to a single role. To cite just one, a Malvolio today might organise his preparation by visiting the discrete acts and scenes in which the majority of his 'lines' appear. Indeed he may think of 'his' part in the play as an interrupted sequence of discrete scenes – the Gulling Scene, the Cross Gartered Scene, the Dark House Scene, etc. – or, as we call them but the first Malvolio would not, 2.5, 3.4, 4.2. He will find these scenes efficiently, since the physique of the book is hospitable to indexical systems including act, scene, line numbers, that allow us to 'find our place' in the text. 'Indexical' acting today conforms, that is, to our relentless logic of systemisation, where an actor has access to the entire play in addition to textual apparatuses that allow him to find his place and function within it, as opposed to the 'scarcity economy' enforced by the individualised part. Malvolio 'by the book' is a collection of disparate sites of reading, many of which do not include the actor at all. The roll of Malvolio, on the other hand, is all sequence and continuity, and there is no place in his part in which his character(s) do not abide. Malvolio's role is *all about him*.

While it is easy to imagine early modern playwrights and audiences thinking of plays as 'bundles of scenes', actors may have possessed a very different concept of the plays in which they took part.[27] Preparing in isolation from individualised and even customised parts might, therefore, have promoted not just idiosyncratic but solipsistic acting. After all, if Edward Alleyn's part of Orlando is a reliable guide, each part included the character's name at the top, so that every actor, from 'Hamlet' to 'first citizen', might imagine himself to be playing, even figuratively, the 'title role'. Such a notion challenges an idea of early modern plays in performance as uniform in style and actors as 'tuned in' to the individual play's genre and tone. Indeed, it can be difficult to intuit something like a play's genre or tone from an isolated part (what kind of play did Osric think he was in?). Did companies spend their limited rehearsal time trying to conform divergent or even aberrant individual performances into a coherent acting approach that might align with a uniformity of presentation dictated by their interpretation of the play in its textual form? Or, alternatively, we could reconceive early English plays in performance as potentially vaudevillian in their presentation, a hurly-burly of performances that cohered only because they were taking place on the same stage on the same afternoon.

In summary, since matter *matters*, handwritten rolls provoked approaches to acting that differ, and probably differed dramatically, from those produced from printed books. While these differences will remain ever elusive to us, we need, wherever possible, to think about a culture of performance informed and enabled – both materially and conceptually – via the infinite quirkiness of the human hand and the hand-held tools required to craft performance.

CODA – AGAINST 'STYLE'

One is a freak, two is a category, three is a style. 'Style', that is, is a product of iteration. As such, style is implicated in the ideologies of the copy. It is therefore the somewhat perverse conclusion of this chapter that the understandable impulse to imagine early modern actors conformed to something as uniform as 'a' style should be rejected. (Of course, the 'idiosyncratic style' of acting that this chapter has tentatively argued for is, in these terms, oxymoronic – 'idiosyncrasy' is antithetical to the conformity on which 'style' depends.) Fortunately, debate today has cooled on the relative 'formalism' or 'realism' of early modern acting styles, a debate that over the years employed such terms as 'rhetorical', 'naturalism' and 'artificial'. It is none the less striking that these terms can all equally describe various literary movements or 'styles'. Indeed, it is certainly from within literary studies that such terms originate. Why, however, did we ever imagine that the early modern community of actors observed something as mono-lithic as *a* single style of acting or were capable of only single 'lines'? I have argued that the answer might be 'print'. To think afresh about acting in the early modern period requires, therefore, that we think anew about the material form and representation of the words that actors received and the ways they read and thought about them. Above all, we might resist an urge to back-project our print-influenced desire for conformity of approach by early modern actors. Perhaps we honour the actors of the past best by allowing them to be as quirky, as strange, as idiosyncratic as ourselves.

PART THREE

THE SENSORY STAGE

CHAPTER EIGHT

WITHIN, WITHOUT, WITHINWARDS: THE CIRCULATION OF SOUND IN SHAKESPEARE'S THEATRE

BRUCE R. SMITH

Even if we have got the acoustical engineering just right – the shapes, the dimensions, the building materials as close as possible to what the documents and archaeological evidence suggest – a number of factors still prevent us from experiencing sound in Shakespeare's Globe in London as Shakespeare and his contemporaries did in the original structure of 1599. The most disabling factor may be our very keenness to hear sound on its own terms. The emergence of 'sound studies' in the past thirty years – most practitioners would date it to R. Murray Schafer's *The Tuning of the World* (1977) – is part of a much larger phenomenon: media studies. At the heart of sound studies is the assumption that sound gives us a purchase on the world that is quite different from vision. Seeing *feels* linear: I cast my gaze out into a world that is 'out there', beyond my body. Listening, by contrast, *feels* round:[1] sound comes to me from the world and engulfs me. Stephen Handel in *Listening: An Introduction to the Perception of Auditory Events* puts the distinction this way: 'Listening is centripetal; it pulls you into the world. Looking is centrifugal; it separates you from the world.'[2] And so it feels to me – sometimes.

Truth be told, my experience of the theatre, like my experience of the world in general, is not really an either/or proposition, even when I am trying hard to 'bracket' sound in the way phenomenologists – those who study the structure of experience – like Husserl counsel me to do. To understand what you are perceiving, Husserl says, you must block out everything but yourself and the object you are coming to know. To know something through sound, for example, you must block out vision. Most of the time, however, I don't choose to look at one moment and listen at another. Especially in the theatre, where looking and listening are aesthetically shaped, intensely concentrated, and forcefully directed activities, looking and listening happen at the same time. Indeed, they are *coordinated* in ways quite particular to theatrical performance as a medium in its own right. Bracketing is well and good for purists. When it comes to human perception, binaries oversimplify a much more complex situation. David F. Armstrong, William C. Stokoe and Sherman E. Wilcox sound this warning in their work on gesture: 'Discontinuities of all types – language versus gesture, language versus general cognitive capacities (such as abstraction, categorization, judgments of similarity, etc.), language as amodal (independent of transmission system) versus language as intermodal (multiply linked to all human transmission systems) – are suspect.'[3]

In that spirit, I am proposing here a model of analysis based, not on difference-marking but on continuities, not on framing but on circulation. I will chart the circulation of sound in Shakespeare's theatre in two stages: first by examining the medium (air), next by surveying the three containers that shaped that medium in Shakespeare's playhouse: the tiring-house, the amphitheatre and the human body. Along the way, I will try to stay true to my own experience by attending to sight as well as sound.

THE MEDIUM

Although it is widely recognised that Shakespeare's theatre was a multi-media affair that combined speech, music and other sound effects, costumes, props and choreography in distinctive site-specific and time-specific ways, it is not so widely recognised that the medium in each case was then – and is now – *air*.[4] It is molecules of nitrogen, oxygen, argon, carbon dioxide, and traces of other gases that transmit the sound waves that reach our ears and impede the light rays that reach our eyes. That is a material condition we share absolutely with Shakespeare and his contemporaries. Within the confines of the Globe's wooden O, players and patrons alike were immersed in a single homogenous medium: a charged, pulsating medium. The charge came partly from light rays. Whether reflected off the players' bodies or projected out into space from the players' eyes (opinions about the source varied in Shakespeare's time), light rays connected watching eyes in the pit and galleries with moving bodies on the platform. The charged quality of bright colours, the pulsing of those hues in the ambient air, is caught in one of Shakespeare's characteristic words, 'glister'. 'All that glisters is not gold', Morocco reads from the scroll in *The Merchant of Venice* (2.7.65).[5] Projective presence, movement of light across space, is even more prominent in Richard II's exclamation 'Down, down I come like glist'ring Phaethon' (*Richard II*, 3.3.178). The 'glistering apparel' brought on by Ariel to dupe Stefano and Trinculo in *The Tempest* (stage direction before 4.1.194) refers to something felt more viscerally by the spectators than the white/yellow hue of the fabric or the jewels that are sewn upon it. The effect is expanded to the entire visual ensemble of the stage in Time's prophecy in *The Winter's Tale* to 'make stale / The glistering of this present' (4.1.13–14). In moments like these, the radiant quality of light, its movement through air, is felt in one's eyes, even perhaps on one's skin.

Let me cite just one example out of many. In the dénouement of *Cymbeline* the King narrates a scene in which looking charges the air with emotional energy and touches bodies with physical force:

> Posthumus anchors upon Imogen;
> And she (like harmless lightning) throws her eye
> On him: her brothers, me: her master hitting
> Each object with a joy: the counterchange
> Is severally in all.

(5.5.394–8)

What the King describes here is a *circuit* of vision, an enclosed space within which beams of vision circulate among the actors on stage. Add the audience to that circularity, and the entire amphitheatre becomes a force field of passions that pass from the onlooker to the persons looked on. In such moments the air became more than invisible gases. It is called into palpable presence and endowed with sound and touch as well as vision. Synaesthesia suffuses the King's speech: he turns images into sounds; he invites the spectator/listeners to *hear* in his words what they *see* with their eyes.

Scientific inquiry into air began, in England at least, with Francis Bacon. Bacon's account of sound in Experiments 124 and 125 in *Silva Silvarum* emphasises the susceptibility of air to external energy that will cause 'eruptions' – movements that, if strong enough, will reach the human ear and be heard as sounds. Several times in the series of experiments Bacon speaks of the air as positively *desiring* these eruptions:

> It is Profound Contemplation in Nature, to consider of the Emptinesse, (as we may call it,) or Insatisfaction of severall Bodies; And of their Appetite to take in Others. Aire taketh in Lights, and Sounds, and Smells, and Vapours; And it is most manifest, that it doth it, with a kinde of Thirst, as not satisfied with his owne former Consistence; For else it would never receive them in so suddenly, and easily.[6]

By considering the effect of humidity on the transmissibility of sound, Bacon directs attention to conditions that obtained in outdoor theatres like the Globe. Lacking a practical means of testing his deduction, Bacon argues more than once that moisture in the air serves to contain and preserve sound, making it more present, while dry air serves to dissipate sound. Modern experiments demonstrate just the reverse. Sound in the Globe would have been 'damped' just as the colours and contours were.

The varying qualities of air – thick or thin, humid or dry, full or empty – are registered not only in philosophy books but in Shakespeare's scripts. '*Why do we heare better in the night then in the day*,' goes one of the problems attributed in the Middle Ages and the Renaissance to Aristotle:

Answer. Because, as *Aristotle* doth say, there is greater quietness in the night then in the day, because the sunne doth not so well draw up vapours in the night as in the day, and therefore the meane is more fit and readie, and the meane being fit, the motion is better done by him, the which is sayd to bee done with sound. Another reason is, because there are more motions of the ayre and sound in the day then in the night, which doe hinder one another. Also in the night there is greater silence which is opposite unto sound, and things opposite put one against the other, shew the better.[7]

This passage is cited with approval by Helkiah Crooke in his medical encyclopaedia *Mikrokosmographia*.[8] The air of the inner ear, Crooke says, is like the night air in being 'thin and pure' and hence able to receive sounds with special acuity. Hermia describes the same phenomenon:

Dark night, that from the eye his function takes,
The ear more quick of apprehension makes;
Wherein it doth impair the seeing sense,
It pays the hearing double recompense.
(*A Midsummer Night's Dream*, 3.2.177–80)

By this standard, listening conditions at the Globe in mid-afternoon, in England's vaporous climate, were less than ideal.

More favourable conditions were available in each listener's inner ear or – could they get there – in the ether that was imagined by most people as connecting the stars and planets beyond the earth's atmosphere. For such thinkers (and they were the majority) there had to be *something* everywhere. Even Robert Boyle in his posthumously published *General History of the Air* cannot bring himself to dismiss the existence of ether. In defining his subject Boyle keeps his sights trained not on interstellar space, but on the material world around him:

> By the *Air* I commonly understand that thin, fluid, diaph-
> anous, compressible and dilatable Body in which we
> breath, and wherein we move, which envelops the Earth
> on all sides to a great height above the highest Mountains;
> but yet is so different from the *Aether* [or *Vacuum*] in the
> intermundane or interplanetary Spaces, that it refracts
> the Rays of the Moon and other remoter Luminaries.[9]

In providing alternatives – *either* ether *or* a vacuum – Boyle nods to
the contemporary controversy between 'plenists' and 'vacuists'.
Taking their cue from the Latin mass ('*Pleni sunt caeli et terrae
gloria tua*'), 'plenists' asserted that interplanetary and interstellar
space was filled with highly refined air in the form of ether. There
had to be *something* everywhere. 'Vacuists' believed these spaces
were empty. As for the sublunary world, it was imagined by Boyle
as a continuous medium. In his experiments he never forgot its
omnipresent, inescapable materiality.

Structuralist, linguistic and post-structuralist critics, by
contrast, prefer the vacuum. For the purposes of this paper at
least, I am a 'plenist', and I invite you to join me out here in the air.
What you are reading is a perhaps perverse experiment in
eco-criticism, an attempt to situate imaginative texts in physical
environments. The result, I hope, will be a changed understanding
not just of air as a medium, but of the human body as an entity
within that medium. The human body is not just *contained* within
a biosphere of air but is *immersed* within that biosphere, like a fish
in water. We can chart the biosphere in Shakespeare's theatre by
attending to three containers of air: tiring-house, amphitheatre
and human bodies. Our entrée into these three containers is
provided by a series of adverbs appropriate to each of the spaces in
turn: 'within', 'without', 'withinwards'.

WITHIN

One cals within, Juliet.
Within. A Saile, a Saile.
Alarum afarre off, as at a Sea-fight.
Enter a Porter. / Knocking within.
A tempestuous noise of Thunder and Lightening heard: Enter a
  Ship-master, and a Boteswaine.[10]

In the macrocosm of the Globe, as in the microcosm of the human
body, meaning-making with sound began – as it always must –
within. In physical terms, speech begins in the lungs, with an
inbreathing of air. Held in place by the diaphragm, that volume of
air is released gradually through the larynx and the mouth, both of
which shape the outbreathed air in certain distinctive ways to
produce phonemes that are heard as speech. If Lev Vygotsky is
right, this body-centred making of meaning happens in psychological terms as well as physical. Thought begins, Vygotsky claims,
as an inchoate whole-body experience. By the time a thought is
spoken or written down it has undergone a metamorphosis.
Sensations have become words in the loose syntax of what Vygotsky
calls 'inner speech' before they are spoken as words in the
tighter syntax of 'external speech' or encoded in the even tighter
syntax of writing. Decoding a theatrical script reverses this process: writing becomes auditory speech that, in the ears of the
listener, becomes inner speech, which in turn becomes sensations.
'*What is contained simultaneously in thought unfolds sequentially in
speech*,' Vygotsky explains. 'Thought can be compared to a hovering cloud which gushes a shower of words.'[11] For spectator/
listeners in the theatre, the experience of drama is like getting
caught out in the rain – which at the Globe must have been the
case often enough.

As speech itself begins within the actor's body, so in the staging
arrangements at the Globe, meaning-making through sound
began within the tiring-house. It was there that all the words were
kept in store, as 'the book' of the play. It was from within the
tiring-house that actors made their entrances before they spoke. It

was there they returned when they had finished speaking. Meanwhile, the tiring-house could make its auditory presence felt, in the form of non-verbal sounds like alarums and thunder or in garbled verbal sounds like shouts and cries. With respect to sight, it is clear enough that Shakespeare's plays emerged from within. My argument is that they likewise emerged from within with respect to sound.

Take, for example, this moment from *Macbeth*:

MACBETH
What is that noise?

[*a cry within, of women*]

SEYTON
It is the cry of women, my good lord.
(5.5.7–8)

The sequence here is repeated again and again in Shakespeare's scripts: first a sound without a visual source, then a verbal identification of that source. Schematically, that sequence might be rendered thus:

sound? → vision → sound+vision

Whether a question mark is correct for the first unit is open to question. To render Macbeth's 'What is that noise?' as a question is to miss a curious slippage between questions and exclamations. In early modern orthography there was as yet no separate punctuation mark for exclamations. Question marks did service for both. Every instance of '*What* is that noise?' was – and still is – 'What is that *noise*!'

A famous example is the knock in *Macbeth*. The uncanny sound begins in 2.2 as interruptions of Lady Macbeth's confident speeches about Duncan's murder. The first knock comes as Lady Macbeth takes her exit, within, to finish the deed that Macbeth has left undone there. Alone on stage, Macbeth is instantly unsettled by the sound: 'Whence is that knocking? – / How is't with me, when every noise appals me?' (2.2.56–7). Taking his cue perhaps from the whiteness implicit in 'appals' (the word means literally 'to turn pale'), he ends his search for a visual source by fixing on his bloody hands. His speech is both a question and an exclamation: 'What hands are here? Ha! they pluck out mine eyes' (2.2.58).[12] In effect, knock = bloody hands. At the second knock, the returning Lady Macbeth is able to contain the sound by identifying its source within the fiction: 'I hear a knocking / At the south entry' (2.2.64–5). Two more knocks in scene two, and six more in scene three fail, however, to lessen the sound's appalling effect, its dissociation of sound from source. Thomas De Quincy was on to something in his essay 'On the Knocking at the Gate in *Macbeth*' (1823). From his earliest years, De Quincy says, this particular moment in the play 'produced to my feelings an effect for which I never could account'.[13] More was going on in the knock, De Quincy realised, than his understanding could explain. Fictionally locating the knock at 'the south entry' does not contain the sound or settle the listeners' imaginations.

'*Knock within*': that stage direction refers to a physical space that was very different from what we casually refer to as 'offstage' or 'backstage'. It is curious that the tiring-house, a space so much associated with aspects of visual performance – with costumes and props, with the making of entrances and exits – should also be a major site for the making of sounds.[14] The prepositions 'back' and 'off' are locators in visual space. They work well enough to indicate what lies beyond the stage's margins in proscenium theatres of the seventeenth, eighteenth, nineteenth and early twentieth centuries. Peter Brook's 'open space' depends on there once having been a backstage and an offstage, even as Brook presumes to move those once hidden locations into plain view. The tiring-house in the Globe was not, however, a space of this sort. In visual terms, 'within' marks a boundary less definite than 'back' and 'off'. 'Within' implies continuity with what can be seen 'without'. The wooden O of the Globe was itself a 'within' relative to the city spaces 'without'.

Experiments by psychologists and physicists have demonstrated that sounds from a source that a listener cannot see tend to be attributed by the listener to a space 'behind'.[15] Macbeth registers a sense of dislocation when, having just stabbed Banquo, he hears the first '*Knock within*' in 2.2. Relative to Macbeth's position on the stage platform, the space within the tiring-house, the source of the knocking sound, is 'behind'. Ten repetitions of '*Knock within*' keep the fictional source of the sound unknown to the theatre's audience/spectators, despite Lady Macbeth's offhand tracing them to the south entry, until the Porter opens the gate and admits Macduff and Lennox several minutes later, at 2.3.20. As I have argued elsewhere, 'behind' remains an axis of orientation in *Macbeth* from beginning to end.[16] Noises of the battle in Act 5 presumably emanate, like the knocks in Act 2, from the tiring house. Macduff, in his pursuit of Macbeth, first heads into the 'behind': 'That way the noise is', Macduff exclaims. 'Tyrant, show thy face!' (5.7.14). It is from that space 'behind' that Macduff emerges moments later when he finally finds Macbeth. Again, the disconnection of sound from vision is dislocating. The audience/spectators get to see the coming consummation, an event of which Macbeth remains ignorant until Macduff's command, 'Turn, Hell-hound, turn!' (5.8.3), adds sound to the picture. Ultimately Macbeth is done in by the unheard noises 'behind' that unnerved him in 2.2.

WITHOUT

In the sequence of sound! → vision → sound+vision, the locatives 'within' and 'without' prove to be interchangeable, at least in terms of the fiction at hand. Most often in Shakespeare's texts an unseeable sound is located 'within', but not always. In *Romeo and Juliet*, for example, the brawl in 1.1 is visibly present to the audience/spectators. With respect to the tiring-house, the brawl is located 'without'. With respect, however, to Capulet, who makes his entrance from the tiring-house, the brawl is located 'within'. 'What noise is this?' Capulet cries as he enters. 'Give me my long sword, ho!' (1.1.75). Similarly, in 4.5 the Nurse's lament, on stage, over the drugged body of Juliet draws Lady Capulet from the tiring house's 'without' to the platform's 'within'. 'What noise is here?' Lady Capulet cries as she makes her entrance (4.5.17). To move into presence, from behind to in front, a noise needs a source and a name. In the space 'without', sound is coordinated with vision. With respect to the circulation of sound, it is this coincidence of sound and source that makes the cylinder of the wooden O, the space in which actors and audience come face to face, different from the space 'within'.

The sound that circulates in the air 'without' turns out not to be the uniform, undifferentiated phenomenon we might expect. Another scene from *Macbeth* will help us get our acoustic bearings in 'without', an environment in which sound is directed and modulated in complicated ways. In 4.3 Rosse brings bad news to Malcolm and Macduff in their exile in England. 'Your eye in Scotland', Rosse tells Malcolm, 'Would create soldiers, make our women fight, / To doff their dire distresses' (4.3.187–9). Malcolm immediately fills this unseen space 'within' – Scotland – with the image of his imminent return, backed by ten thousand Englishmen. But the ominousness of that unseen space within returns as Rosse continues.

ROSSE

        Would I could answer
This comfort with the like! But I have words,
That would be howl'd out in the desert air,
Where hearing should not latch them.
[. . .]
Let not your ears despise my tongue for ever,
Which shall possess them with the heaviest sound,
That ever yet they heard.

MACDUFF

Humf! I guess at it.

            (4.3.192–5, 201–3)

And so follows the terrible tale of Macbeth's massacre of Macduff's wife and children. Five features of these brief exchanges characterise the circulation of sound 'without':

(1) command for attention to what is about to be spoken ('Let not your ears despise my tongue for ever')

(2) a report of what sound *feels like*, especially the experience of sound as siege, invasion, or capture (Rosse's speech will 'possess' Macduff's ears)

(3) hearing as immediate affect (to Macduff's ears Rosse's speech will come as 'the heaviest sound, / That ever yet they heard')

(4) definition of a space for sound that is psychological as well as physical ('I have words / That would be howl'd out in the desert air')

(5) varying alignments of sound and sight ('Your eye in Scotland' is the first of several verbal evocations of Scotland as a visual absence)

Taken together, these five reference points modulate the circulation of sound 'without'. Let us examine each briefly.

(1) *Commands for attention.* Explicit demands to be heard are frequent in Shakespeare's scripts. Prologues ('Open your ears', commands Rumour at the beginning of *2 Henry IV* [Ind. 1]) and formal orations ('Friends, Romans, countrymen, lend me your ears' [*Julius Caesar* 3.2.74]) provide obvious examples. But more casual references *in medias res* suggest that the constant trading in words during the two hours' traffic of the stage demanded special markers along the way. A speech-act theorist might regard them as emphatic perlocutions. Commands to hear in *Hamlet* lay heavy burdens on the hearers. 'Season your admiration for a while / With an attent ear' (1.2.192–3), Horatio advises Hamlet before he follows up his one-line report of the sight of the ghost with a twenty-three-line aural replay of the encounter, ending in the ghost's refusal to speak. When the ghost does speak three scenes later, he lays on Hamlet a command that reverberates through the rest of the play: 'Pity me not, but lend thy serious hearing / To what I shall unfold' (1.5.5–6). If ever there were a serious hearer, Hamlet is he. The murder that the ghost proceeds to narrate involves a perversion of the sense organs, whereby ear is substituted for mouth and 'juice of cursed hebenon' (1.5.62) for airwaves.

It is as if Lear's aural cursing of Goneril ('Thou art a boil, / A plague sore, or embossed carbuncle / In my corrupted blood' [2.2.415–17]) has become 'the leperous distilment' (*Hamlet*, 1.5.64) that produces a 'vile and loathsome crust' (*Hamlet*, 1.5.72) on the king's smooth flesh.

(2) *Reports of what sound feels like*. The phenomenal effect of hearing a speech is registered often in Shakespeare's scripts, but in terms that may not seem intuitive to twenty-first-century listeners. Rosse's reference to 'the *heaviest* sound' that Macduff's ears have ever heard give sound a tactile quality that is repeated in other speeches. Heaviness can't be seen or heard; it can only be felt with the body. Particularly striking is the metaphor Lady Macbeth finds after she laments that Macbeth's nature is 'too full o'th' milk of human kindness, / To catch the nearest way' (*Macbeth*, 1.5.16–17). In almost the next breath she wishes that Macbeth were already present, 'That I may pour my spirits in thine ear, / And chastise with the valour of my tongue' (1.5.25–6). The description here of sound as liquid poured into the hearer's ear is echoed in Juliet's response to Romeo's intrusion in the garden ('My ears have yet not drunk a hundred words / Of thy tongue's uttering' [*Romeo and Juliet*, 2.2.58–9]) as well as in Iago's boast 'I'll pour this pestilence into his ear' (*Othello*, 2.3.345). In *Hamlet* this metaphor becomes a physical fact, an event the spectators actually witness in the dumbshow of 2.3. The notion of sound as liquid poured into the hearer's ears works well with the account of hearing in Galenic medicine. Reverberations in the inner ear were thought to be carried through the entire body via '*spiritus*', an aerated fluid.

(3) *Hearing as immediate affect*. 'Friends, Romans, countrymen, lend me your ears' (3.2.74): the most famous synecdoche in Shakespeare's scripts draws our attention to the whole-body affects that are located at, on and in the ears. The cuckoo's song in *Love's Labour's Lost*, 'unpleasing to a married ear' (5.2.893), is perhaps the most familiar among the phrases in Shakespeare's scripts that locate affects in a hearer's ear: Julia's 'quick ear' in *The Two Gentlemen of Verona* (4.2.61), Edward's 'heedful ears' in *3*

Henry VI (3.2.63), Dido's 'sad-attending ear' in *Titus Andronicus* (5.3.81), Egeon's 'dull deaf ears' in *The Comedy of Errors* (5.1.317), the Princess's 'ear of grief' and Berowne's 'sickly ears' elsewhere in *Love's Labour's Lost* (5.2.749, 5.2.854), Aumerle's 'treacherous ear' in *Richard II* (4.1.53 in 1597 Q), the audience's 'patient ears' in *Romeo and Juliet* (Pro. 13), Lewis the Dauphin's reference to 'the dull ear of a drowsy man' in *King John* (3.3.109), Northumberland's 'greedy ear' in *2 Henry IV* (1.1.78), 'the night's dull ear' in *Henry V* (Chorus 4.0.11), Ligarius' 'healthful ear' in *Julius Caesar* (2.1.318), Ophelia's 'too credent ear' and Laertes' 'knowing ear' in *Hamlet* (1.3.30, 4.7.3), Olivia's 'most pregnant and vouchsafed ear' in *Twelfth Night* (3.1.90), Desdemona's 'greedy ear' in *Othello* (1.3.150), Octavia's 'grieved ear' in *Antony and Cleopatra* (3.6.60), and Ferdinand's 'too diligent ear' in *The Tempest* (3.1.42). In all these instances the ear becomes the site of affects that are felt through the entire body. The immediacy of those affects seems to have much to do with the way they enter the listener's body, through the ear.

(4) *Sonic scene-setting*. Fictional soundscapes constitute still another way in which sound is directed and shaped on stage. By 'soundscape' I mean not just verbal and physical gestures to throne room or battlefield or bedchamber, each of which would, in real life, have different soundmarks and different contours of sound, but here-and-now indications of how far the actors' voices are imagined to carry and who will or will not hear those voices. We might call this phenomenon 'sonic scene-setting'. Hermia does just this when she awakes in the forest and finds Lysander missing:

> Lysander! What, remov'd? Lysander! lord!
> What, out of hearing? Gone? No sound, no word?
> Alack, where are you? Speak, and if you hear.
> > (*A Midsummer Night's Dream*, 2.2.150–2)

Fictionally, the soundscape invoked here is a forest, a place where sources of sound might not always be seen, but what Hermia indicates more emphatically is a *psychological* space, an interpersonal soundscape just big enough, in this case, for two people. Cued by Shakespeare's theatre scripts, we can imagine a range of such soundscapes, extending from small (asides, soliloquies, whispered confidences that the audience does not hear) to vast (supernatural sounds coming from beyond the reach of human speech).

Small soundscapes, in which one or two characters are sequestered from the other interlocutors, are to be found everywhere in Shakespeare's plays, in all genres, in scripts from all phases of Shakespeare's career. More often than not, the audience occupies a privileged position *vis-à-vis* such sonic scenes: the audience gets to hear even when other characters on the stage do not. That privileging of the audience holds true in asides and soliloquies, but also in scenes where a private listening space is marked off amid a more public listening space. In some cases, the aside becomes a beat or a scene in its own right. 'What I am, and what I would', Viola tells Olivia, 'are as secret as maidenhead: to your ears, divinity; to any other's, profanation' (*Twelfth Night*, 1.5.209–11). 'Give us place alone', Olivia commands Maria and other attendants who have been listening, 'we will hear this divinity' (*Twelfth Night*, 1.5.212–13), and off the others go, leaving the audience alone with Viola and Olivia. In other instances, however, the audience does *not* get to hear whispered speeches, as when Prospero passes along to Ariel instructions for charming Ferdinand and leading him to Miranda: 'Hark in thine ear' (*Tempest*, 1.2.319). Another case is presented by exchanges that are cued to happen off stage, in the space 'within'. 'I would commune with you of such things / That want no ear but yours', Duke Vincentio tells the Provost in *Measure for Measure* (4.3.104–5) – a strategy that he repeats at the play's end with Isabella:

> Dear Isabel,
> I have a motion much imports your good;
> Whereto, if you'll a willing ear incline,
> What's mine is yours, and what is yours is mine.
>
> (5.1.530–3)

Whether or not Isabella's ear is willing remains unspoken. Presumably, she will speak up later, when the protagonists have made their exit 'within', into the Duke's palace. There, in the Duke's words, 'we'll show / What's yet behind that's meet you all should know' (5.1.534–5). Is that 'behind' a physical space as well as a temporal space? A psychological space as well as a physical space?

In stark contrast to these scenes of private hearing are scenes in which speeches are directed to 'the public ear', as when Mark Antony delivers his funeral oration. That adjustment of the sonic scene happens right on stage, but it can also happen off stage, within the fiction, as when Duke Vincentio says he has 'strew'd in the common ear' the rumour that he has left Vienna for Poland (*Measure for Measure*, 1.3.15), or when the Provost tells the disguised Duke that Angelo 'hath to the public ear / Profess'd' that he will never pardon Claudio (4.2.99–100). *Hamlet* is another play in which the sonic scene is constantly shifting from the acoustic equivalents of wide-angle to close-up. 'Now, Hamlet, hear', the ghost commands in 1.5. 'The whole ear of Denmark' has been abused by the story that he was killed by a serpent's sting (*Hamlet*, 1.5.34, 36). The Roman plays in particular are spoken within large soundscapes open to 'the public ear'. Larger still is the soundscape invoked in Rosse's spatialisation of 'words / That would be howl'd out in the desert air, / Where hearing should not latch them' (*Macbeth*, 4.3.193–4) – that is to say, close them out or perhaps hold them down. Largest of all are soundscapes whose limits are deep in the earth or high in the air, sonic scenes that are given depth and height by supernatural sounds like the hautboys under the stage when the god Hercules abandons Antony (*Antony and Cleopatra*, stage direction after 4.3.12), or the tempestuous noises (*The Tempest*, stage direction before 1.1.1) and the 'thousand twangling instruments' (3.2.138) that attend Prospero's aerial magic.

(5) *Varying alignments of sight and sound.* Those hautboys under the stage in *Antony and Cleopatra* point up the way sound, even 'without', can be separated from sight. What noise is that? Where is it coming from? 'Music i'th' air', ventures one soldier. 'Under the earth', counters another (4.3.16, 17). Their next impulse is to verify what they have heard – in visual terms. 'Walk', says the first

soldier. 'Let's *see* if other watchmen / Do *hear* what we do' (4.3.22–3, emphases added). As we have observed with the knocks in *Macbeth*, disorientation results when sight and sound are separated in the 'without'. The uneasy sense of disequilibrium presses for resolution.

Consider how many of Shakespeare's comedies reach joyous closure when misalignments of sight and sound are corrected, when Antipholus of Syracuse and Antipholus of Ephesus at last speak in their own persons, when 'Ganymede' speaks as Rosalind, when the 'natural perspective, that is and is not' (5.1.213) is resolved in *Twelfth Night*, when Vincentio speaks again as a duke and not a friar, when events seen in *The Tempest* are told aloud by Prospero to Alonso so that they 'take the ear strangely' (5.1.315). Corrections to the misalignments of vision and voice in Shakespeare's tragedies come with a price: Hamlet's excess of speech is silenced in the moment Claudius is unmasked as a murderer; Iago stops speaking when he can no longer make his listeners confuse verbal appearances with visual realities; imperative Lear becomes a man of few words and then no words at all when he enters with the corpse of Cordelia. However hard Albany and Edgar try to say the right thing, to align vision and voice, *King Lear*, like most of Shakespeare's tragedies, ends with an abandonment of speech. With or without a spoken epilogue, the play is turned over to the watchers and listeners.

WITHINWARDS

Between the dagger and the bell, Macbeth in 2.2 finds himself in sensory limbo. What he says he sees before him, a bloody dagger, was almost certainly not *there* for the spectators at the Globe who watched the actor playing Macbeth and listened to him speak. Nor was it present within the fiction for Macbeth himself: 'Art thou not, fatal vision, sensible / To feeling, as to sight?' (2.1.36–7). The 'feeling' that Macbeth has in mind is, literally, tactility, the dagger's susceptibility to being grasped. But in the next breath 'feeling' metamorphoses into a state of mind: 'or art thou but / A dagger of the mind, a false creation, / Proceeding from the heat-oppressed brain?' (2.1.37–9). The ringing bell that interrupts Macbeth's soliloquy ('*A bell rings*', goes the stage direction before 2.1.62)[17] likewise has a double existence: a summons from Lady Macbeth ('Go bid thy mistress, when my drink is ready, / She strike upon the bell', Macbeth has directed a servant at 2.1.31–2) and an unnerving 'noise within', a sound without a visible source, a sound without a fixable meaning. Macbeth immediately tries to supply that meaning: 'Hear it not, Duncan; for it is a knell / That summons thee to Heaven, or to Hell' (2.1.63–4). But the bell, like the knock, reverberates far beyond the immediate situation. Moments before, Macbeth has imagined his crime in terms of sound, not vision:

> Thou sure and firm-set earth,
> Hear not my steps, which way they walk, for fear
> The very stones prate of my where-about.
>
> (2.1.56–58)

As with the knock, the sound can be placed in two ways: diegetically as the sounds of Macbeth's feet upon the castle's pavements, performatively as the sounds of the actor's feet upon the platform's boards as he stalks towards his exit 'within'. In performance those ominous footsteps work like the bell and the knock, as sounds that exceed the meaning of the words being spoken, as sounds that fix the scene in the perceiver's ears. After the actor has left the stage, all the elements of the scene – words, gestures, blocking, props, non-verbal sounds – vibrate in the perceiver's consciousness. They form, as Vygotsky argues, a whole impression, not a sequence of separate elements. They linger as a 'hovering cloud' (281). The dagger, the bell, the footsteps: it is not just words and non-verbal sounds that are fused and confused but things heard and things seen.

To place this state of inner thought with respect to the Globe's 'within' and 'without' an equivalent word is needed. John Florio provides one in 'withinward', his translation of the Italian *adíntra*, literally 'towards the interior'.[18] Present in 'withinward' is the physical idea of 'ward' as a guarded enclosed space, as within a castle. One of the eight instances that turn up in an *Early English Books Online* ('EEBO') search – all but one of them pre-dating Florio, despite the *OED*'s crediting him with having invented 'withinward' as a nonce word – does refer to the interior precincts of a fortress (Geoffrey Fenton's 1579 translation of Guicciardini's *The Wars of Italy*), but the rest have to do with physiology or with meditation or, in the case of the sores of Lazarus in a sermon by St John Chrysostom, with both. Helkiah Crooke, for example, describes in *Mikrokosmographia* how the '*Ring-shield* muscles' around the larynx arise from cartilage but become implanted in 'the shield-gristle or *Thyroeides* withinward'.[19]

It is just here, in the throat, that the circulation of sound that began in the tiring-house is completed. In the course of performance, air provides the medium through which character is made manifest through costume, speech and locomotion. It is the medium that brings to the outside the illusion of insides, both within the characters' heads and hearts and within the tiring-house, out of which the fiction comes into presence. Air likewise provides the medium through which the perceivers of these dramatic events process what they have witnessed and return those impressions to the outside. Early modern physiology was as much attentive to the circulation of air within the human body as it was to the fluids that have commanded so much attention in recent scholarship. The body's intercommunication system, as we have noted before, was thought to be *spiritus*, an aerated fluid. The air in the inner air, according to Crooke, is 'inbred ayre', so called because it is implanted in the body in the mother's womb at the moment of conception.[20] For Crooke, the air of the inner ear was imagined to be different in quality from the ambient air in which a person drew breath after birth. Hence, perhaps, the anxiety about pestilence and infection that constitutes one of the most frequently invoked characteristics of air in Shakespeare's scripts. Casca in *Julius Caesar* describes to Brutus how the mob reacted when Caesar refused to accept a crown at the hands of Antony: the crowd 'uttered such a deal of stinking breath because Caesar refused the crown that it had almost choked Caesar'. For his own part, says

Casca, 'I durst not laugh for fear of opening my lips and receiving the bad air' (1.2.245–6, 247). Enemies of London's public theatres regarded the air within the Globe as just such an environment. Despite the purity and thinness of inbred air, Crooke insists that ear, mouth and lungs directly communicate with each other, that the air of the inner ear is constantly being replenished through the mouth and lungs. Question 44, following his disquisition on the ear, is devoted to 'the wonderfull simpathy and Consent of the Eaeres, the Palate, the Tongue, and the Throttle'.[21] Why do we hold our breath when we try to hear something? Why does yawning impede our hearing? If you stick something against the tympanum of your inner ear, why do you cough? If you put a resonant material like a Jew's harp between your teeth, why do you hear the sound in your ears? For two reasons, Crooke explains: because of a branch of the auditory nerve that goes to the tongue and glottis, and because of 'a gristly Canale like a water-pipe which is conveighed from the second hole of the Eare unto the Mouth & Pallate'.[22] Modern anatomy knows these canals, only recently discovered in Crooke's time, as the Eustachian tubes. It is absolutely necessary that these tubes exist, Crooke says, so that the violent air of loud sounds can be released through the mouth. In the schema of 'withinwards' that I am proposing here, the Eustachian tubes function like the pineal gland in Descartes' theatre of the mind: they mark the spot where 'within' communicates 'without'. Descartes liked to imagine the soul as a spectator in a theatre, sitting back and observing the sensations presented by the body. Soul and body may be two separate entities, but Descartes realised that there had to be a place where the soul touched the body and the body touched the soul. Was it the brain? The heart? No, Descartes decided, it was the recently anatomised pineal gland, 'situated in the middle of the brain's substance and suspended above the passage through which the spirits in the brain's anterior cavities communicate with those in its posterior cavities'.[23] As important as Descartes may be to the rise of rationalism, he still imagines the body's inner communication system as consisting of air.

With respect to hearing, Crooke envisions just such a system, in which sounds in the air without become sensations in the *spiritus* within. Waves in the external air strike the eardrum, which, in turn, transmits those waves to the pure, thin air of the inner ear:

> This aire is thin, pure, without any sound at all, immoovable, plentifull & separated from the externall aire. *Thin & pure* that it might more readily and more perfectlie admit any externall sound, for through a crasse and cloudy aire the sound is not so freelie caried, but heard with more difficulty; whence it is that a mans voice in winter is baser then in Summer.[24]

From the inner ear the waves, now transformed into immaterial forms or *species*, are carried by *spiritus* through the auditory nerve to the brain, which Crooke regards as 'the first *Sensator*'.[25] In this process, the air of the inner ear works like the crystalline lens in the eye, turning an external material fact into an immaterial form that the brain can receive. But of course the air remains material throughout the process, albeit in the purer form of the 'inbred air' of the inner ear and the aerated liquid of *spiritus*. Any discrepancies between things seen and things heard on the stage are rectified in the brain, which fuses in a faculty called 'the common sense' all the reports of the separate senses. In this kinaesthetic form, sensations from 'without' are delivered up to fancy 'within'. Physical sensations may vanish,

> yet their footsteps and expresse Characters might remaine with us. And this conception or apprehension we call *Phansie*. By this *Phansie* that supreme & soveraign *Intellectual* power of the Soule is stirred up and awaked to the contemplation of the Ideas or Notions of universall things.[26]

In this kinaesthetic, purified form, the entire experience is stored in memory.

The pattern of audition that Crooke describes here has, of course, a Platonic goal: intellection by the soul. What the brain knows and what the perceiver retains in memory, is assumed to be forms and ideas. And yet those 'footsteps and expresse Characters' linger in consciousness, in what Crooke and his contemporaries knew as *imagines*. We would call them 'images'. In the theatre sounds taken in by individual members of the audience never remain ideal forms. At the Globe and early modern London's other amphitheatres, the reactions of audiences could be immediate, and loud. In one of the sonnets in his cycle *Idea* (1605), published the same year that *Lear* was likely first acted, Michael Drayton compares his acclaim as a poet within the metaphorical 'circuit' of his readers to the aural adulation that embraced actors like Burbage within the physical 'proud round' of the theatre:

> I in the circuite for the Lawrell strove,
> Where the full praise I freely must confesse,
> In heate of blood and modest minde might move:
> With showts and claps at everie little pawse,
> When the prowd round on everie side hath rung.[27]

What Drayton describes here is in fact the default mode of performance all over the world: performers and listeners exchange sounds. The oddity is Western insistence, since the late nineteenth century, on the passive reception of sound in classical music concerts and the theatre. Drayton's poem is not the only testimonial from the period that the social air within the Globe, encouraged by the patrons' physical mobility, was anything but what Martin Buzacott describes in *The Death of the Actor: Shakespeare on Page and Stage*. In Buzacott's view, modern audiences more resemble hostages caught up in the Stockholm Syndrome:

> The traditional western theatre is, in design, an efficient but overcrowded space like a bank vault or an aircraft cabin, where individuals are confined for the purposes of mass transformation at the hands of the few [. . .] As much from peer pressure as from physical confinement and social etiquette, theatre audiences are denied the right to speak or stand up, so that their sole attention is focused on the new 'world' transpiring before them.[28]

Globe audiences were not so passive. They were actively encouraged to return sound to the actors in the form of applause.
Prospero's epilogue to *The Tempest* begs for more, shouts as well as
claps:

> But release me from my bands
> By the help of your good hands.
> Gentle breath of yours my sails
> Must fill, or else my project fails.
> (Ep. 9–12)

The audience will supply the air needed to fill his sails for the
voyage back to Milan. Then as now, outside the closed circuit of
the theatre, sounds begin to dissipate like the ripples gradually
petering out around a pebble dropped in a pond.

It was Charles Babbage, the nineteenth-century visionary cred-
ited with inventing the computer, who popularised the notion that
sound waves never dissipate entirely but continue to reverberate,
however faintly, somewhere within the Earth's atmosphere. As
Babbage explains it,

> The pulsations of the air, once set in motion by the human
> voice, cease not to exist with the sounds to which they
> gave rise. Strong and audible as they may be in the imme-
> diate neighbourhood of the speaker, and at the immediate
> moment of utterance, their quickly attenuated force soon
> becomes inaudible to human ears. The motions they have
> impressed on the particles of one portion of our atmos-
> phere, are communicated to constantly increasing
> numbers, but the total quantity of motion measured in
> the same direction receives no addition. Each atom loses
> as much as it gives, and regains again from other atoms a
> portion of those motions which they in turn give up. The
> waves of air thus raised, perambulate the earth and
> ocean's surface, and in less than twenty hours every atom
> of its atmosphere takes up the altered movement due to
> that infinitesimal portion of the primitive motion which

has been conveyed to it through countless channels, and which must continue to influence its path throughout its future existence.[29]

Well before we reach the outer limits of the atmosphere, however, we have the words audience members say to each other as they leave the theatre, the verbalisations of what they have seen, the disagreements over what happened when, the arguments over how good the performance was. It is in the listener's own voice that 'within' and 'without' become 'withinwards'.

CHAPTER NINE

'AS DIRTY AS SMITHFIELD AND AS STINKING EVERY WHIT': THE SMELL OF THE HOPE THEATRE
HOLLY DUGAN

Though few modern adaptations stage it, Shakespeare's *Taming of the Shrew* begins with an induction scene.[1] A nameless lord, returning from a hunt and debating the virtues of his hounds (and their ability to catch 'the dullest scent') with his huntsman, crosses paths with a drunken tinker, 'a monstrous beast', lying 'like a swine' in the road (Induction, 1.23, 33).[2] Disgusted by the sight and perhaps the scent of Sly, the lord plays a cruel and elaborate 'jest' upon him, testing the limits of his class-based sense of self when confronted with the sensorial effects of luxury: 'What think you, if he were conveyed to bed, / Wrapped in sweet clothes, rings put upon his fingers, / A most delicious banquet by his bed, / And brave attendants near him when he wakes, / Would not the beggar than forget himself?' (Induction, 1.36–40). The *Taming of the Shrew* thus begins with a taming of the tinker, staging the sensate effects of performance on a captive audience member: Christopher Sly. The 'swine' is inundated with ambient perfumes: his head is 'balm[ed]' with 'warm distillèd waters', his hands 'cool[ed]' with 'rosewater bestrewed with flowers', while 'sweet wood' burns 'to make the lodging sweet' (Induction, 1.47, 55–7, 48). The olfactory effect of the lord's staged perfumes is powerful. Sly emerges from his intoxicated sleep aroused by his new life (and his new wife): 'Am I a lord? And have I such a lady? / Or do I dream? . . . / I do not sleep: I see, I hear, I speak / I smell sweet savours, and I feel soft things. / Upon my life, I am a lord indeed' (Induction, 1.72–6). The final tool of transformation is the play itself, staged for his pleasure.

Shakespeare's invocation of aromatic stage properties in *Taming* is merely one reference among many in his canon. Others include Fluellen's leek in *Henry V* (5.1.9–11), the dung squibs that caused the thunder and lightening that opens *Macbeth* (1.1),[3] the flowers and sweet water sprinkled on Juliet's tomb in *Romeo and Juliet* (5.3.9), Alarabus' smoking entrails in *Titus Andronicus* (1.1.147–48), and Autolycus' damask-scented leather gloves for sale in *The Winter's Tale* (4.4.223), to name just a few olfactory props. Each of these props emphasises a multi-sensorial realm of theatre, key to staging the imagined worlds of medieval England and Scotland, of tombs in Verona and Rome, and of bucolic Bohemia. Shakespeare's provocative references gesture to the importance of scents as stage properties on early English stages, but he was not alone in harnessing olfaction in stage effects. Like Shakespeare's *Taming*, Ben Jonson's *Bartholomew Fair* begins with an induction scene that examines the role of smell in theatrical performance. He, too, focuses on the relationship between lords and swine in his play, which seeks to re-create the eponymous fair's sensory world on stage, its notorious stench included. Rather than invoke the intoxicating effects of sweet savours, Jonson revels in the seedier aspects of London's smellscape. Whereas *Taming* uses ambient stage perfumes to represent the powerful and ephemeral effect of theatrical representation on audiences, Jonson's *Fair* stages a seedier aspect of performance: how did the smells of audiences influence stage productions and the phenomenological experience of playgoing?

The olfactory effect of Jonson's induction scene is very different from Shakespeare's, achieved not through scents as stage properties, but through the amalgamated smells of the theatre itself. The opening debate in the induction scene between the stage-keeper and the Scrivener emphasises that foul stench. For better or worse, the Hope and its famously foul stench comprise an important part of the play's staged effects. The stage-keeper, for example, complains that the playwright 'has not hit the humours' of the fair and 'does not know them' (15).[4] The fair's usual itinerant suspects are missing from Jonson's staged re-creation along with many famous performers (16–25). Without these 'fine sights', and perhaps the sounds, smells and tactile encounters they engender, the play, in his humble opinion, might as well be set in Virginia rather than Smithfield: that's how badly the stagehand believes it has missed its mark (12–14).[5] The audience is offered only the squalor of the Hope Theatre to conjure the fair: the stage is in desperate need of sweeping; the broken apples, left over from baiting events, are rotting in the dirt; and the savours are awful, it 'being as dirty as Smithfield, and as stinking every whit' (198–9).

Yet such stench, the Scrivener assures the audience, is actually a boon to the play: its vulgar language 'somewhere savours of Smithfield, the booth, and the pig-broth' (187–8). Although the actual 'Fair be not kept in the same region' of London as the Hope Playhouse, the Scrivener argues that the theatre's stench creates what critics today might term a 'Proustian' memory, a powerful and immediate olfactory memory of another time and place.[6] The tension that opens Jonson's play between the 'savours' of the Fair and the stage and between the stage-keeper's and Scrivener's opinions of them emphasise the important role of the senses, particularly smell, to fact and fiction. Jonson's use of the immediate stench of the Hope Theatre as a prompt for cultural memories of Bartholomew Fair is an important aspect of the play. It offers a particularly rich opportunity to examine the role of olfaction in understanding both the history of early modern performance and of Londoners' lived experience of the city's many sensory worlds.[7] By interrogating the relationship between the smell of the Hope Theatre – known for its unique and terrible stench – and the staged re-creation of Smithfield's equally pungent market in Jonson's *Bartholomew Fair*, I will excavate a forgotten part of the historical phenomenology of early modern playgoing: its smellscape. In doing so, I will query how the play's doubled premiere at the Hope theatre and at Whitehall Palace the next day impacts the olfactory effects staged in Jonson's theatrical fair, particularly the gaseous vapours of fairgoers that choke its clime.

'BARTHOLOMEW PIGS': THE SMELL
OF THE FAIR IN SMITHFIELD

The sites of the Hope Theatre, and Bartholomew Fair, defined their sensory realms; both were located on the outskirts of the city in areas associated with noisome industries (like the tanning of leather and the boiling of soap) and with theatrical entertainments. Yet Bankside and Smithfield were distinct realms. Smithfield market, for example, occupied an area north of the original walled city, and had only recently, in 1608, been incorporated into London itself.[8] Long associated with the priory of St Bartholomew and the festive entertainments connected to it, Smithfield's 'smooth field' had been deemed an ideal space for markets as early as the mid-twelfth century (housing a cloth market for St Bartholomew's feast day and animal markets most other times of the year) and for festivals, as well as jousting tournaments, wrestling matches, civic processions and public executions.[9] With its inclusion in the space of London proper, civic concerns about its unruliness grew: by 1614, the 'rude, vast' and 'durtie' field had been confined by being paved, drained and fenced.[10] By 1619, however, it was once again causing notice for its stench, particularly its reeking 'soile'.[11]

The fair's long history in London, as a religious, civic and economic event, made it an important part of the festive life of the city.[12] Celebrated every August in the ex-priory of St Bartholomew and in the adjacent Smithfield market, just outside Aldersgate, Bartholomew Fair was both a religious festival and thriving market. Its famous entertainments, which included Medieval Mystery plays, puppet shows, tumblers and performing apes, connected medieval urban performance traditions with newer forms of entertainment that depended on London's growing economy.[13] Yet the fair was also defined by the spaces in which it was held and their many uses across the sixteenth century. These spaces included both the original enclosed area inside the priory and, as the fair grew in popularity, the adjacent fields surrounding it. The fair's early associations with St Bartholomew's Priory emphasised Catholic rituals of performance, celebrating the patron saint in the festivities surrounding the cloth market. In 1539, the Priory and its adjacent Hospital were dissolved by Henry VIII, who took possession of both, maintaining the Hospital for the city's infirm and selling the Priory's lands to Sir Richard Rich, including the rights to the cloth fair (and its tolls, at least within the enclosed area).[14] In the second year of her reign, Mary restored the Priory's lands to the Catholic Church; seventeen Protestants were burned there that year for heresy. In 1558, Elizabeth I restored the lands to the Rich family. The legacy of these Protestant martyrs, especially those who died in the 'fires' of Smithfield, helped redefine St Bartholomew's Day during Elizabeth's reign as one of Protestant pride.[15] By the early seventeenth century, however, the fair's festive entertainments had eclipsed the cloth market, whose centre was within the enclosed space of the ex-priory. St Bartholomew's fair had become synonymous with Smithfield, celebrating secular aspects of London's licit and illicit economies.

Smithfield's open pasture north and west of the city was vital for the economic trade that came to define the fair: though the area was associated with horse and cattle trading, the fair itself was a cloth market. For up to three days every summer, fair-workers and cloth vendors overtook the field, setting up trading booths in the pervasive muck, mud and excrement of animals (nearby streets that lead to the field, with names such as 'Cow Bridge', 'Cow Cross Street', and 'Chick', 'Cow' and 'Turnbull' lane, suggest the kinds of dung that covered the field and the kind of scents associated with the market). During this time in August, pungent scents were matched by the smell of the fair's unique delicacy: roast pork. That an annual cloth market could become synonymous with the scent of roast pork may seem surprising; however, as the cloth market evolved, so too did the festive entertainments that accompanied it. What began as a convenient practice of selling ready-made pork products to the cloth vendors themselves (a practice as old as the fair itself) soon came to define the fair's festive importance to Londoners, its smell synonymous with the ribald debauchery that accompanied it.[16]

The smell of roast pork every August was thus one more scent that came to define an already overwhelmingly pungent space.

That it could signal the festivity that far surpassed the boundaries of the cloth fair demonstrates the important role of olfaction in navigating a shifting urban sphere.[17] By the early seventeenth century, London's rapid population expansion had changed the boundaries of the city itself; industries that had thrived on its borders were suddenly closer to its heart and to civic purview.[18] By 1608, Smithfield had become part of the city, its economic affairs under the control of the Lord Mayor. London officials needed to balance the space's many uses, including its cattle, horse and cloth markets, with the health hazards that went along with them. Smithfield's mud bore the muck of its markets, particularly its expanding livestock markets. Despite concerns that the space had become too noisome, the demands of feeding the city led to expanded hours of its livestock market.[19] By 1614, however, the mud of Smithfield had become too foul; it warranted both the attention of the King and of the Lord Mayor.[20] Civic attempts to transform both the field and its fairs into an orderly zone of commerce focused on mitigating the mud's noisome stench.[21] Yet the presence of hazardous industries to the north of the market that had been pushed out of the city, like leather tanning and butchery, along with other trades that provided 'shadow econo-mies', like the brothels of Turnbull lane, made regulation difficult to enforce.

Given the dramatic changes made to the space of the market in 1614, it is hard not to interpret Jonson's play as an ephemeral trace of the last fair that took place in the muck of Smithfield. Though St Bartholomew's feast day was 24 August (at the height of the medieval feast calendar), the play's premiere in late October coin-cided with the end of the summer cycle of religious feasts, typically marked by Martinmas (11 November), when surplus livestock would be slaughtered and salted for meat in winter. From Smithfield and Holborn in the north to the tellingly named 'Stinking Lane' in the east, London would be overwhelmed by 'poisonous air'.[22] Jonson's play also debuted after the last fair before the paving of the field in 1614, which occurred late in the year.[23] Such timing suggests that the fair most 'fresh' in the memories of Jonson's audience was anything but. Jonson's depiction of the fair's celebration of all things ribald, bodily and vaporous exploits such timing; it is connected to the rituals of memory associated with Allhallows Eve, the feast of All Saints, and the coming sobriety of preparing (and fasting) for the Christmas season.[24] It is also, in many ways, an occasional play, celebrating the last fair in Smithfield's 'durtie' field.[25]

The play thus seems to serve two ideological purposes at once: celebrating an ephemeral trace of the city at its foulest, while also celebrating the return of temperance and the coming regulation over such ribald feasting. Yet olfaction and its idiosyncratic triggers of personal or cultural memory rarely serve ideological purposes alone. One scent in particular emphasises this point: the scent of roast pork. Its smell is everywhere in Jonson's play, linking his 'sprawling vision of the puppet-littered, pork-mad' fair to the audience's seasonal desires.[26] As in Jonson's play, the desire for pork cuts through London's hierarchies of class: a delicacy associated with the festival, it fed itinerant performers, textile merchants and aristocratic fairgoers alike.[27] Its scent was overwhelming and not necessarily pleasant: Ned Ward, in his *London Spy* (a late seventeenth-century commentary on London's seedier aspects), described the 'singeing of pigs' as 'odiferous effluvia'. It drew more than just consumers: Burgundy in Shakespeare's *Henry V* derisively describes French maids as being as plentiful as 'flies at Bartholomew-tide' (5.2.304–5).

Another source notes how the extreme heat made the many Bartholomew Fair 'pig-dressers', 'cooks' and 'dames' that consumed it resemble the 'roasted' wares.[28] Despite this, Londoners had an almost violent desire for the delicacy. The flesh of a roasted pig was described in one early modern cookery source as 'moist' and thus 'excrementiall', yet also 'very pleasant to the taste and easily digested'.[29] Longings for it were culturally associated with symptoms of pregnancy, but also with other kinds of carnality associated with the fair. In Jonson's play, Win Littlewit suffers from 'the natural disease of women', which in this instance is both pregnancy and a 'longing to eat pig', namely 'a Bartholomew pig in the fair' (1.6.46–51). A later source, Rowley, Dekker and Ford's *Witch of Edmonton* (1621), posits that the meat itself could be bewitched, describing a sow cast under a witch's spell to farrow a day early so that her pigs might be sent to London and served as 'Westminster dog-pigs at Bartholomew Fair as ever great-bellied ale-wife longed for' (5.3.36–40).[30]

Such site-specific desire emphasises the multifaceted pleasures of the space: in Jonson's play a Bartholomew pig is both a consumable good, a hawker of such goods and one who indulges too much in the fair's 'flesh'. Desire for it cuts across class lines and its complicated layering of meanings gestures to the complex systems of regulation within the fair itself. As Busy notes, roast pork itself is not the problem, but the gluttony of the fair is. Even to call the meat 'Bartholomew Pig' is a 'spice of idolatry', for the phrase itself conflates the scent of the pork with the Catholic history of the fair (1.6.46–65). Yet Busy himself longs to go 'and eat exceedingly'. Though Busy rationalises that his consumption will allow him to disassociate his Puritanism from Judaism, his companions see through his proselytising. The overwhelming desire to eat roast pork transcended most Londoners' social differences, including gender, class and religion.

Given the attention paid to the scent of Bartholomew pigs in accounts of the fair (and in Jonson's play), it is likely that pork, pigs' heads, and grease were used as props in *Bartholomew Fair*. Blisset hypothesises that the smell of pork (like the scent of tobacco) would have masked the 'bear' scent of the Hope Theatre, helping to transform the space from the reality of Bankside in October to the fiction of Smithfield in August.[31] Yet were this olfactory stage effect employed, it would have had a doubled meaning, for the play anyway fuses the scent of pork with the scent of bear. In Act 2, Ursula, 'the pig-woman', is described by another character as a great 'she-bear' presiding over a 'litter of pigs', who wields a firebrand (2.3.2–3, 2.5.67). Ursula and her canvas booth, located on the makeshift stage, would have towered over the pit where an actual bear had been baited earlier in the month. So the smells of the Hope would have mingled with the stage effects of the fair, creating an olfactory mélange unique to Jonson's play, which links the absurdity of Puritan zealotry over eating pork with their zealous objections to the theatre. The play will have provided its own unique sensory realm were it to have staged key scents associated with the fair.

DOUBLED DEBUTS: THE FAIR AT
THE HOPE AND AT WHITEHALL

Gifted at creating elaborate sensory delights in his masques, as well as ribald, raunchy sensory jokes in his city comedies, Jonson, many critics have argued, masterfully 'fitted' his plays to the particularities of the stages in which they were to be performed.[32] *Bartholomew Fair* reflects his acumen: staged at Whitehall Palace the day after its premiere at the Hope, his play raises questions about the effects of performance in these decidedly different olfactory environments: did the stage effect of roast pork change in these two venues? Was it materially present in one and not in the other? What about the scent of bears? Do such differences in aroma affect the meaning of the play? To begin to answer such questions, it is necessary to grapple with the temporal aspects of performance and the ways in which the audience itself contributes to the sensory realm of the theatre.

Jonson's *Bartholomew Fair* was one of the first plays written specifically for the Hope Theatre and its uniquely moveable stage; it is likely that its debut marked the first theatrical performance in the new arena.[33] Kathleen Lynch, Alison Chapman and Leah Marcus have deftly unpacked the way in which the date of the two performances, on Allhallows Eve at the Hope Theatre and on Allhallows Day at Whitehall Palace, affected the play's staging of the fair.[34] Its 'doubled première' was unusual and Jonson seems to have been well aware of how such differing performance conditions could affect audience responses, offering the induction for those at the Hope (who were undoubtedly intimately familiar with the fair and its stench) and the prologue for those at court (who, it has been posited, would have had less knowledge of the more

unseemly aspects of urban life).[35] Whereas the induction at the
Hope warned the audience to link their criticism to their own
experience of the fair, the prologue 'invite[d]' its royal audience to
delight in the author's 'fairing', a small gift commemorating the
fair, which includes the sensory hazards of such 'place, such men,
such language, and such ware', namely the zealous 'noise' of puritan 'factions' (1–12). The first emphasises to the audience what is
lacking in this theatrical re-creation of the fair, even as it stages a
few, key olfactory stage effects associated with it; the second
suggests that the play (and its scents) are a product of the fair itself.

Critics such as Kathleen Lynch and Alison Chapman have also
queried how the imagined setting of the play may have materially
resonated with the audience of the Hope; they have connected
Bartholomew Fair with medieval religious drama and with audience members' phenomenological experiences of the fair and of
urban life.[36] According to such readings, the foolish Bartholomew
Cokes' journey through the fair mocks St Bartholomew's hagiographic tradition by simulating the raucous festivities that
commemorated his feast day.[37] The saint's purported 'odour of
sanctity' is mocked by the smells that surround Cokes in the play
(and the audience in the theatre), which would traditionally link
the saint's icon of a knife and flayed skin to the fair's economic
focus on cloth and leather. The Skinners of London, who worked
nearby on the Fleet and had St Bartholomew as their patron,
undoubtedly staged religious performances that highlighted just
such connections.[38] Jonson's play, in contrast, satirically mocks
such links, using only a few symbolic goods associated with the fair
as props, including the fleshliness of roast pork. Expanding earlier
trade connections latent in medieval pageant plays, while also
mocking them, Jonson's play depends on sensory substitution
between the smell of Smithfield and the Hope and between the
smell of sanctity and that of festive, urban debauchery.

Such substitution is inherently theatrical: the play's many references to the scent of livestock, pork, leather, tobacco, stale
gingerbread, ale, farts, belches, sweat and urine conjure both the
material realm of the fair and the stage. Like Smithfield market,

the Hope, located to the south on Bankside, had its own uniquely foul stench, connected to that of the surrounding area: the aroma of the pike stews, soap-boiling yards, rose gardens, mud and the flooded, polluted ditches of the surrounding area, were combined with the smells of the theatre – its structure (its oak frame, thatch and hazelnut-strewn yard) and its occupants (the sweat, urine, belches, perfume of the actors, animals and crowd, along with the apples, oysters, ale and tobacco that they undoubtedly consumed inside).[39] These scents, to name just a few of them, defined the smellscape of the Hope. They were not a deliberate part of staged theatrical productions, yet they were often associated with them, particularly in anti-theatrical critiques, plague commentaries and descriptions of London.

Designed as both a playing- and baiting-arena, the Hope Theatre attempted to capitalise on two of Bankside's popular entertainments: playgoing and animal-baiting. In concept, the differences between the two kinds of performances were seen as an economic perk: plays staged four days a week and baiting perform-ances two days a week would, Henslowe undoubtedly hoped, draw more paying customers to the arena. Occupying the site of the former Bear Garden, the new arena was believed to be capable of filling a temporary void in Bankside after the Globe theatre had burned to the ground in 1613. Attempting to rival the King's Men and the Globe, Henslowe seized this opportunity, while drawing on the theatre's historic association with baiting to expand its focus. Though it was similar in size and shape to other London theatres (its contract specifically recommends copying aspects of the tiny Swan playhouse), it had a removable stage, together with a removable cantilevered roof and heavens; these were technological marvels. The roof allowed the audience an unobstructed view of both the heavens, which were unsupported by posts, and the stage beneath them. In practice, however, the arena's dual focus altered the effects of performance, particularly of plays. The smell of bait-ing lingered past its scheduled days of performance, providing the playgoing audience with a strong olfactory reminder of previous entertainments.

Given its animal smell, the Hope was ideally suited for staging Jonson's play: the ephemeral festive world of the fair is like that of this particular theatre. The bare stage of Act 1, most likely representing a public street outside Littlewit's home, quickly becomes crowded with props and various booths as characters enter the fair and the location subtly changes to that of the fair.[40] Though some argue that the play uses the fair as a microcosm of London life – the characters and audience enter the world of the fair and remain within it for the entirety of the play – it is hard to believe that the material conditions of the Hope could be truly forgotten.[41] The open pit where the audience stood was the arena where the most violent baiting occurred: playgoers stood in the mud that had absorbed the blood, urine and sweat of baited animals. The Hope, with its animal smells and sounds, undoubtedly contributed to the festive 'ambiance' of the Jonson's staged fair, the desirable smell of pork mingling with the fearful odour of the bear.

Such amalgamated scents link the sensory world of the fair (and its hierarchies and rituals) with the space of the new theatre through the cultural associations of the audience. Jonson's play staged at the Hope draws upon the powerful role of olfaction in defining certain zones of the city while celebrating its ability to flout such clear-cut spatial, class and hierarchical boundaries. Smells, like those of roast pork or of bears, waft and linger in the fair, the play and the playhouse. Jonson himself seemed to delight in such sensory associations, particularly those that accrued in spatial zones where strangers and animals mixed. Staged at the Hope, his play revels in such theatrical devices and their relationship to the sensory world of the stage, such as the smell of Ursula and her pork staged among the effluvium of bears. But it also drew upon the collective exhalations of that audience during the performance itself, connecting the debilitating atmosphere of the fairgrounds with that of the theatre itself, an effect that would have been intensified within an indoor realm like Whitehall.

If the stench of the Hope was critical to the stage effects of Jonson's play, then what of the scent of Whitehall? Did it smell 'better' than the Hope and, if so, in what way did that olfactory difference shape the meanings of Jonson's play? Though some characters within the play emphatically insist that 'wellborn' people of 'fashion' do not traverse the muck of the fair (1.5.153–5), it is widely noted that Londoners of all classes attended the fair, including royalty and the aristocracy. Jonson himself dedicates the play to the King in its first published edition in 1631; it is the only one of his published plays to carry such a dedication, which Curtis Perry argues suggests its particular relevance to the King.[42] Though Perry focuses on the play's representation of law and Puritanism, his claim raises questions about the extent to which the differences between the two performances of *Bartholomew Fair* shaped its ideological meanings.

James I himself had been notoriously unwilling to engage with urban crowds and his dislike of pork was widely known; critics William Blisset and Ian Donaldson have posited that Jonson's induction, 'welcoming his majesty to a fair', thus offers the play to the King as a 'safe' way of engaging with the seedier aspects of city life, including smells.[43] In such an environment, the play's vapours could only be metaphorical. Yet that is to ignore the fact that the King was, particularly after discovering and foiling the Catholic 'Gunpowder Plot', renowned for his 'sagacity', a term associated with olfaction as well as wisdom, and used to describe acute discernment of fragrant *and* foul scents.[44] As one ballad proclaimed, James I was an 'excellent smeller'; thus James' olfactory acumen in discovering the dungy smell of gunpowder was seen to relate to his display of political power in the face of Catholic threats. And given James' interest in regulating London's unprecedented population growth, he presumably had intimate experience with the fouler scents of city life, including those associated with the fair and with the stage. Rather than staging unknown horrors of pedestrian London, Jonson's play offers itself as a comedy to a King who is well versed in the exigencies of urban life and of its theatres. He licensed public plays, invoking his royal power over city regulations against them.[45] He certainly knew the scents associated with animal baiting.[46] Jonson's play was thus fitted for Whitehall as much as it was for the Hope. Like the Hope, Whitehall too was a multi-use entertainment venue. The doubled premiere of *Bartholomew Fair* demonstrates not only how smells of urban life defined London but also how certain ones came to signify urban space in distinct ways, transcending clear-cut class differences between high and low entertainment venues. Jonson's play, fitted for the Hope and for Whitehall in November, relies on the unique mélange of each to conjure forth the festive atmosphere of Smithfield in August.

Indeed, though there was certainly more than one way to smell 'rank' in early modern London, Jonson's play mocks attempts to discern class status through olfaction, thus linking the pleasures of the fair with its uniquely urban environment and its heterogeneous inhabitants.[47] The experience of playgoing, whether at the Hope or at the cockpit at Whitehall, simulates this sensuous experience. For Jonson, the city comprises an olfactory zone that engages all who navigate its terrain. His poem, 'On the Famous Voyage', charts the journey of two noblemen up the polluted Fleet sewer, where excrement 'rains' on them as they near Holborn Bridge (and the brothels nearby).[48] In his later play, *The New Inn* (1629), the theatre is itself valued for its sensory engagement with all of society. In it, Lord Lovel, an aristocratic guest at the titular inn, registers surprise at his host's occupation, noting 'a man of [his] sagacity, and clear nostril, should have made another choice than of a place so sordid as the keeping of an inn' (109–12). Yet the host refuses such logic, offering a different definition of sagacity than merely that of maintaining a 'clear' nostril. The inn, and its smells, are a kind of theatre where 'all the world's a play' in which he can 'laugh and chuck at the variety of humours and throng of humours and dispositions that come jostling in and out still' (128, 133–5).[49] The theatre is entertaining not only for its staged theatrical devices, but also for the wide variety of 'humours' latent in its audience and their vaporous, bilious exhalation. It is a space where one can experience, first hand, all the sights, sounds and smells that collectively define London.

VAPOROUS EFFECTS OF PERFORMANCE

Given the extent of London's population and health crises, even aristocrats would have had some exposure to the smells that abound in Jonson's play, including roast pork, urine, sweat and the 'vaporous' exhalations associated with London's neighbourhoods. The city was a dynamic space and anyone traversing it was porously linked to its environment. The play's many 'games' of 'vapours' trade on that fact: characters at the fair repeatedly pun on the fact that even the most witty exchanges can involve vaporous belches of bad breath. Smells, dungy or otherwise, connected the atmosphere of the Hope playhouse and Whitehall during performance with the imagined setting of the play. Though the induction emphasises the play's humours as a metaphor for its inhabitants, its ending focuses on a collective experience described as 'vapours'. Renaissance 'vapours', maladies caused when the body's effluvia (especially its bilious humours) pollute themselves and their environment, were thought to be caused by excessive heat and crowding. Vapours were thus individual and collective disorders, aptly suited to development in the environment of the fair. Smelling such 'vapours', Jonson's play seems to argue, is a critical component and effect of performance, a point that many of the characters make about the fair itself. Each character's presence changes the realm, adding more and more 'vapours' to an already polluted space.[50] By Act 4 of the play, the fair's entertainments cause their own kind of festive 'madness' linked to the cumulative environmental hazards of traversing the ribald and polluted space. The fairgoers' vapours emphasise the goods consumed at the fair, like roast pork. Intoxicated by such festivity, more and more characters attempt to display their wit to one another through verbal competitions that descend into more and more belches and farts. Such cumulative staged effects invite the audience at the Hope and at Whitehall to consider their own material connection to other playgoers.

Though vapours were theoretically 'steamy, imperceptible particles' exhaled by the body, the smell of the crowd was an all too perceptible reminder of other kinds of bodily exhalations released into the air.[51] Thus, as Gail Kern Paster has recently argued, vapours connected humoral theory with spatial practice as well as with the metaphoric language of Jonson's play.[52] Jonson famously captures the sounds of the fair, but he also captures its smells, merely by drawing attention to the sensory world of the stage. As the day progresses, the olfactory realm of the fair is changed by the vapours of its participants, both workers and fairgoers alike. Inebriation aids this process; though the term vapours is ostensibly used by the characters in the play as a synonym for breath, it quickly expands to include other kinds of bodily 'winds', namely belches, farts and other kinds of 'shtink' (77). As Wasp and Knockem joke, by the end of the game, characters seem to have more than just metaphorical 'turds' in their 'teeth', their game of vapours having become more and more 'gross' and 'noisome' (4.4.119, 137).[53]

Likewise, the verbal 'vapours' exchanged between Ursula and the ramping punk Alice equally suggests that an embodied funk descends on the fair, though it is the women's bodies rather than their speech that stinks. Knockem, for example, refers to 'green' women as 'vapours' in this play, which described loose, wild or inexperienced women, indeed almost all in the play (4.5.75). Ursula's pig-booth, introduced early in Act 2, is a metaphorical and material centre of the play. She is the source in the play of the fair's famous 'Bartholomew pigs' and, as such, she embodies the dangers and delights of both the fatty delicacy and of the theatre: a great 'she-bear' presiding over the fair, her presence on the stage (in both venues) playfully drew connections between the bear baiting and playgoing. As Gail Kern Paster argues, the steam erupting from her booth is likened to the steam erupting from her body, both of which threaten all who encounter it (equally in the social world of the play and the material realm of the theatre).[54]

Smell signifies other kinds of bestial pleasures. Like the scent of roasted pork, which defines Ursula's booth, the scent of roasted tripe defines other kinds of social practices, namely wife-hunting. If there are clear links between spatial and social meanings of olfaction in Jonson's *Bartholomew Fair*, they refer more to gendered meanings of class. Men 'nose' women (and their wealth) in this play. So, too, does the audience. In Act 1, Quarlous jokes that Winwife's courting is akin to hunting: 'there cannot be an ancient tripe or trillibub i' the town but thou art strait nosing it [. . .] and 'tis a fine occupation thou'lt confine thyself to when thou hast got one – scrubbing a piece of buff, as if thou hadst the perpetuity of Panier-alley to stink in' (1.2.77–80). Comparing Winwife's ability to discern a rich old woman to his ability to nose the entrails of an ox, as well as to buff leather, Quarlous mocks both transitive and intransitive meanings of the verb 'to smell'. To marry well, one must be willing to suffer sensory hardships, to 'rake [. . .] a fortune in an old woman's embers' (95–6) and then to 'brook the noise' that results from life lived with her (111). Winwife himself concludes that he is quite 'off that scent,' displaced by a rival (127).

Ursula, too, invokes this metaphor, referring to the play's prostitute Alice as 'tripe' of Turnbull street, associating her both with consumable animal entrails and with a known red-light district in early modern London.[55] Alice, in turn, addresses Ursula as a 'bawd in grease' and 'a sow of Smithfield' (4.3.94–5). Both phrases target the women's bodies, quickly moving beyond bestial slurs to more site-specific hazards: Ursula refers to Alice as 'tawed' (i.e. steeped in alum and salt for whitening purposes) leather, while Alice calls Ursula a 'night-tub' (a tub used collect and haul away sewage sludge that collected in the middle of early modern London streets). Like Quarlous' misogynist jokes about Winwife's courting practices, these new insults emphasise the stench of the fair, of Smithfield, and of its nearby surroundings, particularly the area just to the north, which was occupied by leather tanners and horse traders (as well as prostitutes). These industries required a water source to sluice away hazardous industrial remains; Turnbull street was adjacent to a particularly noxious segment of the famously foul Fleet ditch.[56] The insults thus work on multiple levels: the women insult one another's femininity and class status while also associating one another with particularly noisome industries and industrial hazards associated with the area.

Inundated by such 'vapours', the audience (whether at the Hope or at Whitehall) would undoubtedly be reminded of the vulnerability latent in sniffing. Sitting and standing in close proximity to one another, the audience members, like the fairgoers, were more than the sum of their individual bodies; they collectively changed the atmosphere in which they were located. The Hope playhouse, like Smithfield market (and Turnbull street), was a heterogeneous space, where rich and poor men and women congregated.[57] The play's emphasis on the changed atmosphere of the fair was thus both a festive reminder of the pleasures of group entertainment and its dangers. Jonson's play, after all, was two and a half hours long; by the time the play has staged the many 'vapours' of Act 4, the audience will long since have acclimated to the smell of the theatre, and of its surrounding areas, foul or not. Such a reminder would (at least momentarily) draw attention back to the place's stench. The scene ends by reminding the characters of other urban olfactory hazards: as Knockem searches for a coach to parade his new wards, he remarks casually to Win Littlewit that coaches are as plentiful as 'wheelbarrows where there are great dunghills', a phrase that, like Littlewit's earlier references to London's 'rag-rakers', draws attention to the growing health crises caused by the rapidly expanding population of London (1.3.5–6).[58]

CONCLUSION

If we ignore the history of the doubled premiere of *Bartholomew Fair*, it is possible to interpret Jonson's play – and its dependence on a certain kind of theatrical stench – as marking the end of an era in early modern stage history. It is tempting to argue that Jonson 'fitted' the humours of his play a bit too closely to those of the Hope. For the Hope playhouse, as a venue for playgoing, was a stunning failure: though its contract stipulated that animal-baiting was to occur only on Tuesdays and Thursdays, the labour required to move the stage was substantial.[59] And, while the pungent aroma worked well for Jonson's play, the lingering stench of the animals baited in the arena made it impossible to mount certain kinds of plays. Simply put, the Hope was no Rose (by any stretch of the imagination, including the olfactory). By the time the theatre opened in late 1614, playgoing had emerged as very different kind of entertainment from animal baiting.[60]

Rather than end on this point, however, it is useful to consider what the doubled premiere of *Bartholomew Fair* suggests about the role of theatre in the expanding metropolis, a built environment increasingly defined by crowding – of industries, infrastructures, animals, waste and people.[61] The smell of early modern London comprised these individual scents as well as their interconnected complexity, which formed a unique (and sometimes toxic) mélange. Jonson drew on both to create his own uniquely urban kind of play. Jonson's fair thus comprised a sensory realm in own right, composed of the scents associated with Smithfield, mingled with those of the stages in which it was performed and the vaporous exhalations of audiences watching the performance. And like Shakespeare's *Taming of the Shrew*, *Bartholomew Fair* argues that olfaction is an important aspect and effect of performance, though one not easily controlled or directed. Ultimately, in Shakespeare's play, the Lord's use of perfumes on Sly works against his use of the play-within-the play as a tool of ideological control: Sly famously sleeps through the performance. Jonson's play makes a similar point, though his use of olfaction expands beyond that of the stage, dwelling in the murky space of the theatre itself where the smells of the play and those of the audience collide, inextricably linked through performance. *Bartholomew Fair* thus illustrates the importance of understanding the material conditions of London's theatrical entertainments, for the theatre shaped its then audience's collective understanding of the changing, crowded space of London, smells and all, through the plays performed and crowds breathing within it.[62]

CHAPTER TEN

TOUCH AND TASTE IN
SHAKESPEARE'S THEATRES
FARAH KARIM-COOPER

In his study of Shakespeare's audiences, Andrew Gurr observes that 'English lacks an adequate word for the feast of the senses which playgoing ought to provide'; he goes on to argue that 'auditor' and 'spectator' are the two terms most popularly used in the period to refer to those attending plays, both of which address specific senses.[1] Meanwhile, Carla Mazzio points out that some writers used the term 'assembly' to describe playgoers, 'a word worth reintegrating into the sensory dimensions of theatrical experience, because it implied not only a coming together of persons, but a physical touching of bodies in space'.[2] When we think of this word etymologically, we recall its original meaning: to assemble from parts, an implicitly tactile endeavour. Other more derogatory terms for audience also existed, including 'rabble', which refers to a throng or crowd, and 'multitude', often coupled with 'rude' and used to describe the supposedly uneducated masses who attended plays. Both 'rabble' and 'multitude' conjure a visual image of an aggressive crowd of people, pushing, shoving and buzzing with sounds, smells and tactile energy. Indeed, one aim of this chapter is to emphasise that contact among the audience was a condition of performance in Shakespeare's theatres, which raises the question as to how tactility might affect the reception of plays; another is to show how the very words used for audience emphasise the sensory dimension that was such a crucial part of attendance at the theatre.

Early modern sensory theory had it that to know the world one needed to sense it first.[3] Thus performance effects rely upon the notion that all of the senses would be in use by an audience during a performance, including touch and taste. In 1579, Stephen Gosson's infamous excoriation of plays makes this point abundantly clear: he wrote that players

> set [. . .] abroach strange consortes of melody, to tickle the eare; costly apparel, to flatter the sight; effeminate gesture, to ravish the sence; and wanton speache, to whet desire to inordinate lust.[4]

This passage refers to sensation in a typically early modern fashion. The idea that music can 'tickle' the ear, apparel 'flatter' the eye and speech 'whet desire' for sex, suggests that the early moderns did not think of the senses as singularly functional; rather, all of the senses were mutually receptive to touch, taste, sound, smell and sight. This notion of synaesthesia or a 'commingling of the senses' is crucial to understanding how touch and taste operate on more than one level in the Shakespearean theatre.[5] In this chapter I will examine the different categories of touch and taste as they were perceived by playwrights, audiences and anti-theatrical writers, in order to argue that the effects of performance were contingent not only upon the more obvious senses of sight and hearing but, crucially and conceptually, on touch and taste as well. Though this chapter's emphasis is primarily on the sense of touch, it will conclude with a brief section on taste proposing that, within the idiom of early modern theatrical discourse, plays, conceptually, could be consumed by, as well as touch, audiences in the playhouse.

TOUCHING MOMENTS IN SHAKESPEARE'S THEATRE

In recent years, critics who have written about 'touch' in Shakespearean or early modern culture (Marjorie O'Rourke Boyle,[6] Evelyn Tribble,[7] Elizabeth Harvey,[8] Carla Mazzio,[9] Bruce Smith[10] and Katherine Rowe[11]), have observed its position as lowest in the Renaissance hierarchy of the five senses, and have pointed out the influence of Aristotle's work on the senses, such as his designation of touch at the bottom of the sensory scale and his identification of the important relationship between touch and knowledge.[12] In doing so, they have shown that there were conflicting viewpoints in early modern sensory theory: touch was simultaneously described as the basest sense, and an ennobling mark of human identity. Most current work on the senses has focused on poetic or dramatic literature, but Carla Mazzio, discussing the resistance of touch to representation, raises the question of how touch works in the theatre itself. Patricia Cahill, even more specifically, in a critical survey of Renaissance studies and the senses, asks: 'what would happen if we were to think of the interactions between early modern players and playgoers as a tactile encounter? [. . .] what might it mean to be touched by a play?'[13] Part one of this chapter seeks to address Mazzio's and Cahill's questions by examining touch not just as a sense at work in the theatres, but as a physical and conceptual effect of performance.

An examination of early modern discourse about the senses reveals that there were numerous theories of knowing and perceiving developing at the time, and that these were used as regulatory discourses designed to warn against the vulnerability of the soul through the body. In *Essaies Upon the Five Senses* (1620), poet and moralist Richard Brathwait sets out to anatomise the senses, but his academic mode of enquiry is consistently undercut by his anxious tone. The senses are necessary gateways to knowledge and understanding, but they must be used responsibly to activate reason, which is distinguished from sense: 'Let my *Taste* be directed by reason, and not by sence.' He equates touch with the original sin (as do most writers in this period), but refuses to deny its essential dignity, calling it the 'living Sence' and 'vitall faculty'.[14] He then identifies the relationship between the sense of touch and understanding as 'the *Intelligible*, the *Irascible*, and the *Concupiscible*'; in other words he recognises the variety of functions and the multiple meanings the sense has: verification (or determining the world through touch), emotional effect and what Brathwait refers to as 'lustfull satisfaction'.[15] It is this last meaning that concerns the author the most: 'O how many fall by this *sence of life*, making it their sence of death?'[16]

Thomas Wright also distinguishes between sense and reason, arguing in 1601 that the passions were aligned with the senses and that therefore sensual activity could stir them, at times, to produce dangerous humours. Citing the ancient ecclesiastical writer Valefius, for example, Wright warns that '(sayth hee) the sight of redde things (according to the common opinion of *Galen*, and other physitians) stirreth and inflameth the blood', producing anger and possibly violent action.[17] The idea that objects or actions perceived through the senses could have a penetrative effect on human emotions, psychology and behaviour also preoccupied the anti-theatrical polemicists of the early modern period. Although physicians such as Helkiah Crooke (1615) attempted to dispel certain myths associated with sense perception, such as dubious claims about the haptic[18] nature of sight – 'we also deny that a Basilisk or menstruous woman do by their looks infect anything' – anti-theatrical writers, in particular, saw the senses as being uniquely vulnerable to theatrical performance.[19] Tanya Pollard has shown how opposition to theatre was grounded in fears about the body's permeable quality; plays can 'seduce' as well as 'produce a wide range of powerful affective and physiological sensations in their audiences and actors'.[20] It was this affective 'touch' of theatre that worried anti-theatrical moralists. By examining a range of play-texts and anti-theatrical tracts, we can identify the categories of touch that early modern performance constructed: physical contact (between audience members), scenes of touching (on stage) and affective touch, meaning the presumed emotional or physiological effects of performance on members of the audience.[21] To feel things deeply or be moved emotionally is to be *touched* in Shakespeare; for example, in the opening scene of *Cymbeline*, the first Gentleman reports the misfortunes that have already taken place and observes that 'all is outward sorrow, though I think the king / Be touch'd at very heart' (1.1.9– 10).[22] All of these modes of touching in the theatre stimulated an anxious response from the writers who feared that through the porous body, plays would corrupt the minds and actions of spectators.

CONTACT

The topic of playhouse dimensions is much debated among theatre historians, but Andrew Gurr argues that the 1599 Globe was

> roughly 100 feet (30 metres) in its outside diameter, markedly larger than the approximately 72 feet (22 metres) of the Rose. The outer and inner gallery walls enclose a space a little over 11 feet (3.4 metres) deep, much the same as the Rose's gallery bays. The Globe's yard must therefore have been nearly 78 feet (24 metres) in diameter.[23]

We also know from several sources, that the playhouses often packed in anywhere from 2,500 to 3,000 people during a performance.[24] At the new Globe in London, the dimensions are roughly the same as its 1599 ancestor; however, due to modern health and safety regulations, the theatre has a maximum capacity of 1,500 people, which means the audience there, though experiencing intimacy-in-a-crowd, is not tactile in the way it would have been in the early modern playhouse. To be audience in those theatres meant to be jostled, shoved and pressed in with roughly 2,999 others. The extensive archaeological report by Julian Bowsher and Pat Miller, published by the Museum of London in 2009, provides an account of the shape, size and age of the theatre buildings and the vast range of objects (pins, aglets, beads, pipes, clay pots, shoes etc.) discovered on the sites of the Rose and Globe playhouses. Having examined some of the objects associated with clothing found among the detritus at the foundations of the Rose, dress historian and theatre designer, Jenny Tiramani, described the use of the numerous pins and aglets found there; they were employed to fasten clothes together and 'were "essential" everyday objects, used by all men and women from every social class'.[25] The prosthetic nature of Renaissance clothing, which was 'a composition of detachable parts, so garments could be disassembled',[26] also suggests how tactile the playgoing experience must have been: objects associated with clothing could easily fall away from a person's body when congregated with others in such close proximity.

When discussing players in his chapter on Sloth in *The Seuen Deadly Sinnes of London* (1606), Thomas Dekker writes that 'their houses smoakt everye after noone with Stinkards, who were so glewed together in crowdes with the steames of strong breath, that when they come foorth, their faces lookt as if they had been perboylde'.[27] Here Dekker satirically observes the multi-sensory conditions within the yard of the playhouses. This portrait of the 'stinkards' or groundlings is created by the vivid synaesthetic image of steaming breaths sticking them together; Dekker underscores the moral depravity of the throng of tradesmen and -women, implicitly calling to mind a grotesque image of London's citizenry. Dekker's satirical portrait of interaudience contact participates in the moral discourse that admonishes readers to regulate their sensory activities. Another example of this argument comes from *A Third Blast from Plaies and Theaters* (1580): 'Whosoever shal visit the chapel of Satan, I meane the Theater, shal finde there no want of young rufins, nor lacke of harlots, utter-lie past al shame: who presse to the fore-front of the scaffolds, to the end to showe their impudencie, and to be an object to al mens eies.'[28] Having to 'press' to the front suggests that the experience of being part of an early modern audience, at times, may have been a hostile one. Gosson takes this idea a step further, insinuating that the theatre is a sexually licentious environment with people 'heaving' and 'shooving' in the pursuit of lust: 'In our assemblies at plays in London, you shall see [. . .] heaving, and shooving, [. . .] ytching and shouldring, too sitte by women.'[29] Mazzio's observation that playhouse audiences were also referred to as 'assemblies' is underlined by commentaries such as these. A couple of years later, Gosson recycles his argument:

> In the playhouses in London, it is the fashion of youthes
> to go first into the yarde, and to carry their eye through

> every gallery, the like unto ravens where they spye the
> carrion thyther they flye; and presse as nere to ye fairest as
> they can.[30]

Obviously, we have to keep in mind that anti-theatrical writers would often paint exaggerated pictures of the playhouses to deter people from attending plays. However, when we turn to the play-texts, we can see useful parallels between onstage action and, potentially, audience behaviour. In particular, Shakespeare writes moments into some of his plays that reflect upon the prospective danger of crowds, perhaps to exacerbate the concerns of the city authorities opposed to theatrical performance. In *Coriolanus* (3.1) a '*rabble*' of Plebeians appears on stage and is incited to seize upon Coriolanus: '*They all bustle about Coriolanus*', and shout 'Down with him! Down with him!' (182).[31] What is particularly revealing about juxtaposing this moment from Shakespeare's play with anti-theatrical concerns about tactile crowding is the effect it may have on the reception of such scenes. Being shoved and pressed in an audience at the same time as there is a 'bustling' violence enacted on stage, creates a mirroring effect, that, as Amy Cook puts it 'does not reflect, though, it predicts and warns'.[32] In a play like *Coriolanus* where the impact of a crowd proves fatal, the close contact and volatility within the audience would have intensified the effects of the drama. The word 'touch', for example, has interesting connotations when we read the play in this light. In 2.1 Brutus and Sicinius discuss plans to antagonise the crowd against Coriolanus. Brutus proposes,

> We must suggest the people in what hatred
> He still hath held them: that to's power he would
> Have made them mules, silenc'd their pleaders, and
> Dispropertied their freedoms; holding them,
> In human action and capacity,
> Of no more soul nor fitness for the world
> Than camels in their war, who have their provand
> Only for bearing burthens, and sore blows
> For sinking under them.

SICINIUS

   This (as you say) suggested
   At some time when his soaring insolence
   Shall touch the people – which time shall not want,
   If he be put upon't, and that's as easy
   As to set dogs on sheep – will be his fire
   To kindle their dry stubble; and their blaze
   Shall darken him forever.

                     (245–59)

In this exchange, the word 'touch', meaning to stir feeling, high-lights the relationship between crowding and emotions. The line between fiction and reality becomes somewhat blurred as this is a play in which being audience means to be co-opted into the drama. A Roman play, *Coriolanus* exploits the conditions within the play-house which produces such close contact between audience members; the play contains many scenes involving Roman citi-zenry, which, when we consider the atmosphere within a crowded playhouse, draws in the spectators, transforming them momentar-ily into the very people whom Coriolanus, reluctantly, has had to work so hard to win over. The protagonist needs the people's voices as much as the actor playing him needs the approval of the audi-ence. Thus it is hard to miss the irony when Coriolanus remarks that he doesn't like to speak to the people – 'It is a part / That I shall blush in acting, and might well / Be taken from the people' (2.2.143–5). Sicinius and Brutus exploit Coriolanus' lack of sincer-ity towards the people by galvanising the citizens to stage a crowded mutiny, while denying Coriolanus their support. Sicinius remarks:

               To th' Capitol, come:
   We will be there before the stream o'th'people,
   And this shall seem, as partly 'tis, their own,
   Which we have goaded onward.

                  (2.3.258–61)

The word 'goaded', in the early modern period, was synonymous with 'prick' and 'sting' or 'spur', which meant to incense.[33] In this moment, the sense of touch has a double significance as Brutus and Sicinius demonstrate the power words have to touch or 'goad' an already volatile and tactile crowd. Crowding was not an unusual phenomenon in early modern London, a city that by 1600 had a population of roughly 500,000.[34] Anxieties about overcrowding in theatres may seem odd in light of the fact that crowding in streets, on bridges, at church, at markets was a common occurrence. But the theatres with their round shapes enclosing their spectators, pushing them up against one another, body against body, all the senses attuned to performance, was a different thing from crowding in the street. In *Coriolanus*, Shakespeare explores how the particular anxieties about interaudience contact and the potential violence of crowds are further exacerbated by the belief that the senses could be abused by theatre, thereby producing excessive passions and potentially destructive behaviour either in the service of lust (as anti-theatrical writers suggest) or politics.

TOUCHING ON STAGE

In some respects, all plays contain scenes involving physical touching: friends greeting each other by shaking hands; lovers embracing or kissing; enemies duelling and fighting; villains murdering; martyrs committing suicide; masters beating their servants. Even the feel of costumes against actors' bodies, the cosmetics on their faces, the gloves on their hands and hats on their heads, constitute onstage tactility. Since there is no single organ of touch (meaning the entire body can experience touch through the skin; it is not isolated in the hand), as Aristotle had argued in his explanation of sense perception, *De Anima*, experiences of touching are constant both on and off stage.[35] Therefore this section will focus on a form of onstage touching that carried particular cultural and moral significance for audiences, actors and anti-theatrical writers alike: the polluted kiss.

Karen Harvey's study of the kiss in history focuses predominantly on two types of kisses: the kiss of peace (used in medieval Catholic ritual) and the kiss of shame (a perversion of the former and associated with the diabolical, specifically 'the placing of a kiss on the anus of the Devil'): the kiss, therefore, was often presented in the early modern period as 'polluting, sinful and shameful'.[36] More broadly, Harvey's work examines the cultural history of the kiss, a romantic gesture that was at the centre of important debates in early modern culture. 'Confusion arose', writes Harvey, 'over kissing in social situations, and a taxonomy of kissing developed which was part of a wider attempt to codify practices of civility and politeness.'[37] Within this broader cultural context, one can see how the thrilling enactment of the (often shameful/polluted) kiss on stage would be subject to theatrical exploitation, moral debate and anxiety.

Critics who have written about cosmetics in theatre (myself included) have considered the ways in which scenes involving cosmetics or face painting are designed to demonstrate the dangers of female sexuality, visual artifice and the permeable boundaries between appearance and reality. However, what has not been explicitly drawn out by these studies is that in addition to providing visual theatre, scenes where cosmetics are applied to characters who are then kissed are also examples of tactile theatre. It is not just the kiss, but its texture and its effects that are crucial to this particular type of spectacle. Makeup, with all of its associations in the moralistic literature of the period with sin, the devil, witchcraft and female toxicity, is used as a theatrical prop, tangible in itself as a material that is applied to the body. The cosmetically poisoned kiss is an important tactile motif in the drama of Shakespeare and his contemporaries. Tanya Pollard has astutely recognised the parallels between tactile moments on stage and imagined fears about the effects of theatrical performance: 'The direct physical contact of the kiss [. . .] at the liminal boundary of the mouth, calls attention to the instability of the boundary between spectator and spectacle, and the idea of spectators as passive onlookers.'[38] Similarly, in my own work on cosmetics, I argue that the 'poisoned kiss motif stems from the popular notion that the tongue was a dangerous member of the body, specifically the female body'.[39] But neither Pollard nor I make much of this particular motif as a unique sensory spectacle.

Although most anti-theatrical writers spoke out against actors touching each other in a sexual way, there was a particular concern about kissing, which was rooted in the belief that disease and unhealthy humours could be transmitted uniquely and quickly through the kiss. In turn, playwrights wrote poisoned kisses into the drama, first to embody this cultural fear symbolically, second to exploit anti-theatrical anxieties about theatre as a morally poisonous entity. Such moments on stage also challenge assumptions about kissing in society: should it be public or private, for example, or should it take place between two male actors, particularly when one is often much younger than the other? In Shakespeare's *Romeo and Juliet*, we see the poison kiss motif somewhat turned on its head. When Romeo poisons himself and kisses Juliet's presumed dead lips – 'Thus with a kiss I die' (5.3.120)[40] – we see an anticipation of the poisoned kiss; later on, when Juliet wakes up and finds her lover dead, she kisses him deliberately in an attempt to steal some poison from his lips, referring to them as a 'restorative' (166). Shakespeare stages here a version of the poisoned kiss that proves to be ineffective at bringing about death, perhaps gesturing to the implicit virtue of their married bond. Generally, however, the spectacle of two actors kissing (particularly if it leads to the death of one of the characters) on such a public platform is designed to elicit an emotional response, whether governed by morality, or the debates surrounding kissing in the courtesy literature of the period. Either way, the kiss on stage was a tangible or haptic force seen to have potentially irrevocable effects on those who witness it. Famously, Henry Crosse worries about such erotic, tactile moments: 'groping, colling, kissing, amorous prattle, and signes of Venerie, whereby the maidenly disposition is polluted with lust'.[41] This anxiety, again, relies upon early modern notions about the permeability of the flesh: that it was permeable enough as to enable the sight of lovers touching to enter into a spectator's body and change it. The stage picture of the poisoned kiss was very popular, particularly in Jacobean tragedy, but there are earlier examples, such as the one in the final moments of *Romeo and Juliet* cited above.[42] By the time Thomas

Middleton was writing *The Revenger's Tragedy* in the early seventeenth century, the poisoned kiss had taken on a much more macabre character and required the explicit use of cosmetics in order to complete the spectacle. To the horror of anti-theatrical and anti-cosmetic polemicists (many of whom wrote both kinds of text), what is often staged is the topical application of the makeup first. In the case of Middleton's *The Lady's Tragedy* (1611), the poisoned kiss takes place within a planned theatrical spectacle, a contrived sequence in which the dead, recently exhumed, body of 'the Lady' is brought out in state (5.2), painted by the Lady's lover (disguised as an artist), and then used as a trap to ensnare the necrophiliac Tyrant – who kisses the poisoned lips only to die moments later from their contamination:

> *Govianus straightens the Lady's body.*

TYRANT
> Does she not feel warm to thee?

GOVIANUS
> Very little, sir.

TYRANT
> The heat wants cherishing, then. Our arms and lips
> Shall labour life into her. Wake, sweet mistress,
> 'Tis I that call thee at the door of life!

> *[He kisses her.]*

Ha!
> I talk so long to death, I'm sick myself.
> Methinks an evil scent still follows me.

$$(5.2.116–23)^{43}$$

Anti-theatrical writers interpreted such moments as designed to provoke sexual desire in theatre audiences, and contaminate vulnerable minds. They argued that inordinate lust was deliberately induced by performance, and was, in particular, a direct result of witnessing physical touching on stage. This emphasis on the polluted kiss gestures here, not only to the idea of corrupt female sexuality, but also to the Tyrant's own overzealous and taboo desire to kiss the dead. This assessment correlates with a much earlier version of the polluted kiss, though one that does not involve cosmetics explicitly. Christopher Marlowe's *Dr Faustus* stages a similar moment in 5.1 when Faustus' vain desires are satisfied by the entrance of a devil as Helen of Troy at the order of Mephistopheles, inspiring Marlowe's most famous lines: 'Was this the face that launched a thousand ships / And burnt the topless towers of Ilium?' (93–4). When Faustus kisses her – '[*They kiss*]' – he reveals, 'Her lips suck forth my soul' (96).[44] This line shows how charmed he is by his erotic encounter, but the eventual outcome for Faustus resembles what happens to Middleton's Tyrant: death and damnation come to both of them as a consequence of their excessive misuse of power and, in this instance, the socially codified kiss. Since the cosmetics in Middleton's kiss embody the diabolical associations that are explicit in Marlowe's play, both can be seen as polluted kisses and deliberately troubling instances of onstage touching that provoked anti-theatrical anxieties about the soul's susceptibility to threat through the sensuous body.

AFFECTIVE TOUCH

At the end of the rude mechanicals' version of 'Pyramus and Thisbe' in Shakespeare's *A Midsummer Night's Dream*, Theseus sends the newly married couples to bed as the night has been spent on watching a play that was much too long:

> The iron tongue of midnight hath told twelve.
> Lovers, to bed; 'tis almost fairy time.
> I fear we shall outsleep the coming morn
> As much as we this night have overwatch'd.
> This palpable-gross play hath well beguil'd
> This heavy gait of night.

$$(5.1.357–61)^{45}$$

What stands out in this passage is the reference to the play as 'palpable-gross'. Most obviously, the phrase implies that the meaning of the play is tangible or comprehensible. But 'palpable-gross' also has the sense of being doubly tangible, as the *OED* lists 'palpable' as one of the meanings of 'gross'.[46] So why does Shakespeare refer to the play as tangibly tangible? On a comic level, this phrase is a value judgement, implying that the Mechanicals' play had a simplistic plot and that it was performed by simplistic actors. Alternatively, it suggests the play or performance was rough or crude. But what if the sense is, rather, touchingly touching? Perhaps Theseus infers that the performance of the play has surprisingly 'touched' them on an emotional level, a sense of the word that would have been in use in the 1590s when the play was written and first performed. Having witnessed an apostrophe to a dead lover on an evening that celebrates their own love, the court spectators may indeed have taken in more of the performance than met their eyes. What we can be sure of is that the play the lovers have just witnessed has palpability or touchability, so we ought to ask in what ways a play can touch its audience? To conclude the first part of this chapter, I will focus on the affecting forms of touch in the playhouse and show how the idiom of touch is embedded in play texts and in the various responses to theatrical performance.

Drawing upon Gail Kern Paster's observations about the early modern notion of the humoral body, Nancy Selleck adds that, as 'a model of influence and absorption, it suggests a self not only permeated but changed, reconstituted, by what had been outside the self'.[47] Equally, as Selleck observes, 'humoral theory posits no Cartesian split between mind and body, so that these susceptibilities and assimilations are psychological as well as physical'.[48] Thus the notion that the senses are a portal to the soul is inextricably linked with the Galenic model of bodily absorption.[49] The sense of touch not as active but as receptive provides the idiom through which the emotional and psychological impact of performance is expressed. In Ben Jonson's *Volpone*, Celia asks Volpone to save her honour, appealing to his sensual capacity to be moved by her story: 'If you have ears that will be pierced – or eyes / That can be opened – a heart may be touched. Or any part that yet sounds man – about you' (3.7.240–2). As I have shown, the anti-theatrical writers were collectively nervous about the absorptive nature of the body, seeing the body as vulnerable to the sights and sounds of performance, which had the ability to 'touch' human bodies in such a way as, potentially and damagingly, to alter humoral and thereby moral constitution. So, within this model, objects, sights, sounds, vapours or ideas can enter into the ear and the eye and touch the deeper parts of the self. Anthony Munday, for example, argues that at the theatres 'There cometh much evil in the eares, but more at the eies, by these two windows death breaketh into the soule.'[50] The soul can be touched and therefore morally tainted, leading to its eternal damnation. John Northbrooke shares Munday's concerns about the capacity for performance to break through the body's surface and penetrate the heart:

> All such spectacles and shewes [. . .] are therefore to be avoyded, not onelye because vices shall not enter our heartes and breastes, but also lest the custome of pleasure shoulde touche us, and converte us thereby both from God and good workes.[51]

Conversely, being able to touch the audience and influence each individual's emotions would have been an important aim of theatre makers; it would have been a desired effect. Shakespeare's and Fletcher's Prologue to *Henry VIII*, for example, guides the audience as to the ways in which the ensuing performance should touch them:

> I come no more to make you laugh: things now
> That bear a weighty and a serious brow,
> Sad, high and working, full of state and woe,
> Such noble scenes as draw the eye to flow,
> We now present. Those that can pity here
> May, if they think it well, let fall a tear:
> The subject will deserve it.
>
> (Prologue, 1–7)[52]

But as Charles Whitney has pointed out, audiences were not homogeneous even though there was a 'tremendous advance in the theatre's power to move audiences collectively'.[53] Thus the emotional responses to performance would have been complexly varied, individual and wide-ranging. Shakespeare knew this, as we see in the disparate effects the play-within-a-play has on each of its spectators in *Hamlet*. Hamlet is pleased with the performance, but Claudius is deeply troubled by it, causing him to rush out of the hall in anguish. Hamlet celebrates Claudius' emotional outburst because it signals to him that his production of the play-within-a-play has unearthed Claudius' guilt. Hamlet sings [italics mine]:

> Why let the *stricken* deer go weep,
> The hart *ungalled* play,
> For some must watch while some must sleep.
> Thus runs the world away.
>
> (3.2.263–6)[54]

Here the way a play touches its audience is represented as targeted and individualised as Hamlet describes the tangible effects of the play upon Claudius using a hunting metaphor from an unknown ballad. He imagines the play as an arrow and Claudius as its 'stricken' victim; the term 'ungalled' here means untouched or not struck by an arrow. Elizabeth Harvey argues that the sense of touch for most early moderns had a double quality; although usually 'associated with the surface of the body, it becomes a metaphor for conveyance into the interior of the subject, particularly the capacity to arouse emotion (registered in the figurative sense of "touching" as kindling affect)'.[55] This 'conveyance into the interior' is exemplified in Hamlet's ballad. Shakespeare's pun on 'hart'/'heart' in this passage recalls anti-theatrical imaginings about the effects of theatre on individual 'harts'. Anthony Munday highlights the tactile effects of performance when he characterises weeping as 'a pricking of the hart',[56] while Stephen Gosson argues that plays 'by the privie entries of the eare, slip downe into the hart, & with gunshotte of affection gaule the minde'[57] ('gaule' indicating touching or rubbing a sore, so with implications of moral corruption).

It is not just the sights of theatre that touch the body; the sounds of poetry could touch the ear as well: 'because the sweete numbers of Poetrie [. . .] do wonderfully tickle the hearers eares, the devil hath tyed this to most of our playes'.[58] We see the reference to tickling the ear emerge again in this discourse, suggesting that the metaphor was a common one. Thus the interior effects of theatrical performance, whether manifesting as weeping, laughing or moral laxity are often imagined in tactile terms, and the seeing and hearing of plays are frequently characterised as synaesthetic activities with the capacity to penetrate and transform the self: a result feared by the anti-theatrical writers, but desired and seen as essential to the playgoing experience by the playwrights and actors. Shakespeare's language is replete with references to touching, and once we consider the ways in which touch worked or operated in the early modern theatres, we can read Shakespeare's plays with new insight into the importance of this sense not only as an experience but as a metaphor. Take *Othello*, for example. When Iago describes the effect that his manipulation of people has had, he frequently describes it as a type of touching or contact; speaking about Roderigo, Iago notes: 'I have rubbed this young quat [pimple] almost to the sense / And he grows angry' (5.1.11–12).[59] Here, Iago draws attention to the effect his lies have had on Roderigo, suggesting metaphorically that it has been like rubbing a wound or pustule to the point where it has become angry. Sir John Davies' *Nosce Teipsum* (1599) is useful in drawing our attention to another example of Shakespeare's diverse use of touching metaphors. Davies writes, 'So in th'Eares larbyrinth the voice doth stray / And doth with easie motion touch the braine' (67). These lines describe a voice, penetrating ears and moving into the body through some type of tangible or physical process; effectively, and 'with easie motion', the disembodied voice 'touches' the brain. Davies suggests that sounds have haptic qualities, but more than this, the body consumes sounds through the ear and the result is an affective motion to the brain or soul. The ear is a very important image in *Othello*, its frequent appearance as idea, image or word, gestures towards the play's concern with hearing, listening and interpreting words. Iago is keenly aware of the effects of persuasive language, and in his confessional, suggests he will disease Othello's mind through his ear: 'I'll pour this pestilence into his ear: / That she repeals him for her body's lust' (2.3.344–5). Thus Iago's effectiveness in driving Othello mad with jealousy is imagined as tactile. Iago touches, rubs, scratches, pulls, pushes, pours with words and the play stages the terrible effects of his tactile strategy.

TASTING PLAYS

Plays enter in at the mouth as well as the ear and the eyes. This brief section will address the notion that plays can be tasted in more ways than one. In *Hamlet* 2.2, when Hamlet meets the players he reminds them about a speech one of them had recited:

> I heard thee speak me a speech once – but it was never acted, or, if it was, not above once for the play I remember pleased not the million, 'twas caviar to the general. But it was, as I received it, and others whose judgements in such matters cried in the top of mine, an excellent play, well digested in the scenes, set down with as much modesty as cunning. I remember one said there were no sallets in the lines to make the matter savoury nor no matter in the phrase that might indict the author of affection, but called it an honest method, as wholesome as sweet, and by very much more handsome than fine.

> (2.2.372–82)

Hamlet describes the ideal dramatic speech using a food metaphor, suggesting that a speech that is as aesthetically pleasing as it is intellectually stimulating is like a perfectly wholesome meal. This metaphor becomes more poignant when we consider what Ken Albala refers to as the 'doctrine of similarities': 'the characteristics of any given food [. . .] are directly transferred into the consumer. You literally become what you eat.'[60] To take in good poetry according to Albala and Shakespeare is to enable some form of moral nutrition, which is, of course, a popular notion in Elizabethan and

Jacobean literary theory. But if we extend this principle into the domain of theatre, then the tasting of theatre (as theatregoing is often described) is an essential component in the formation of moral identity. You become what you consume. Apart from the technologies of theatre that created sound, visual, olfactory and tactile effects, the language of the plays – i.e. the speeches and poetry – and the play itself as a constituted whole are often figured in the period's theatrical literature as food, to be tasted, digested or consumed. Prologues, in particular, draw upon the idiom of taste to allude to the range of 'palates' that playwrights are attempting to satisfy, as does the Prologue to Jonson's *Volpone*:

> Now, luck God send us, and a little wit
> Will serve, to make our play hit;
> According to the palates of the season,
> Here is rhyme, not empty of reason.[61]

The metaphor of playgoing as tasting was particularly popular with Jonson, a playwright who, it is known, was concerned with the reception of his plays as works. The most explicit example comes from the prologue of his *Epicoene, Or the Silent Woman* (1609):

> Truth says, of old the art of making plays
> Was to content the people; and their praise
> Was to the poet money, wine, and bays,
> But in this age, a sect of writers are,
> That only for a particular likings care,
> And will taste nothing that is popular.
> With such we mingle neither brains nor breasts;
> Our wishes, like to those make public feasts
> Are not to please the cooks' tastes, but the guests.

Jonson suggests that playwrights are cooks, the plays food, and the audience's palates judge the value of the dramatic feast to be had. This vocabulary of taste is deliberate on the part of the playwright. Anti-theatricalists use the same vocabulary to warn audiences against surfeiting their appetites with the theatre. In *A third blast of retrait from plaies and Theaters* (1580), the author declares that those who see plays are 'despisers of GOD, looke where they take anie pleasure, and find sweetnes, and find sweetnes, there they hold, themselves, and feede their greedie humors; & it falleth out, as Salomon saith, that he who is throughlie anhungered, thinks the meate which he eateth to be sweete, although it be as bitter as wormewood'.[62]

Like touch, the sense of taste was ranked one of the lowest in the hierarchy of the senses. Tasting is conducted with the tongue, but the tongue has associations with sexual licentiousness, gluttony and loquaciousness, all of which are linked literally and metaphorically to appetite. Taste is closely associated with touch and many writers spoke of the two as conjoined, not least because of taste's Biblical associations with the Fall: Eve had to pluck the apple before she tasted it. Richard Brathwait laments the original sin when writing about the sense of taste, 'sith hence came our greefe, hence our miserie: when I represent her before my eyes, my eyes become blinded with weeping, remembering my granddame Eve, how soone she was induced to *taste* that shee ought not'.[63] Here taste is linked to metaphorical death: damnation of the human race was thus ever linked to excess, Epicureanism, gluttony, consumption and sexual voraciousness. We might be tempted to ask how one could eat anything and escape the judgement of the sensory moralists. Needless to say, there were very strict parameters about tasting, such as what flavours and foods should be consumed depending on class, humoral predominance, gender and a variety of other conditions that distinguished individuals from one another.[64] Throughout the middle ages and Renaissance the experience of tasting was heavily regulated and organised. C. M. Woolgar shows how taste was determined by the fact that there were distinctive categories of flavour: '"tastelessness" (insipidus) [. . .] sweet (dulcis), greasy (unctuosus), bitter (amarus), salty (salsus), sharp (acutus), harsh or styptic (stipticus), vinegary (acetosus)'.[65] Naturally these categories also extend metaphorically to judgement of performance, and, in one form or another continue to characterise the language of aesthetic value up to the present moment. In Shakespeare, this is illustrated clearly in *Hamlet*, when the prince asks one of the players to say a speech: 'We'll have a speech straight. Come, give us a taste of your quality. Come, a passionate speech' (2.2.431–2).

It might be useful at this stage to reflect upon the act of eating in the theatres, for it can be argued that literally tasting food or ale in the playhouse impacts upon the experience of tasting plays. In Bowsher and Miller's report on the Rose and Globe excavations, evidence of food and drink residue is documented. The authors add to this the written evidence available showing that that the 'association of the playhouses with eating and drinking was made clear in 1599 by Thomas Platter, who recorded that "during the performance food and drink are carried around the audience, so that for what one cares to pay one may also have refreshment"'.[66] They argue that evidence for the consumption of alcohol substantiates arguments for the existence of tap houses attached to playhouses in the period.[67] In addition to locating on the theatre sites pottery and glass vessels that were used in food preparation and consumption, the archaeologists found the remains of plants, cereals, vegetables, fruits, nuts and animals, suggesting that a range of food might have been consumed in the early modern playhouses. Although the preponderance of animal waste is not necessarily indicative of consumption (it may simply supply evidence about local waste depositories nearby), the authors observe that animal bones 'suggest that a selection of meat and fish was being prepared in or near the playhouse'.[68] We know that early modern play-texts, especially Shakespeare's, are replete with banquets, scenes of eating and drinking as well as numerous witty references to food and drink, which allude to consumption and the rituals of eating as socially coded; they may gesture towards the habit of eating and drinking among the playhouse crowds.[69] And tasting foods affects the reception of the dramatic content being tasted.

For there is no question that attending plays was viewed as a consumptive activity; this notion is ubiquitous in the anti-theatrical discourse, which time and again refers to theatres as food-producing entities: 'in all our recreations we shoulde have an instructer at

our elbowes to feede the soule. If wee gather Grapes among this-
tles, or seeke for this foode at Theaters, wee shall have a harde
pytaunce.'[70] Feeding and tasting plays, like touching them, can
occur through the eyes and ears as well: 'we leave Christ alone at
the aultar and feede our eyes with vaine and unwholesome sights,
and with filthie and unclean plays'.[71] Poetic language is seen as
immodest and deceptive to the ear, presenting itself as 'sweet'.
Shakespeare himself even applies an eating metaphor to criticise
overwrought poetry. In *Much Ado About Nothing*, describing the
traits of a lover, Benedick says 'his words are a very fantastical
banquet, just so many strange dishes' (2.3.20–1).[72] Henry Crosse
sees plays as able to 'feed the eare with sweete words, equally
balanced, the eye with variable delight'.[73] Munday insists the spiritual symbolism of the word of God is the only appropriate
linguistic food for consumption: 'Those unsaverie morsels of
unseemlie sentences passing out of the mouth of a ruffenlie plaier
doth more content the hungrie humors of the rude multititude,
and careth better relish in their mouthes, than the bread of the
worde, which is the foode of the soule.'[74] Within this gustatory
allegory players and playwrights are sometimes imagined as
diabolical chefs serving up sumptuous dishes of entertainment to
be consumed greedily by crowds of gaping spectators; in return,
their souls are somehow fed to Satan: 'the devil is fed by Theaters'.[75]
Food has always been consumed in theatres, but curiously for
authors of anti-theatrical tracts, consuming words and consuming
food are parallel activities. Shakespeare plays upon the idea that
reading is a type of tasting, as it is perceived in the early modern
imagination. As Nathaniel points out in *Love's Labour's Lost*, 'he
hath never fed of the dainties that are bred in a book. / He hath not
eat paper, as it were, he hath not drunk ink. His intellect is not
replenished; he is only an animal, only sensible in the duller parts'
(4.2.25–7).[76] The relationship between food and entertainment is
materialised by the fact that food and drink was sold at the playhouses and has been ever since; but the metaphorical link between
consuming food and consuming words is a moral one. One's bodily
appetite must be governed by virtue and reason – and one's

intellectual appetite should follow suit. Playwrights, therefore, attempted to shape the intellectual appetites of their consumers by determining the importance of cultivating a 'taste' for theatre.

'Cookes did never shewe more crafte in their junckets to vanquish the taste, no Painters in shadowes to allure the eye, then Poets in Theaters to wounde the conscience.'[77] This synaesthetic image demonstrates aptly the assault on the senses, including touch and taste, that theatre presented to its audience. In Shakespeare, to be called 'senseless' is, then, one of the most damning judgements. It insinuates incapacity for feeling, the inability to be touched, the inhumanity of being resistant to sensation. Murellus' damning outburst in 1.1 of *Julius Caesar* — 'You blocks, you stones, you worse than senseless things!' (36)[78] – to the fickle citizenry of Rome articulates, perhaps, a veiled frustration that playwrights may have felt towards their own audiences whose tastes could change quickly enough to dictate the careers of playwrights and influence reportorial trends. It also suggests that an important function of the senses is not just to direct reason, but to provoke the passions. As I have been arguing, touching and tasting were conditions as well as effects of performance. Categories of touch and taste were constructed by theatres that enabled a coming together of bodies and a range of intellects at close proximity. As part of a wider network of sensory moralising, the anti-theatrical discourse is most notably anxious about the reception of theatre through the senses. The fear that plays could touch people to the core, arouse passions, stir humours and alter moral behaviour is, however, counteracted by the desire of playwrights and theatre companies to move their audiences through the deliberate provocation of the complex sensory network, to penetrate into the body and enable theatre to do its work of emotionally invigorating those who come to feed upon it, inciting the most thrilling of tactile effects: the sound of clapping hands.

CHAPTER ELEVEN

'SIGHT AND SPECTACLE'
EVELYN TRIBBLE

Sight is simultaneously a physical, biological, cognitive, material and cultural phenomenon. The paradox of seeing is that our 'hardware' is very limited – our visual field is very gappy and patchy – but our visual experience is extraordinarily rich. Our brains and our environment bridge the gap through a process of 'predictive coding'. As the author of a recent paper on vision and cognition argues, the brain 'is not a passive organ simply waiting to be activated by external stimuli [. . . Rather, it] continuously employs memory of past experiences to interpret sensory information and predict the immediately relevant future'.[1] We use the patchy, incomplete data we receive to create rich predictions and beliefs about the world – a rabbit behind a picket fence is seen holistically as a rabbit, not as slices of animal interspersed with wooden slats. Most of the time these mechanisms work efficiently and well; indeed, as the noted philosopher of mind Andy Clark suggests, such short cuts are 'hugely beneficial when the sensory data is noisy, ambiguous, or incomplete – situations that are, in fact, pretty much the norm in daily life'.[2] Seeing is always a creative, constructionist act; by the same token, it is fundamentally subject to manipulation and error. These twin attributes of sight were actively exploited by Shakespeare and by the early modern players for whom he wrote.

Sight is also historically and materially situated, and it is important to recognise that contemporary assumptions about sight and light are profoundly conditioned by experiences with visual technologies, including the ubiquity of artificial lighting and mediated forms of seeing. The most obvious difference between contemporary and early modern theatre is the nature of the lighting. Shakespeare's players performed in the same ambient light as their audiences. This fact is widely recognised, but there is not full agreement about its implications. Some scholars have assumed that such conditions must inevitably have lessened the illusionistic effect. Jenn Stephenson has argued for 'a strongly self-aware theatrical effect' in these circumstances, suggesting that

> a confluence of historical performance conditions on the early modern English stage, including a daylight performance, the bare minimally adorned stage and boy-players in female parts, demanded significant interpretive work on the part of the audience to manage the relationship between the actual [. . .] and the fictional [. . .] Subject to such conditions the perceptual gap between the fictional and the actual is wide and inescapable.[3]

Commenting on the experience of seeing plays at the new Globe theatre, Andrew Gurr similarly claims that

> acting at the new Globe in broad daylight shows what an anachronism the modern tradition of stage realism is on such a stage. The inherent and manifest artifice of playing in such a venue makes attempts at realistic and psychologically plausible acting ineffective, and certainly misconceived [. . .] We talk now about the danger on stage of breaking the illusion. Setting up any kind of illusion was a concept the Elizabethans were extremely wary of.[4]

According to these lines of argument, early modern spectators differed from contemporary theatre, cinema and television audiences in their 'awareness of the illusion',[5] both because of the visibility of the audience 'to the players and to themselves' and because 'the spectacle was always relatively parsimonious'.[6]

I will return to the question of the parsimony of the spectacle in due course. For now, I will examine the claim that the lack of lighting effects necessarily reduces the audience's immersion in the fiction, resulting in the 'perceptual gap' Stephenson describes.

Audiences accustomed to modern theatres or cinemas may well experience a distancing effect at the new Globe, but this effect might well be as much a result of the collision of modern assumptions and conventions with early modern practices as any inherent distancing effect of full visibility. As R. B. Graves notes, 'inevitably, each age interprets the sparse information about Shakespeare's stage based in part on its own aesthetics and theatre practice'.[7] A Shakespearean audience had no other competing visual regimes with which to compare its experience of playgoing. What Gurr and Stephenson seem to register here is the *difference* between most contemporary experiences of playgoing and the 'lights-on' practice of the new Globe and of other reconstructed playhouses such as the American Shakespeare Center's Blackfriars playhouse. As Cynthia Marshall writes, one of the first reviewers of the new Globe's production of *Henry V* in 1997 noted the difficulty of adjusting to '"dull, samey afternoon light"' and reflects upon '"how much we have come to rely on lighting designers to concentrate our attention on this actor or switch it to that one"'.[8]

Indeed, every entertainment mode has its own visual logic that is swiftly absorbed by its consumer. The filmic convention of shot/counter-shot, in which the camera continually cuts between two speakers to establish that they inhabit the same space, is anything but 'realistic', but has become generally accepted as a visual convention, to the extent that it has become naturalised by contemporary audiences. Such conventions are a moving target, and our acceptance of them is relational. Older films with sequences shot inside a car, painfully obvious as rear-projected studio shots, are greeted with howls of laughter today, but this is because of a mismatch between older visual technologies and our expectations; we can take comfort in the notion that today's innovative CGI technologies will seem equally risible in the near future. Thus visual technology and audience expectation is always relational – and therefore always subject to change and revision, as today's cutting-edge technology becomes hopelessly dated and stagy in the future.

A similar point might be made about the question of the visual parsimony of the stage; this, too, is relational and depends upon the larger set of expectations and experiences of the audience. It has become common to argue that Elizabethan audiences preferred to 'hear' rather than 'see' a play.[9] In fact, as Gabriel Egan has shown, the phrase to 'hear a play' was actually somewhat unusual: most Elizabethans spoke of 'seeing' a play. Shakespeare used the term 'hear a play' in three of the eight instances which Egan has discovered; however, references to 'seeing' a play outnumber those to 'hearing' a play 12 to 1.[10] Certainly Shakespeare and early modern playing companies were keenly attentive to the acoustic dynamics of their plays, and the pioneering work of Bruce Smith on the 'acoustic world' of early modern England has rendered critics much more aware of the auditory dimension of theatregoing and to the ways that early modern players participated in a distinct soundscape, an idea he develops further in this collection.[11] Nevertheless, attention was lavished upon the visual dimensions of the play. While the visual spectacle of Shakespeare's outdoor theatre might seem stingy in comparison to the immersive visual technologies of cinema, or to the lavish displays at the entertainments of the Jacobean court, the resources outlaid for visual display were extensive. In the sensory ecology of the early modern stage, sight held a predominant place.

Detractors, defenders and observers of the theatre all attest to its powerful effect upon the senses, particularly the sense of sight. Sight was simultaneously the most elevated of the senses and potentially the most dangerous. Early modern writers inherited a suspicion of vision from Plato's warnings about the deceptiveness of appearance, as mediated through the writings of St Augustine, who was wary of temptations proffered through the senses.[12] Although a playwright himself, the writer Anthony Munday invoked this tradition in his warning about the dangerous side of vision: 'There cometh much evil in at the eares, but more at the eies, by these two open windows death breaketh into the soule. Nothing entereth more effectualie into the memorie, than that which commeth by seeing.'[13] Such warnings were echoed by many anti-theatrical writers. The polemicist Stephen Gosson notes the avidity with which playgoers sought after spectacle: 'in publike Theaters, when any notable shew passeth over the stage, the people arise in their seates, and stand upright with delight and eagernesse to view it well.'[14] The desire for a good vantage point for consuming sights is also testified to by the Swiss visitor Thomas Platter, who notes that 'The playhouses are so constructed that they play on a raised platform, so that everyone has a good view [. . .] The actors are most expensively and elaborately costumed.'[15]

Defenders of the theatre agree with Munday that sight is the most 'effectual' of the senses, but it is for that reason that they argue for its effectiveness as a didactic tool. The prolific playwright Thomas Heywood responded to anti-theatricalists such as Gosson by arguing that bodies in motion on the stage were a particularly effective educational tool: seeing heroic action on the stage could rouse equally heroic impulses within the audience. Heywood contrasts the 'action' of the players, who present not just static images but living bodies, to the technologies of two-dimensional printing or portraiture:

> A Description is only a shadow received by the eare but not percevied by the eye: so lively portraiture is meerely a forme seene by the eye, but can neither shew action, passion, motion, or any other gesture, to moove the spirits of the beholder to admiration: so bewitching a thing is lively and well spirited action, that it hath power to new mold the harts of the spectators and fashion them to the shape of any noble and notable attempt.[16]

A similar defence was mounted by pamphleteer and playwright Thomas Nashe. Nashe compares the inert historical representation in books and monuments to its full-bodied living presence on stage:

> First, for the subject of them [plays] (for the most part) it is borrowed out of our English Chronicles, wherein our forefathers valiant acts (that have line long buried in rustie brasse, and worme-eaten bookes) are revived, and they themselves raised from the Grave of oblivion, and

brought to pleade their aged Honours in open presence: than which, what can be a sharper reproofe to these degenerate effeminate dayes of ours. How would it have joyed brave Talbot (the terror of the French) to thinke that after he had lyne two hundred yeares in his Tombe, hee should triumphe againe on the Stage, and have his bones newe embalmed with the teares of ten thousand spectators at least, (at severall times) who in the Tragedian that represents his person, imagine they behold him fresh bleeding.[17]

Both detractors and defenders of the theatre, then, focused on the potential affective response that might result from the spectacle before them.

These accounts describe the overwhelming impact of sight upon the audience, but they do little to tell us precisely what the spectators saw. However visually spare the Elizabethan stage may seem to contemporary audiences accustomed to immersive visual environments, early modern theatre companies invested in cutting-edge visual technologies and materials to create visually sumptuous effects. Among the most costly and impressive of these were costumes, which as Thomas Platter noted were elaborate and expensive. It might seem odd to count costumes as a major compo-nent of visual spectacle, but these costumes were often sumptuous in fabric, beautifully worked and sometimes remarkably exotic. Moreover, the high cost of clothing in this period meant that the clothing could create a 'wow factor' out of proportion to that achieved by any costuming today (see Figure 7). Susan Cerasano notes that the value of the costumes held by an early modern company would have been nearly equal to the value of the building itself.[18] While Thomas Platter notes that the companies bought the cast-off clothing of noblemen, there is also ample evidence that companies also spent considerable sums of money on particular visual effects through costume.

Our primary source for the materials and practices of playing companies in this period comes from the so-called 'diary' of Philip Henslowe, a record of expenditure, inventory and income of the

Figure 7 Mark Rylance (Vincentio) in *Measure for Measure*, Shakespeare's Globe (2004), photograph by John Tramper. With kind permission of The Globe Theatre

Admiral's Men. While we do not possess such records for Shakespeare's company (the Lord Chamberlain's Men, later the King's Men), most scholars concur that their practices were comparable.[19] Henslowe's diary records numerous lavish outlays for costumes. Examples include seven pounds for a 'dublett of whitt satten layd thicke with gowld lacke, and a payer of raowne pandes hosse of cloth of sylver, the panes layd with gowld lace' ['a doublet of white satin laid thick with gold lace and a pair of round paned hose of cloth of silver, the panes laid with gold lace'];[20] '[b]ryches of crymson velvet' for Tamberlaine; a 'black satten dublet layd thycke with blacke and golwde lace', and for *Henry V* (presumably the *Famous Victories of Henry V*, originally performed by the Queen's Men, rather than Shakespeare's play) a 'velvet gowne' and a 'satten dublet layde with gold layce'.[21] As these records indicate, considerable sums were laid out to clothe the central characters in stunning style, using sumptuous materials that would show up well against the neutral light that Graves describes. This lavish expenditure for prominent roles fits with one of the few pieces of visual evidence we have for costuming in the Elizabethan theatre: the 1595 'Peacham drawing' (so named as it is said to be by Henry Peacham, 1578–c.1644) of *Titus Andronicus*.[22] (See figure 8.) The drawing, in the manuscript papers of the Marquesse de Bath in Wiltshire, shows a grouping of characters from Shakespeare's early play *Titus Andronicus*. The characters in the sketch include Titus, Roman soldiers (or Titus' sons), Tamora the Queen of the Goths and her sons, and Aaron the Moor. The characters are dressed in a variety of styles, from simple baldrics gesturing at Roman costuming for the soldiers, to a sumptuous gown for Tamora, to what seems to be elaborate, perhaps purpose-designed costumes for Aaron and Titus. Susan Cerasano argues that this evidence suggests that companies deployed their resources strategically, investing in costumes for major characters and using existing resources, perhaps with a few additions, for less prominent characters. [23] By so doing, the companies could create an exotic flavour by producing 'effects foreign to contemporary England'.[24]

Probably written around 1590, *Titus* participates in the vogue at the time for exotic locales and costumes. Such visual effects were gained in part by strategic outlays on distinctive costumes, but were also produced by stage processions and the use of portable properties and movables. *Titus* uses such means to create visual spectacle freely, as shown by this stage direction:

> *Sound drums and trumpets, and then enter two of Titus's sons, and then two men bearing a coffin covered with black, then two other sons, then Titus Andronicus, and then, as prisoners, Tamora, the Queen of Goths, and her three sons, Alarbus, Chiron, and Demetrius, with Aaron the Moor, and others as many as can be* (1.2.73ff).[25]

Thus a major element of the sight and spectacle in the theatre were the bodies of the actors themselves, costumed, holding or carrying properties, and using their physical training in gesture and movement to move across the stage individually, or in the practised patterned movements of fencing, dancing, processing or martial display. The phrase '*and others as many as can be*' shows Shakespeare's awareness of the effect of crowding the stage and

Figure 8 *Titus Andronicus*, drawing by Henry Peacham. © Reproduced by permission of the Marquess of Bath, Longleat House, Warminster, Wiltshire, Great Britain

creating a sense of abundance and variety with limited resources. Shakespeare used such tactics throughout his career; examples include '*Dead march. Enter the funeral of King Henry the Fifth, attending on by the Duke of Bedford, Regent of France; the Duke of Gloucestor, Protector; the Duke of Exeter; the Earl of Warwick; the Bishop of Winchester; and the Duke of Somerset*' (*1 Henry VI*, 1.1sd); '*Enter King Richard and his train, including Catesby, marching with drums and trumpets*' (*Richard III*, 4.4.136sd); '*Enter in conquest with drums and colours Edmund [with] Lear and Cordelia as prisoners, soldiers [and a] Captain*' (*King Lear*, 5.3.1sd); '*Enter a company of mutinous Citizens with staves, clubs and other weapons*' (*Coriolanus*, 1.1sd).

Such visual displays were relatively invariant; that is, they were the essential and portable elements of the stage, since actors' bodies, costumes and hand-held properties were constant across outdoor amphitheatres, indoor theatres, court appearances and touring venues. Overall, the time and money invested in properties and movables was considerable.[26] Henslowe's diaries and the internal evidence from the plays of Shakespeare and others attest to additional substantial investments in such items as beds, cauldrons, thrones, chariots and musical and martial panoply, as well as specialised equipment for particular plays, such as 'a tombe for Dido', a 'paire of stairs for Phaeton', 'one wheel and frame for the *Siege of London*'.[27]

Depending on venue and available technologies, more elaborate visual spectacles could be achieved by use of stage technologies discussed in Stern's chapter, such as the trap below the stage and, in some theatres, the 'heavens' above, which used winches for the descent of supernatural characters. Shakespeare's later plays, especially the romances, employ such devices frequently. The final act of *Cymbeline* features a spectacular descent using such stage machinery: '*Jupiter descends in thunder and lightning, sitting upon an eagle: he throws a thunderbolt. The Ghosts fall on their knees*' (5.4.92sd). Perhaps Shakespeare's most extravagant use of visual and aural spectacle occurs in *The Tempest*. One of his latest plays, and perhaps purpose-written to exploit the visual and aural potential of the King's Men's indoor theatre, the Blackfriars, *The Tempest* employs the full panoply of early modern theatrical technologies.[28] The play calls for elaborate costumes, including Prospero's 'magic robes' (5.1.1); a variety of outfits for Ariel, including a disguise as a 'water nymph' (1.2.317) and as a 'Harpy' (3.3.52), as well as fantastic costumes for the numerous 'strange shapes' and spirits which inhabit the island: '*Enter diverse spirits in shape of dogs and hounds*' (4.1.255ff). Like *Cymbeline*, this play features a supernatural descent from above, in this instance of Juno in the midst of the marriage masque Prospero performs for Ferdinand and Miranda. *The Tempest* also calls for one of the few examples of overt visual trickery in Shakespeare: '*Thunder and lightning. Enter Ariel, like a harpy, claps his wings upon the table, and with a quaint device the banquet vanishes*' (3.3.53sd). While we cannot tell with certainty what this 'quaint device' was, it is likely that it was some form of revolving table of the kind that jugglers (magicians) of the time would have used. These examples show the eagerness with which Shakespeare could embrace spectacular visual technologies, particularly in creating the other-worldly effects so crucial to *The Tempest* and other late romances. (For visual compared with sound effects in *The Tempest*, see Jones' chapter in this volume.)

Shakespeare and other playwrights did not need to resort to such overt visual trickery often, however. For the most part they could rely upon their audiences to be willing if unwitting partners in a range of cognitive illusions, as a result of the ease of manipulating human attention. Paradoxically, our visual fields are both highly reliable, in that they are 'good enough' most of the time, and yet easily subject to manipulation. Con men, magicians and actors have always relied upon the ease with which human attention can be manipulated. Our attention is focalised; as psychologist William James wrote, '[attention] implies withdrawal from some things in order to deal effectively with others'.[29] The easy manipulation of attention is attested to by the famous 'gorilla study' which vividly demonstrates 'inattentional blindness', or the unconscious tendency to screen out visual stimuli to which we are not directly attending. In that experiment, conducted by psychologists Christopher Chabris and David Simons, subjects were told to count the passes in a basketball game; while concentrating on this task, roughly half of subjects miss the fact that a person in a gorilla suit enters the frame, beats her chest, and exits.[30] This experiment strikingly shows that spectators have an 'attentional spotlight' that is easily manipulated by a variety of devices, including preoccupation with a particular task; social cues such as gaze and gesture; the use of motion and contrast to render objects and events salient; the use of sound to direct attention in a particular direction; and laughter. Magicians, pickpockets and actors use overt and covert misdirection to 'manipulate the awareness and attention of their marks'.[31]

Early modern players were expert at manipulating the attentional spotlight of the spectators. A good example is the use of supernatural effects, particularly the appearance of ghosts, apparitions, gods and witches. These can employ high-tech stage machinery, such as the descent of the deities on a winch from the ceiling just described, or the sinking of the cauldron under the stage in *Macbeth*. But such effects can also be gained through manipulating and misdirecting audience attention. The exits of the Ghost in *Hamlet* 1.1. provide a pertinent instance. How, for instance, does the ghost exit in the opening scene of *Hamlet*? The first exit seems clearly to be via a stage door, since Barnardo says that the ghost 'stalks away' (1.1.53). But the mechanism of the second exit is more ambiguous, and the dialogue is written in such a way as to confuse the issue deliberately, in order, presumably, to convey a sense of a mysterious disappearance rather than a simple exit. In a theatre equipped with a space 'below' the stage, the Ghost may well descend through the trap. But he may equally simply exit virtually unnoticed via a stage door, his exit masked by the general confusion and chaos of the scene, as each character in turn takes charge of audience gaze: ''Tis here!' / ''Tis here!' / ''Tis gone!' (1.1.145–7). With each phrase, the actor, armed with halberd and almost certainly rushing about the stage, directs attention to a different portion of the stage and, in the confusion, the ghost can easily leave the stage unnoticed. It is the simplest of attentional manipulations.

Moreover, in this scene and in others, Shakespeare uses another common technique to manipulate perception: the so-called misinformation effect. Psychologists use this term to describe 'the tendency for misleading information presented after the event to reduce one's memory accuracy for the original event'.[32] While scientists interested in the forensic uses of memory in legal testimony view this effect as primarily pernicious, it could be seen instead as the inevitable consequence of the inherently social nature of remembering.[33] In discussing the ghost's disappearance, Horatio relates that 'it started like a guilty thing / Upon a fearful summons' (1.1.153–4), while Marcellus notes that 'It faded on the crowing of the cock' (1.1.163). These accounts do not jibe with one another, as fading and starting are rather different actions; taken together, they further shape and modify the audience's memory of the ghost.

A similar instance involving the supernatural takes place in *Macbeth* 1.3 when the witches exit after making their prophecies to Banquo and Macbeth. Like the ghost in *Hamlet*, they refuse the solicitations of the mortals to stay and speak; the stage direction reads *'Witches vanish'* (1.3.77). This exit may well take place through the trap, which almost certainly would have been used when the play was performed at the Globe; the use of the trap is also in keeping with the general high level of machinery and effects in the play, especially in the revised and interpolated scenes with Hecate (4.1). However, in 1.2 the supernatural effect is not created solely by visual trickery, but by the retrospective commentary of Banquo and Macbeth:

BANQUO

The earth hath bubbles, as the water has,

And these are of them. – Whither are they vanish'd?

MACBETH

Into the air; and what seem'd corporeal,

Melted as breath into the wind.

(1.3.79–82)

The two accounts are actually inconsistent, as Banquo seems to indicate that the witches have disappeared into the 'bubbles' on the earth, while Macbeth has seen them vanish 'into the air'. No audience will notice the discrepancy, since the ambiguous descriptions serve primarily to accentuate the retrospective impression of supernatural effects. Language itself retrospectively transforms full-blooded actors into airy nothings.

Playwrights and players, like magicians, trade upon the malleability of vision. Shakespeare seems to have been particularly interested in the susceptibility of sight to manipulation and error; it is a recurrent thematic preoccupation in his plays. In *A Midsummer Night's Dream* the young lovers comment upon the seemingly arbitrary nature of vision. Helena, bemoaning her rejection by Demetrius, notes that 'throughout Athens' she is reputed as 'fair' as Hermia and concludes that 'Love looks not with the eyes but with the mind / And therefore is wing'd Cupid painted blind' (1.2.234–5). The action of the play depends upon the manipulation of sight through the 'little Western flower' (2.2.166), and characters subject to its influence comically comment upon its effect. Upon having the herb removed, Titania sees Bottom for what he 'really' is and exclaims, 'O, how mine eyes do loath his visage now!' (4.1.78). However, Helena's lament shows us that the organ of sight is subject to the whims and desires of the mind even without such trickery.

Shakespeare fully explores the sinister aspects of the susceptibility of sight to error in *Othello*. Iago prides himself on his ability to manipulate vision. He is particularly adept at employing the same 'misinformation' effect used in *Hamlet* and *Macbeth* to revise Othello's view of Cassio's action. When Cassio exits after pleading his suit to Desdemona in 3.3, Iago easily recasts Cassio's 'ill at ease' (32) departure into something far more unsettling:

> Cassio, my lord? No, sure, I cannot think it
> That he would steal away so guilty-like
> Seeing you coming.

> (3.3.37–9)

Just as Macbeth and Banquo ask the audience to 'see' the witches sink into solid earth or dissolve into thin air retrospectively, so too does Iago deftly manipulate Othello's memory of Cassio's departure from innocent embarrassment to 'guilty' subterfuge. This moment is the first in a long line of 'misinformation effects' that demonstrate the ease with which sight is manipulated. The entire play, of course, is preoccupied with 'ocular proof' (3.3.362). Iago advises Othello simply to observe: 'Look to your wife, observe her well with Cassio / Wear your eyes thus, not jealous nor secure' (3.3.200–1), knowing full well that his vision has already been tainted by doubts of his wife's fidelity. So powerful is the effect that the staged encounter with Bianca and Cassio easily convinces Iago that Cassio laughs 'at his vice' (167) with Desdemona. Through to tragic end, Shakespeare continually presents to the audience the pernicious effects of a naïve trust in sight.[34]

The Chorus in *Henry V* presents perhaps the most famous example of Shakespeare's overt preoccupation with the mechanics of visual illusion. Each act begins with apologies for the parsimony of the spectacle, contrasting the magnitude of the historical victory of Henry V at Agincourt with the necessarily impoverished onstage representation of it:

> But pardon, gentles all
> The flat unraised spirits that hath dared
> On this unworthy scaffold to bring forth
> So great an object. Can this cockpit hold
> The vasty fields of France? Or may we cram
> Within this wooden O the very casques
> That did affright the air in Agincourt?
> (Prologue, 8–14)

Critics have long debated the implications of these apparent elaborate excuses for the failure of verisimilitude. In Samuel Johnson's 1765 notes to his edition of the play, he comments:

> The lines given to the chorus have many admirers, but the truth is, that in them a little may be praised, and much must be forgiven; nor can it be easily discovered why the

> intelligence given by the chorus is more necessary in this
> play than in many others where it is omitted.[35]

This observation is certainly pertinent, for Shakespeare does not frame other plays that are equally copious in subject matter in such a way; *Antony and Cleopatra* oscillates rapidly between Rome and Egypt, to take just one example. More recent critics have suggested that in the chorus the play foregrounds its 'theatrical anxieties'.[36]

But does the Chorus really reflect a true theatrical anxiety or disenchantment with the visual resources of the theatre? I suggest, rather, that the Chorus' disclaimers are a form of boasting, if anything. Thus we may read the Chorus as saying: 'So skilled are my actors, so vivid is my writing, so easily will you yield to our suggestions, that we are able to lay bare all our devices before you, and you will *still* cheer Henry's St Crispin's Day speech. You will leave the theatre with the impression that you have seen the Battle of Agincourt itself, even though I will literally show you nothing of it.' This account might be fanciful, but I will conclude with an analogy from film. In the 1952 musical comedy *Singin' in the Rain*, a film about movie-making in the transition from silent films to talkies, Don Lockwood (Gene Kelly) woos the ingénue Kathy Seldon (Debbie Reynolds) by singing her a love song in an empty sound set in a Hollywood studio. The audience sees him manipulate the spotlight so that she appears in the flattering light of a sunset, helps her up a ladder which represents a balcony, and directs a fan at her so that her hair flutters alluringly in the wind. All the tricks that Hollywood uses to convince its audience of the verisimilitude of their films are laid open before the filmgoers. Yet the effect does not undermine or distance the audience because of its awareness of the illusion; rather, admiration at the skill with which the visual spectacle is manipulated only increases the pleasure of the scene. In his willingness to expose 'trade secrets', Shakespeare in *Henry V* perhaps exploits a similar dynamic.

NOTES

PREFACE

1. In *Unediting the Renaissance* (London, 1996), 41–64, she adroitly analyses the radically variant substantive texts, from 1604, 1616 and 1663, identifying the three distinct religious positions these different versions of the play illustrate.
2. W.B. Worthen, 'Intoxicating Rhythms: Or, Shakespeare, Literary Drama, and Performance (Studies)', *Shakespeare Quarterly*, 62 (2011), 309–39.
3. Mariko Ichikawa has made careful notes of the time allowed for exits, noting that central characters, who would normally speak from the front centre of the stage, normally took two lines of dialogue more than messengers, who, from a standing start when positioned by an exit door, usually vanished immediately. See her *Shakespearean Entrances* (New York, 2002), 39–41.
4. The manuscript is BL C.142.d.18, London, 1630; in the standard edition of Massinger's plays, 1.2.173–4. *The Plays and Poems*, eds. Philip Edwards and Colin Gibson, 5 vols, Clarendon Press, Oxford, 1976, 3.210.
5. John Marston, *The Malcontent*, in *The Malcontent and Other Plays*, ed. Keith Sturgess, World Classics (Oxford, 1997).

INTRODUCTION

1. George Wilkins, *The Historie of Justine* (1606), sig. A4r.
2. John Stoughton, *XI. Choice Sermons preached upon Selected Occasions, in Cambridge* (1640), 87.
3. Stephen Gosson, *Plays Confuted in Five Actions* (1582), sig. D8v.
4. David Leslie, First Lord Newark, *A Coppy of Generall Lesley's Letter to Sir John Suckling with Sir John Sucklings Answer* (1641), sig. A3r.

1: 'THIS WIDE AND UNIVERSAL THEATRE': THE THEATRE AS PROP IN SHAKESPEARE'S METADRAMA

1. Andrew Gurr, *Playgoing in Shakespeare's London*, 3rd edn (Cambridge, 2004), 108–10.

2. William Gouge, *A Learned and very Useful Commentary on the Whole Epistle to the Hebrews* (1655), 513.

3. John Stockwood, *A Sermon Preached at Paules Crosse* (1578), 134; Ben Jonson, *Execration Against Vulcan* (1640), sig. B2v; John Chamberlain, *The Letters*, ed. Norman E. McClure, 2 vols (Philadelphia, 1939), 1: 544; *Sharers' Papers* (1635), quoted in E.K. Chambers, *The Elizabethan Stage*, 4 vols (Oxford, 1923), 2: 508; Francis Lenton, *The Young Gallants Whirligigg* (1629), 14.

4. Anne Righter, *Shakespeare and the Idea of the Play* (London, 1962), 155–6.

5. Lionel Abel, *Metatheatre: A New View of Dramatic Form* (New York, 1963).

6. Tom Pettitt, 'Midsummer Metadrama: "Pyramus and Thisbe" and Early English Household Theatre', *Charting Shakespearean Waters: Text and Theatre*, eds. Niels Bugge Hansen, Sos Haugaard (Copenhagen, 2005), 31–44. See also James L. Calderwood, *Shakespearean Metadrama* (Minneapolis, 1971); James L. Calderwood, *Metadrama in Shakespeare's Henriad: Richard II to Henry V* (Berkeley, 1979); James L. Calderwood, *To be and Not to be: Negation and Metadrama in Hamlet* (New York, 1983).

7. Andrew Gurr, 'Metatheatre and the Fear of Playing', in *Neo-Historicism: Studies in Renaissance Literature, History and Politics*, eds. Robin Headlam Wells, Glenn Burgess and Rowland Wymer (Cambridge, 2000), 100–1.

8. For further discussion of this point, see Charles Edelman, 'Shakespeare and the Invention of the Epic Theatre: Working with Brecht', *Shakespeare Survey*, 58 (Cambridge, 2005), 130–6 (133).

9. Paul Edward Yachnin and Patricia Badir, *Shakespeare and the Cultures of Performance* (Aldershot, 2008), 3.

10. Thomas Dekker, *Newes from Hell* (1606), sig. G2v.

11. Thomas Heywood, *An Apology for Actors* (1615), sig. D2v.

12. John Stoughton, *The Heavenly Conversation* (1640), 24; 'What is Our Life?', Bodleian Library MS, Eng. Poet f. 27, 91.

13. John Bulwer, *Chirologia, or, The Naturall Language of the Hand* (1644), 135.

14. Ben Jonson, *The Works*, eds. C.H. Herford and C. and E. Simpson, 11 vols (Oxford, 1947), 8: 439.

15. See Tiffany Stern, *Making Shakespeare* (London and New York, 2004), 26. Naturally this space was also associated with the classical underworld, as is usefully explored by Andrew J. Power, 'What the Hell is Under the

Stage? Trapdoor Use in the English Senecan Tradition', *English*, 60 (2011), 276–96. The fact, however, that it is referred to as 'hell', not 'hades', in the early modern professional theatre, suggests how prominent its hellish qualities will have been in the minds of the audience.

16. Thomas Dekker, *Newes from Hell* (1606), sig. B1v.

17. William Drummond, *The Poetical Works* ed. L.E. Kastner, 2 vols (New York, 1968), 1:30; Thomas Middleton, *The Blacke Booke* (1604), sig. B1r.

18. Thomas Nashe, *'Somewhat to reade for them that list'*, in *Syr P.S. His Astrophel and Stella* (1591), sig. A3r.

19. Barnabe Barnes, *The Divils Charter* (1607), sig. F3v.

20. William Kemp, *Kemps Nine Daies Wonder* (1600), sig. B1r.

21. Philip Gawdy, letter of 16 November 1587, in *Letters*, ed. Isaac Herbert Jeayes (London, 1906), 23.

22. Melchior de Marmet, Seigneur de Valcroissant, *Entertainments of the Cours: or, Academical Conversations* (1658), 182; Edmund Gayton, *Pleasant Notes upon Don Quixote* (1654), 94.

23. Thomas Blount, *Glossographia or a Dictionary* (1656), sig. 2M5r-v.

24. See Henry S. Turner's suggestive interpretation of Shakespeare's similar use of 'plot' as story and stage space in *The English Renaissance Stage: Geometry, Poetics, and the Practical Spatial Arts, 1580–1630* (Oxford, 2006), 173.

25. Sir Philip Sidney, *The Defence of Poesy* (1595), sig. H1r. For more on scene-boards see Tiffany Stern, 'Watching as Reading: The Audience and Written Text in the Early Modern Playhouse', *How to Do Things with Shakespeare*, ed. Laurie Maguire (Oxford, 2008), 136–59.

26. Richard Brathwait, *A Solemn Joviall Disputation* (1617), 171; Richard Brathwait, *A Survey of History* (1638), 217; Nathaniel Ingelo, *Bentivolio and Urania in Four Bookes* (1660), 39; Archie Armstrong, *A Banquet of Jests* (1633), 111.

27. Henry Vaughan, *Flores Solitudinis Certaine Rare and Elegant Pieces* (1654), 119; George Wither, *Britain's Remembrancer* (1628), sig. N9v; Henry More, *The Immortality of the Soul* (1659), 490.

28. 'Indenture of 2nd October, 1639', Folger Shakespeare Library MS, z.c.22 (39).

29. Thomas Middleton and Thomas Dekker, *Blurt Master-Constable* (1602), sig. F3v; John Marston, *Insatiate Countesse* (1613), sig. D4v.

30. John Fletcher, *Maid in the Mill*, in Francis Beaumont and John Fletcher, *Comedies and Tragedies* (1647), sig. 4b4v; George Chapman, *May-day* (1611), 46–7; Robert Tailor, *The Hogge hath Lost his Pearle* (1614), sig. B4v; *The Partiall Law* (c.1625), 39, in Folger Shakespeare Library MS, v.a.165.

2: STORM EFFECTS IN SHAKESPEARE

1. J.C., *A Pleasant Comedie Called The Two Merry Milke-Maids or The Best Words Weare the Garland* (London, 1620), sig. A2v.

2. See, for example, Andrew Gurr, *Playgoing in Shakespeare's London* (Cambridge, 1987), 189–96. Mark Bayer has recently argued, persuasively, for a more nuanced approach to the Red Bull's status from today's perspective, but demonstrates that the playhouse maintained a popular reputation while it was in operation. See 'The Red Bull Playhouse', in Richard Dutton, ed., *The Oxford Handbook of Early Modern Theatre* (Oxford, 2009), 225–39.

3. *Two Merry Milke-Maids*, sig. A2v.

4. John Melton, *The Astrologaster, or, the Figure-Caster* (London, 1620), 31.

5. Much of this information has been collated by Phillip Butterworth, whose *Theatre of Fire: Special Effects in Early English and Scottish Theatre* (London, 1998) also provides further examples.

6. The tiring-house was the backstage space in which actors dressed for performance and through which they entered to the main level of the stage. The heavens was a canopy over the stage, supported by columns, which acted as an occasional entry point from above. See Tiffany Stern's chapter in this volume in which she identifies these structural features as significant fixtures of the playhouse, p. 25.

7. John Bate, *The Mysteres of Nature and Art: The Second Booke, Teaching most plainly, and withal most exactly, the composing of all manner of Fire-works for Triumph and Recreation* (London, 1634), 76–7. Bate's work is the earliest entry for Swevel in the *OED*: I use the term as a matter of convenience to distinguish from those rockets and squibs which are not run along 'lines'.

8. See Butterworth, *Theatre of Fire*, 99–129.

9. Thomas Dekker, *If this be not a good Play, the Diuell is in it* (London, 1612), sig. E2r. This play, acted by Queen Anne's company at the Red Bull, provides one example of what the Company of Revels later attempted to 'reform'. The identity of those charged with lighting the rockets is uncertain; only Melton describes them as 'hirelings' (which simply means 'hired actors', i.e. not a principle actor in the company).

10. There is, unfortunately, little evidence either to refute or corroborate this speculation, but Melton's hirelings are 'in their Heavens' and the architect Serlio, who died in 1554, writes that for lightning the 'wyre over the Scene . . . must hang downewards' (see Butterworth, 44).

11. Dekker, *Diuell*, sig. E2r. If the lines which follow this extract are taken literally, then these swevels were ignited from below the stage:

> KING
> from whence flew they?

BRISCO
    Hell, I thinke.

12. I am grateful to Julian Bowsher for alerting me to the fact that a cannon-ball was found at the site of the Rose playhouse, during archaeological excavations. For some time after those excavations the cannonball was a mystery, as evidenced by its account in the catalogue: 'Stone cannon ball [. . .] Diam 6in (150mm), weight 101b (4.53kg). Almost certainly a sixteenth-century cannon ball, probably to be fired from a perier or a culverin [. . .] [I]ts presence on the playhouse site is puzzling.' Julian Bowsher and Pat Miller, *The Rose and the Globe – Playhouses of Shakespeare's Bankside, Southwark. Excavations 1988–90* (London, 2009), 218.

13. See Butterworth, *Theatre of Fire,* 152 n.25.

14. See Bernard Hewitt, ed., *The Renaissance Stage: Documents of Serlio, Sabbattini and Furttenbach*, trans. Allardyce Nicoll, John H. McDowell and George R. Kernodle (Miami, 1958), 172. The stepped thunder-run is described by Sabbattini, whose work was published in Ravenna in 1638. It is unclear when the technique was adopted in England, although several of the techniques described by Sabbattini were used by Inigo Jones, if not before.

15. Ben Jonson, *Every Man in His Humour* in *The Workes of Benjamin Jonson* (London, 1616), sig. A3r.

16. Thunder-runs are simple to reconstruct, and so their effect is easily eval-uated. There is one in the permanent theatre exhibition in the Victoria and Albert Museum.

17. See '"Thus much show of fire": Storm and Spectacle at the Opening of the Globe', in *The Spectacular in and Around Shakespeare*, ed. Pascale Drouet (Cambridge, 2009), 3–16. See also Gwilym Jones, *Shakespeare's Storms* (Manchester, forthcoming 2013).

18. All quotations, unless otherwise noted, are from the Arden 3rd Series, William Shakespeare, *Julius Caesar*, ed. David Daniell (London, 2005). Line references are included in the text.

19. Leslie Thomson, 'The Meaning of *Thunder and Lightning*: Stage Directions and Audience Expectations', *Early Theatre*, 2 (1999), 11–24 (14).

20. For an account of the play's early staging, and arguments for the produc-tion at Blackfriars, see Andrew Gurr, '*The Tempest*'s Tempest at Blackfriars', *Shakespeare Survey*, 41 (1989), 91–102.

21. 1.1.0sd-8. All quotations from William Shakespeare's *The Tempest*, unless otherwise noted, are taken from the Arden 3rd Series edition, eds Virginia Mason Vaughn and Alden T. Vaughn (London, 1999). Line references are included in the text.

22. See Gurr, '*Tempest*'s Tempest'.

23. Gurr, '*Tempest*'s Tempest', 102.

24. Sarah Dustagheer, *Repertory and the Production of Theatre Space at the Globe and the Blackfriars, 1599–1613* (Unpublished PhD thesis, University of London, 2012), 181.

25. See Vaughn and Vaughn, *Tempest*, 126–30.

26. Vaughn and Vaughn, *Tempest*, 130.

27. Gurr, '*Tempest*'s Tempest', 95.

28. Ioris Staell, *Strange newes from Antwarpe*, trans. I. F. (London, 1612), 4; John Foxe, *Actes and Monuments of Matters most Speciall and Memorable, happenyng in the Church* (London, 1583), 279; Leo Africanus, *A Geographical historie of Africa*, ed. and trans. John Pory (London, 1600), 43.

29. As such, the phrase allows for visible thunder, just as it does audible lightning, as in Lloyd Lowick's *The First Part of the Diall of Daies* (London, 1590), 164: 'where they sawe the thunder and lightning'. This means that the stage direction requires 'noise' and 'heard' to specify it as an auditory effect.

30. A.F. Falconer, *Shakespeare and the Sea* (London, 1964), 39. Falconer, himself a naval officer, also provides a detailed appraisal of the validity of the emergency procedures which the play's crew attempt.

31. I have not been able to find any similar examples in extant plays of the period. It remains, of course, possible that texts that have not survived provided the same level of authentic nautical detail.

32. The most famous example of this is in William Shakespeare's *The Winter's Tale*: 'our ship hath touched upon the deserts of Bohemia' (3.3.1–2), Arden 3rd Series edition, ed. John Pitcher (London, 2010), although his *The Two Gentlemen of Verona* seems fancifully to suggest a naval route between Verona and Milan (1.1.71). In *The Tempest* itself, it might be charitably suggested that Prospero's account of the Milanese bark that 'Bore us some leagues to the sea' (1.2.145) is just about feasible, but it would be a stretch to conclude that Shakespeare is as accurate with his geography as with his naval manoeuvres.

33. See Falconer, *Sea*, 36–40.

34. Quoted by Falconer, *Sea*, xii.

35. Timothy Morton, *Ecology without Nature: Rethinking Environmental Aesthetics* (Cambridge, MA, 2007), 35.

36. John Fletcher, *The Sea Voyage*, in *Comedies and tragedies written by Francis Beaumont and John Fletcher* (London, 1647), sig. A5r.

37. Gurr, 'Tempest', 100.

38. Christopher Cobb, 'Storm versus Story: Form and Affective Power in Shakespeare's Romances', in *Shakespeare and Historical Formalism*, ed. Stephen Cohen (Aldershot, 2007), 95–124 (103).

39. As chronology is uncertain, it is possible that either *The Winter's Tale*, *Pericles* or both may post-date *The Tempest*. However, the important factor is that both of those plays embody a particular dramatic tradition: they use the present tense, and employ extensive imagery and pathetic fallacy. This is the tradition that Miranda's speech fits into, and which is avoided in the first scene. Other examples can be found in *King Lear* (3.1.8–15) and *Othello* (2.1.1–17).

40. The relevant sections of Strachey's work are reprinted in Vaughn and Vaughn, 287–302. I quote here from page 290. For the most recent account of the evidence for Shakespeare's reading of Strachey, see Alden T. Vaughn, 'William Strachey's "True Repertory" and Shakespeare: A Closer Look at the Evidence', in *Shakespeare Quarterly*, 59 (2008), 245–73. As well as presenting a clear challenge to doubts over Shakespeare's use of Strachey, Vaughn provides a thorough history of the debate.

41. Arthur Golding, *The. xv. bookes of P. Ouidius Naso, entytuled Metamorphosis, translated oute of Latin into English meeter, by Arthur Golding Gentleman, a worke very pleasaunt and delectable* (London, 1567), sig. T7r.

42. Thomas Churchyard, *The Three First Bookes of Ovid de Tristibus Translated into English* (London, 1580), sig. A6r.

43. Golding, *Metamorphosis*, sig. B5r. It is possible that Shakespeare had this passage in mind when writing this scene as, in these preceding lines in Golding's translation, the South wind is described as having a 'dreadfull face as blacke as pitch'. Along with the juxtaposition of sea and sky – and with their characterisation as Jove and Neptune in Ariel's speech – this may seem only to be a coincidence of clichés. However, nowhere else does Shakespeare use 'pitch' in the description of a storm.

44. I have opted to use 'reimagining' here, as I think it suggests (more than, for example, 'redescribing') the process through which the audience is compelled to consider differently what has already been seen.

45. Indeed, the curses of Caliban and Lear are very similar, a point often overlooked in current editions of *The Tempest*. See especially, *King Lear*: 'Infect her beauty, / You fen-sucked fogs, drawn by the powerful sun / To fall and blister!' (2.2.358–60), Arden 3rd Series edition, ed. R.A. Foakes (London, 1997).

46. For a fuller understanding, see S.K. Heninger, *A Handbook of Renaissance Meteorology, with Particular Reference to Elizabethan and Jacobean Literature* (Durham, NC, 1960). Caliban's lines quoted here are not the first example of his meteorological curse. At his first appearance, we have: 'As wicked dew as e'er my mother brushed / With raven's feather from unwholesome fen / Drop on you both. A southwest blow on ye / And blister you all o'er' (1.2.322).

3: PERFORMING MATERIALITY: CURTAINS
ON THE EARLY MODERN STAGE

1. Lena Cowen Orlin, *Locating Privacy in Tudor London* (Oxford, 2008), 188–92.

2. See Alan C. Dessen and Leslie Thomson, *A Dictionary of Stage Directions in English Drama 1580–1642* (Cambridge, 1999), and David Carnegie, 'Stabbed Through the Arras: The Dramaturgy of Elizabethan Stage Hangings', in *Shakespeare: World Views*, eds Heather Kerr, Robin Eaden and Madge Mitton (Cranbury, 1996), 181–199.

3. The name is derived from the city of Arras, situated in Flanders, which became French after 1659. Arras was the trading centre for tapestries coming from all over Europe and also from the Orient.

4. Henslowe's papers, reproduced in R.A. Foakes, ed., *Henslowe's Diary*, 2nd edn (Cambridge, 2002), 9, feature the purchase of painted cloths which could have been used on the stage: 'bowght the Jemes is head the 24 of aguste 1595 for xxxli & bowghte more as foloweth: [. . .] Itm paynted clothe in the halle, xvj yrdes at vjd per yrd; [. . .] Itm paynted cloth in the parler, v yrdes at vjd yrdes'. The painted cloths could have been used as doors or could have been fitted to a four-poster bed. As Henslowe employed such devices, presumably other companies did likewise.

5. Walter Montagu, *The Shepherd's Paradise*, ed. Sarah Poynting, Malone Society Reprints (London, 1997), 63.

6. See Richard Southern, *The Staging of Plays Before Shakespeare* (London, 1973), 266–71.

7. Author's translation of Victor Bourgy, 'Ecriture Dramatique et Conventions', *Tudor Theater: 'Let There be Covenants. . .'* (Tours, 1998), 9.

8. R.C. Rhodes also recalls the opposition of sixteenth- and seventeenth-century staging with Restoration drama where curtains became pure adornment and thus were deprived of their strategic role as dramatic machines. See *The Stagery of Shakespeare* (Birmingham, 1922).

9. Sasha Roberts, '"Let me the Curtains Draw": the Dramatic and Symbolic Properties of the Bed in Shakespearean Tragedy', in *Staged Properties in Early Modern English Drama*, eds Jonathan Gil Harris, Natasha Korda (Cambridge, 2002), 153–76.

10. Stuart Clark, *Vanities of the Eye: Vision in Early Modern European Culture* (Oxford, 2007), 39.

11. In *De Animae Quantitate* (*Of the Greatness of the Soul*), 27.53, Augustine defines reason as the gaze of the mind and reasoning as the movement of that gaze over objects. He associates an abstraction and a concrete physiological ability and defines seeing as a threefold experience: identifying an object, recapturing that object's history and deducing that object's impact.

12. Andrew Sofer, *The Stage Life of Props* (Ann Arbor, 2003), 29.

13. Marvin Carlson, *The Haunted Stage* (Ann Arbor, 2001), 165.

14. See p. 12. Andrew Gurr recalls how 'black stage hangings were as precise a signal to the audience of what they were to expect as the generic name "tragedy" on a playbill'. See *The Shakespeare Company, 1594–1642* (Cambridge, 2004), 45–6. Moreover, the 2003 Globe production of *Richard III* chose to adorn the railing of the first balcony with black velvet draperies; a similarly simple strategy could have been used in early modern theatres, since valances would have been used on four poster-beds and would therefore have been available in the tiring-house.

15. See the prelude to Thomas Goffe's *The Careless Shepherdess* (1618–29), where two characters recall this comic convention. The recurrence of the comic use of the curtain is confirmed by the frontispiece of Francis Kirkman's *The Wits: or, Sport upon Sport* (1662). It presents several depictions of stage characters and shows the theatrical practices of the past three decades; it includes a Fool poking his head through an arras.

16. Andrew Gurr, *The Shakespearean Stage, 1574–1642* (Cambridge, 1980), 151.

17. William Shakespeare and John Fletcher, *King Henry VIII*, ed. Gordon McMullan, Arden Series 3 (London, 2000), 283.

18. Carlson, 165.

19. Author's translation of Georges Banu, *Le Rideau, ou la Fêlure du Monde* (Paris, 1997), 42.

20. E.K. Chambers, *The Shakespearean Stage*, 4 vols (Oxford, 1923), 3: 65–6.

21. William Shakespeare, *Cymbeline*, ed. J.M. Nosworthy, Arden 2nd Series reprint (Walton-on-Thames, 1997). All quotations from this play are from this edition.

22. The play was performed at the Globe theatre in 1609, a venue whose tiring-house wall featured a central opening flanked by two doors. See Tiffany Stern's chapter in this volume for more about the structural features of the playhouse, p. 11.

23. The figures in the painted cloths or tapestries would then have become echoes of the figures in Iachimo's verbal tapestry.

24. The Italian word *paragone* means 'comparison' or 'debate'. Curtains are the instrument of a debate between different forms of artistic expression. They play a similar role to that of the statue of Hermione in *The Winter's Tale*.

25. Lucrece was a Roman noblewoman who was celebrated for her beauty and her chastity. She offered her hospitality to the lustful Sextus Tarquinus while her husband Collatinus was away, but was raped by her guest. Having recounted her ordeal to her husband and some Roman noblemen she stabbed herself. See William Shakespeare's narrative poem *The Rape of Lucrece* (1594) and its sources, Titus-Livi's *History of Rome*

and Ovid's *Fasti*. She became an emblem of offended chastity and feminine virtue.

26. According to Ovid in Book VI of *The Metamorphoses*, Philomela (poetically abbreviated as Philomel), a princess, was raped by Tereus, her sister's husband, and King of Thrace. To prevent Philomela from telling her tale, Tereus cut out her tongue and hid her. He told her sister Procne that Philomela was dead. Unable to speak, Philomela wove a tapestry depicting her story and arranged for an old woman to take it to Procne. When Procne saw the weaving, she asked the woman to lead her to Philomela. After rescuing her sister, Procne planned revenge on her husband. She killed Itys, the son she had had with Tereus, and served him to Tereus for supper. At the end of the meal, Philomela appeared and threw the boy's head on the table. Realising what had happened, Tereus chased the women and tried to kill them. But before he could catch them, the gods transformed them all into birds. Tereus became a hawk while Procne became a nightingale and Philomela a swallow. In subsequent versions of the myth, authors made Philomela a nightingale and Procne a swallow.

27. The scene within the curtains ultimately comes to resemble a fixed monument. Imogen in bed is depicted as a funeral statue: the book she is holding makes her visually recall the funeral effigies in which characters are depicted with an open book in their hands as though in prayer. The curtain, here, is the expression of *living death* scenes which can be found both in theatre and painting. Graves were adorned with curtains as a way of showing the appearance and actions of the dead. See Jean Wilson, *The Shakespeare Legacy, the Material Legacy of Shakespeare's Theatre* (Stroud, 1995), 82.

28. Carlson, 166.

29. Carlson, 165. The tales of Lucrece and Philomela were recurring narratives in early modern visual culture as reflected in domestic needlework and carvings of the period. A wall panel entitled 'Lucrecia flanked by Chasteti and Liberaliter' can be still seen in the Entrance Hall at Hardwick Hall. The story of Lucrece's banquet is illustrated on a table carpet kept at the Victoria and Albert Museum (T125–1913), and bed valances there tell the tale of Philomela. See Plate 34 in Preston Remington's *English Domestic Needlework* (New York, 1945).

30. Veltrusky, 84.

31. Joseph Roach, *Cities of the Dead: Circum-Atlantic Performance* (New York, 1996), 36.

32. Nathalie Rivère de Carles, 'The Curtained Stage: Inside and Outside the Elizabethan Playing Space', *Theta VII, Théâtre Tudor* (Tours, 2007), 218–22.

33. William Shakespeare, *Hamlet*, eds. Ann Thompson and Neil Taylor, Arden Series 3 (London, 2006), 334.

34. Characters point at the dead body regularly until the end of the act: 'Pandulph Feliche, I have stabbed thy son; / Look, yet his lifeblood reeks upon this steel. / Albert, yon hangs thy friend' (1.4.11–13); 'Why laugh you, uncle? That's my coz, your son, / Whose breast hangs casèd in his cluttered gore' (1.5.59–60); 'Behold! [*Pointing to Feliche*] / Good morrow, son; thou bid'st a fig for cold. / Sound louder music; let my breath exact / You strike sad tones unto this dismal act' (1.5.101–4).

35. See Christopher Marlowe, *Tamburlaine*, ed. J.S. Cunningham, The Revels Plays (Manchester 1981). During the siege of Babylon, Tamburlaine threatens the citizens with reprisals and shows his ruthless strength by turning the body of the governor into what might be seen as an edifying cloth of pain in 5.1. The body was probably suspended from the gallery or at least shot in the gallery when it represented the city's battlements. Tamburlaine's comment on the martyred body equates the governor's body with the city's wall as well as with a hanging: 'So, now he hangs like Bagdeth's governor, / Having as many bullets in his flesh / As there be breaches in her battered wall' (5.1.157–9). Thus reduced to an inert materiality that can be endlessly destroyed, the performing body is the *locus* for the performance of Tamburlaine's blind violence.

4: 'THEY EAT EACH OTHER'S ARMS':
STAGE BLOOD AND BODY PARTS

1. *The Statelie Tragedie of Claudius Tiberius Nero, Romes Greatest Tyrant* (London, 1607), sig. M3v. Because this essay draws heavily on stage directions, all quotations except those from the works of Shakespeare are taken from early editions; u/v and i/j have been modernised.

2. A dedication to Sir Arthur Mannering in the printed text refers to the play as '*This young Scholler*' and says that '*by his speech it should seeme that his Father was an Academian*' (sig. A3r).

3. Unless stated otherwise, all company attributions and dates of first performance are based on Alfred Harbage, rev. S. Schoenbaum, *Annals of English Drama 975–1700* (London, 1964). On the date and auspices of *Doctor Faustus*, see David Bevington and Eric Rasmussen, eds, *Doctor Faustus* (Manchester, 1993), 1–3, 48–9. The inclusion of a question mark indicates that the ascription or date is uncertain.

4. 'Dismemberment and Forgetting in *Titus Andronicus*', *Shakespeare Quarterly*, 45 (1994), 279–303 (279). Earlier treatments of dismemberment in the play include Albert H. Tricomi, 'The Aesthetics of Mutilation in "Titus Andronicus"', *Shakespeare Survey*, 27 (1974), 11–19; Gillian

Murray Kendall, '"Lend Me Thy Hand": Metaphor and Mayhem in *Titus Andronicus*', *Shakespeare Quarterly*, 40 (1989), 299–316.

5. *Stages of Dismemberment: The Fragmented Body in Late Medieval and Early Modern Drama* (Cranbury, NJ, 2005), 20.

6. '"Take Up the Bodies": Shakespeare's Body Parts, Babies, and Corpses', in *The Prop's The Thing: Stage Properties Reconsidered*, ed. J.K. Curry (Tuscaloosa, AL, 2010), 135–48 (148) (his emphasis).

7. See *Powers of Horror: An Essay on Abjection*, trans. Leon S. Roudiez (New York, 1982), esp. ch. 2.

8. 'Theatrical Introduction [to *Appius and Virginia*]' in John Webster, *The Works*, ed. David Gunby, David Carnegie and MacDonald P. Jackson, 3 vols (Cambridge, 2007), 2: 481; Clifford Ronan, *'Antike Roman': Power Symbology and the Roman Play in Early Modern England, 1585–1635* (Athens, GA, 1995).

9. See Gunby et al., *Works*, 443–5.

10. *Appius and Virginia: A Tragedy* (London, 1654), sig. H1r.

11. 'Dismemberment and Forgetting', 280, 286 (her emphasis).

12. *A Choice of Emblemes* (Leyden, 1586), 87.

13. *The Revengers Tragœdie* (London, 1607), sig. F3v.

14. *Ben Jonson, Dramatist* (Cambridge, 1984), 96. On *Claudius Tiberius Nero* see also Lisa Hopkins, *The Cultural Uses of the Caesars on the English Renaissance Stage* (Aldershot, 2008), 43–5.

15. Shakespeare's Globe, 30 July 2006, co-ordinated by Jason Morell. A similarly ambivalent effect is created in the anonymous *King Leir* (?Queen Elizabeth's Men, c.1588–94), in which Perilus '*strips up his arm*' and offers it to the starving Leir to eat, commenting 'Ile smile for joy, to see you suck my blould' (*The True Chronicle History of King Leir, and his Three Daughters, Gonorill, Ragan, and Cordella* [London, 1605], sig. H2r). I am very grateful to Tiffany Stern for calling this moment to my attention.

16. W.W. Greg, ed., *Dramatic Documents from the Elizabethan Playhouses: Stage Plots: Actors' Parts: Prompt Books*, 2 vols (Oxford, 1931), 1: 149.

17. In addition to the works cited above, valuable studies of the use of blood and body parts in the early modern stage include Leo Kirschbaum, 'Shakespeare's Stage Blood and Its Significance', *Publications of the Modern Language Association of America*, 64 (1949), 517–29; Gail Kern Paster, '"In the spirit of men there is no blood": Blood as Trope of Gender in *Julius Caesar*', *Shakespeare Quarterly*, 40 (1989), 284–98; Cynthia Marshall, 'Portia's Wound, Calphurnia's Dream: Reading Character in *Julius Caesar*', in *New Casebooks: Julius Caesar*, ed. Richard Wilson (Basingstoke, 2002), 170–87; Andrew Sofer, *The Stage Life of Props* (Ann Arbor, 2003), chs 2–3.

18. For summaries and relevant examples see the entries on 'bloody, bleeding', 'body', 'corpses', 'cut', 'ear', 'eyes', 'hand', 'head', 'heart', 'hurt',

'leg', 'limbs', 'nose', 'skull', 'stab', 'thrust', 'tongue' and 'wound' in Alan Dessen and Leslie Thompson, eds, *A Dictionary of Stage Directions in English Drama, 1580–1642* (Cambridge, 1999).

19. Dessen and Thompson make this point in relation to 'hurt' and 'wound': see *A Dictionary of Stage Directions*, s.v. 'bloody, bleeding'.

20. Thomas Kyd, *The Spanish Tragedie* (?Strange's Men, c.1587; London, 1592), sig. H2v; *A Pleasant Commodie, Called Looke About You* (Admiral's Men, 1598–1600; London, 1600), sig. E1r; George Wilkins, *The Miseries of Inforst Marriage* (King's Men, c.1605–6; London, 1607), sig. E4r; Francis Beaumont and John Fletcher, *The Maid's Tragedy* (King's Men, c.1609–11), in *Fifty Comedies and Tragedies* (London, 1679), 19 (this text has fuller stage directions than the 1619 quarto edition); Richard Brome, *The Antipodes: A Comedie* (Queen Henrietta Maria's Men, 1638; London, 1640), sig. H3v.

21. *The Divils Charter: A Tragœdie* (London, 1607), sig. G2r.

22. Avarice and Homicide appear '*bloody*' in *Two Lamentable Tragedies* (London, 1601), sig. C3r; Cruelty and Murder 'with bloody hands' in Thomas Preston's *A Lamentable Tragedy Mixed Ful of Pleasant Mirth, Conteyning the Life of Cambises King of Percia* (auspices uncertain, c.1558–69; London, c.1570), sig. D2v; Tragedy with '*a bowle of bloud in her hand*' in *A Warning for Faire Women* (Chamberlain's Men, c.1598; London, 1599), sig. C3v; Envy '*his armes naked besmeared with bloud*' in *A Most Pleasant Comedie of Mucedorus* (auspices uncertain, 1588–98; London, 1598), sig. A2r; and Atë 'all in black, with a burning torch in one hand, and a bloodie swoord in the other hand' in *The Lamentable Tragedie of Locrine* (auspices uncertain, c.1591–95; London, 1595), sig. A3r; Nemesis is described as appearing 'bloudie whip in hand' in the narration that accompanies the Act 2 dumbshow in *The Battell of Alcazar* (London, 1594), sig. B2v.

23. I cite David Bradley's reconstruction of British Library MS Add. 10449, fol. 3, published in *From Text to Performance in the Elizabethan Theatre* (Cambridge, 1992), 122–3. On the date of the revival see Martin Wiggins, 'A Choice of Impossible Things: Dating the Revival of *The Battle of Alcazar*', in *Shakespeare et Ses Contemporains: Acts de Colloque 2002 de la Société Française Shakespeare*, ed. Patricia Dorval (Montpellier, 2002), 185–202.

24. See, for instance, W.J. Lawrence, 'Elizabethan Stage Realism', in *Pre-Restoration Stage Studies* (Cambridge, MA, 1927), 237; Andrew Gurr, *The Shakespearean Stage, 1574–1642*, 2nd edn (Cambridge, 1980), 166.

25. *The Discoverie of Witchcraft* (London, 1584), 350. Sheep's blood is also recommended in *Hocus Pocus Junior* (London, 1634), sig. D3r, E2v.

26. *A Lamentable Tragedy* [. . .] *of Cambises*, sig. D3r.

27. Philip Butterworth, *Magic on the Early English Stage* (Cambridge, 2005), 166.

28. James M. Gibson, ed., *Records of Early English Drama: Kent: Diocese of Canterbury* (Toronto, 2002), 137 ('a new leder bag for ye blode [. . .] x ow*nces* of vermyl*ion*'); see also Butterworth, 171.

29. Butterworth, 171–2. See also Andrea Stevens' chapter in this volume, where she discusses the possibility of face paint being used to create the effects of stage blood, p. 96.

30. Tiramani, Presentation at 'Stage Blood: A Roundtable', Shakespeare's Globe Theatre History Seminar, 13 July 2006; Stevens, 'Drama as Text and Performance', in *A New Companion to English Renaissance Literature and Culture*, ed. Michael Hattaway (Oxford, 2010), 502–12 (510).

31. For recent accounts of the work of early modern laundresses see Douglas Biow, *The Culture of Cleanliness in Renaissance Italy* (Ithaca, NY, 2006), esp. ch. 2, and (with sustained discussion of the role of the tirewoman in the theatre) Natasha Korda, *Labors Lost: Women's Work and the Early Modern English Stage* (Philadelphia, PA, 2011), ch. 3.

32. *The Faire Maide of Bristow* (London, 1605), sig. D2v; *The Politician: A Tragedy* (London, 1655), 57–8.

33. *A Warning for Faire Women*, sig. D1v–D2r. The final direction is missing, but the stage must be cleared before the entrance of '*Sanders, and one or two with him*' (sig. D2r).

34. *Comedies and Tragedies Written by Thomas Killigrew* (London, 1664), 48.

35. *Comedies and Tragedies Written by Thomas Killigrew*, 377. On the dates of *The Princess* and *Thomaso* see G.E. Bentley, *The Jacobean and Caroline Stage*, 7 vols (Oxford, 1941–68), 4: 706–8, 710. A copy of the 1664 Folio in Worcester College, Oxford, includes Killigrew's notes on casting and revisions for production. Sponges are also mentioned in the stage directions of John Dryden and Henry Purcell's operatic *King Arthur: Or the British Worthy* (United Company, 1691; London, 1691), 44 ('*They Fight with Spunges in their Hands, dipt in Blood; after some equal Passes and Closeing, they appear both Wounded*'). D'Urfey's *Trick for Trick* (King's Company, 1678; London, 1678) includes the direction '*Maid within shoots a squirt of blood in's face, and lets off a Pistol*' (44). For brief discussion of Killigrew and Dryden's directions see Lawrence, 238.

36. *The Tragedy of Orestes* (London, 1633), sig. G4r.

37. *The Rebellion of Naples, or the Tragedy of Massenello* (London, 1649), 73.

38. 'What Calphurnia Knew. *Julius Caesar* and the Language of Dreams', in *Questioning Bodies in Shakespeare's Rome*, ed. Maria Del Sapio Garbero, Nancy Isenberg and Maddalena Pennacchia (Göttingen, 2010), 171–90 (183–4). On the thematic and theatrical use of blood in *Julius Caesar* see also Kirschbaum, 'Shakespeare's Stage Blood'; Paster, 'Blood as Trope of

Gender'; Coppélia Kahn, *Roman Shakespeare: Warriors, Wounds, and Women* (London and New York, 1997), ch. 4; Marshall, 'Portia's Wound'.

39. 'Shakespeare's Stage Blood', 520.

40. *The Battell of Alcazar*, sig. A2r.

41. Bradley, 122–3. The direction for the vials of blood and sheep's gather appears in the margin against this direction.

42. Taymor describes these sequences as depicting 'in abstract collages, fragments of memory, the unfathomable layers of a violent event, the metamorphic flux of the human, animal and divine' (*Titus: The Illustrated Screenplay* [New York, 2000], 183). For a persuasive reading of their effect see Lisa S. Starks, 'Cinema of Cruelty: Powers of Horror in Julie Taymor's *Titus*', in *The Reel Shakespeare: Alternative Cinema and Theory* (London, 2002), 121–42 (129–32).

43. R.A. Foakes, ed., *Henslowe's Diary*, 2nd edn (Cambridge, 2002), 317–21.

44. *Henslowe's Diary*, 206. Scot describes a trick 'To cut off ones head, to laie it in a platter, &c: which the jugglers call the decollation of John Baptist' (*Discoverie*, 349).

45. *The Tragicall History of the Life and Death of Doctor Faustus* (London, 1616), sig. F1v–F2r.

46. On the date of *The Devil's Law-case* see Bentley, *Jacobean and Caroline Stage*, 5: 1250–1.

47. For an illuminating detailed discussion of the skulls in *Hamlet*, *The Honest Whore* and *The Revenger's Tragedy* see Sofer, *Stage Life of Props*, ch. 3.

48. *The Tragedy of Selimus Emperour of the Turkes* (London, 1638), sig. F2v.

49. *The Tragicall History of D. Faustus* (London, 1604), sig. E2v (the direction appears in the 1616 text as 'He puls off his leg' [sig. F3v]).

50. *Andronicus: A Tragedy* (London, 1661), 78.

51. *The Faithfull Shepheardesse* (London, ?1609), sig. ¶2v.

52. *The Historie of Orlando Furioso, One of the Twelve Pieres of France* (London, 1594), sig. D4r. Perhaps this was a prop body part fashioned out of wax.

53. 'The Part of Orlando', in Greg, ed., *Dramatic Documents*, 2:11. 101–2.

54. This section is damaged in Alleyn's part, but it clearly included an additional speech after the first five lines. See Greg, ed., *Dramatic Documents*, 11. 104–18.

55. That is, a rhetorical technique in which the whole represents a part, or *vice versa*.

56. On the importance of clothing here see Ann Rosalind Jones and Peter Stallybrass, *Renaissance Clothing and the Materials of Memory* (Cambridge, 2000), 200–1.

57. See, for instance: Daniel Sullivan's 1999 production at the Old Globe, San Diego, California, in which David Lansbury doubled these roles; the

2001 production at Shakespeare's Globe, London, directed by Mike Alfreds, in which they were played by Mark Rylance; and the 2007 Cheek By Jowl production, directed by Declan Donnellan, featuring Tom Hiddleston as Cloten and Posthumus.
58. Martin Butler, ed., *Cymbeline* (Cambridge, 2005), 195.

5: COSMETIC TRANSFORMATIONS

1. Bruce R. Smith, *The Key of Green* (Chicago, IL, 2009), 212. All quotations from Shakespeare taken from the Arden Shakespeare Complete Works (most recent editions up to 1998) accessed via the UIUC online Shakespeare Collection. For *Hamlet*, I've quoted from the Arden 3rd Series edition *Hamlet: The Texts of 1603 and 1623*, eds Ann Thompson and Neil Taylor (London, 2007).

2. Klaus Theweleit, 'Male Bodies and the "White Terror"', in *Body and Flesh: A Philosophical Reader* (Malden and Oxford, 1998), ed. Donn Welton, 306, 313. See also *Male Fantasies*, 2 vols (Minneapolis, MN, 1987), 1: 362.

3. See M. C. Bradbrook, 'Shakespeare's Recollections of Marlowe', in *Shakespeare's Styles: Essays in Honour of Kenneth Muir*, eds Philip Edwards, Inga-Stina Ewbank, and G. K. Hunter (Cambridge, 1980), p. 203. Bradbrook focuses upon Shakespeare's indebtedness to Marlowe in terms of language rather than staging, although she does observe that 'this enormous icon, much bigger than life, with "sable arms / Black as his purpose", foreshadows, with his arrested action as he stands over Priam, his sword held aloft, an image we are to see, of Hamlet himself standing over the kneeling Claudius . . . in its primitive violence and rhetorical emphasis quite un-Shakespearean, though of course well suited to stand out from the text of this play'. See also Gail Kern Paster's richly suggestive discussion of this passage in *Humoring the Body: Emotions and the Shakespearean Stage* (Chicago, IL, 2004). Paster observes that 'Shakespeare's version of the fall of Troy' comes in red, black, and white, which is to say in 'the key colors and thermal markers of early modern humoralism', 29–30.

4. Thomas Heywood, *An Apology for Actors* (London, 1612), sig. D1v. Sir Thomas Overbury, *New and Choise Characters of Several Authors* (London, 1615), sig. M6r. For other accounts of face painting in Renaissance culture, see for example Farah Karim-Cooper, *Cosmetics in Shakespearean and Renaissance Drama* (Edinburgh, 2006) and Tanya Pollard's chapter on 'Cosmetic Theater' in *Drugs and Theater in Early Modern England* (Oxford, 2005). For a comprehensive discussion of the issues raised in this chapter, see my *Inventions of the Skin: The Painted Body on the Early English Stage* (forthcoming Edinburgh, 2013).

5. Phillip Stubbes, *The Anatomie of Abuses* (London, 1583), 64.

6. Related key terms therefore include 'fucus', 'tincture', 'enamel', 'vermilion', 'oil of hell', 'gild', and 'cosmetics', to list but a few; the semantic field for the verb 'to paint' includes 'represent', 'limn', 'decorate', 'prick', 'touch', 'daub', 'adorn', 'beautify', 'disfigure', 'transfigure' and 'adulterate'.

7. Meg Twycross and Sarah Carpenter, *Masks and Masking in Medieval and Early Tudor England* (Farnham and Burlington, 2002), 317.

8. Erika Lin, 'Performance Practice and Theatrical Privilege: Rethinking Weimann's Concepts of *Locus* and *Platea*', *New Theatre Quarterly*, 22.3 (2006), 284.

9. See Bruce Smith's richly provocative analysis of stage curtains in his chapter on 'The Curtain Between the Theatre and the Globe' in *The Key of Green*, especially 242.

10. Alice Rayner, *Ghosts: Death's Double and the Phenomena of Theatre* (Minneapolis, MN, 2006), 75–9.

11. All citations from *Look About You* taken from Tudor Facsimile Texts ed. Richard M. Hirsch (New York, 1980). I have expanded and regularised speech-headings.

12. See Peter Hyland's discussion of the play's multi-disguise plot in 'Face/off: Some Speculations on Elizabethan Acting', *Shakespeare Bulletin*, 24 (2006), 23, and again in *Disguise on the Early Modern English Stage* (Farnham and Burlington, 2011).

13. Suggesting an interesting circulation of objects between court and public theatre (even if imaginary), one scene mentions a 'beard and haire' left over from a court masque, line 1195.

14. Lucy Munro discusses the implications for and effects of staging this moment in this volume, p. 83.

15. John Ripley, *Coriolanus on Stage in England and America, 1609–1994* (Cranbury, NJ, London, Mississauga, 1998), 46. Confirming that Martius is indeed effectively masked and mantled in blood in 1.9, Aufidius fails to recognise him: when they meet again in Antium:

> CORIOLANUS
> If, Tullus,
> Not yet thou know'st me, and seeing me dost not
> Think me for the man I am, necessity
> Commands me name myself.
>
> AUFIDIUS
> What is thy name?
>
> (4.5.54–7)

This lapse only makes sense if this is the first time Aufidius is seeing Martius' bare face.

16. Lucy Munro's contribution to this volume refers to bloodied props, p. 86.

17. See for example *Records of Early English Drama* (*REED*): York, ed. Alexandra F. Johnston and Margaret Rogerson, 2 vols (Manchester, 1979), 676, 707, 722; for her account of the Mercers' inventory, see Alexandra Johnston, 'The York Mercers and Their Pageant of Doomsday, 1433–1526', *Leeds Studies in English*, 6 (1972), 11–35.

18. See Peter Meredith and John E. Tailby, *The Staging of Religious Drama in Europe in the Later Middle Ages: Texts and Documents in English Translation* (Kalamazoo, MI, 1983), 109 [trans. Meredith and Tailby].

19. Bert O. States, *Great Reckonings in Little Rooms* (Berkeley and Los Angeles, CA, 1985), 31.

20. Anthony Dawson and Paul Yachnin, *The Culture of Playgoing in Shakespeare's England* (Cambridge, 2001); see Dawson's chapter on 'Performance and Participation', 34.

21. See Michael Shapiro's analysis of the boy actor and his concept of 'theatrical vibrancy', or the audience's awareness of the layering of gender identity and the actor's oscillations between these layers, in *Gender in Play on the Shakespearean Stage* (Ann Arbor, MI, 1994), 7.

22. Natasha Korda and Jonathan Gil Harris, eds, *Staged Properties in Early Modern English Drama* (Cambridge, 2002), 1. Andrew Sofer, *The Stage Life of Props* (Ann Arbor, 2003), 10.

23. The only revival of this play since the seventeenth century, the American Shakespeare Center's 2011 production, omitted the blood disguise altogether, a decision the actor John Harrell explained to me as follows: 'I played Skinke. No blood. Too much trouble' (Personal communication, 15 December 2011). *Look About You* was staged as part of the ASC's Actor's Renaissance Season in which the actors, rather than a single director, make all the performance decisions.

24. Clifford Davidson, 'Sacred Blood and the Late Medieval Stage', *Comparative Drama*, 31 (1997), 186.

25. See, for example, Andrew Gurr's discussion of the realism of blood effects in *The Shakespearean Stage, 1574–1642* (Cambridge, 1992), 182–4; for Tiffany Stern's view that that the prevalence of blood in early modern plays is especially striking 'given that so much else is left to the poetry', see *Making Shakespeare: From Page to Stage* (London and New York, 2004), 19.

26. Twycross and Carpenter, 8. For an additional example of the use of blood as a disguise device, see 4.5 of James Shirley's *The Politician* (1639).

27. For his concept of 'ghosting', see Marvin Carlson, *The Haunted Stage: The Theatre as Memory Machine* (Ann Arbor, MI, 2001).

28. All citations are taken from Thomas Heywood, *Love's Mistress*, edited for *Jacobean Drama Studies* by Raymond C. Shady (Salzburg, 1977).

29. See Shady's introduction, xxiv.

30. For an excellent survey of blackface performance, see Virginia Mason Vaughan, *Performing Blackness on English Stages, 1500–1800* (Cambridge, 2005).

31. In 1605, the black paint was insufficiently flexible to be removed during the performance; blackface disguises that are removed during the course of a performance can only be found in performances dating from 1621 or so. For my discussion of this, see '"Assisted by a Barber": The Court Apothecary, Special Effects, and Ben Jonson's *The Gypsies Metamorphosed*', *Theatre Notebook*, 61 (2007), 2–11.

32. In *The History of the Tryall of Chevalry* (1605), sig. D2r, D3r, for example, a woman is described as 'spotted like a Panthers skin' and as a 'leper'.

33. See David Bevington, '"Blake and wyght, fowl and fayer": Stage Picture in *Wisdom Who Is Christ*', *Comparative Drama*, 19 (1985), 136–50.

34. Karim-Cooper, *Cosmetics*, 46; see also Pollard, *Drugs and Theater*.

35. See Frances Dolan, 'Taking the Pencil out of God's Hand: Art, Nature, and the Face-Painting Debate in Early Modern England', *PMLA*, 108 (1993), 224–39.

36. Thomas Jeamson, *Artificiall embellishments* (London, 1665), 5.

37. It is hard to determine the amount of time taken backstage for Psyche's various costume changes without knowing how long breaks were between scene changes, since the action of this play – given the use of changeable painted scenic backdrops – was not rapid and continuous.

38. John Donne, 'That a Wise Man is Known by Much Laughing', from *Juvenilia, Or Certaine Paradoxes, and Problems* (London, 1633), original emphasis, printed in *The Complete Poetry and Selected Prose of John Donne*, ed. Charles Coffin (New York, 2001), 301.

39. Sophie Tomlinson, *Women on Stage in Stuart Drama* (Cambridge, 2005), 3.

40. See, for example, Hero Chalmers, Julie Sanders and Sophie Tomlinson in their Introduction to *Three Seventeenth-Century Plays on Women and Performance* (Manchester, 2006), 25: 'Shirley's handling of female theatricals in *The Bird in a Cage* is full of ambivalences and contradictions, and cannot as a result be read as a straightforward defence of women and performance', despite his association with the Queen's circle.

41. All citations from *The Lost Lady* are taken from the Malone Society Reprint prepared by D.F. Rowan (Oxford, 1987). For an account of this anxiety, see Katharine Maus, *Inwardness and Theater in the English Renaissance* (Chicago, IL, 1995).

42. For her discussion of this counter-discourse of praise, see Kim F. Hall, *Things of Darkness: Economies of Race and Gender in Early Modern England* (Cornell, 1995), 117–18; 132; 240.

43. For her discussion of the backstage management of racial change, see Farah Karim-Cooper, '"This alters not thy beauty": Face-paint, Gender, and Race in *The English Moor*', *Early Theatre*, 10 (2007), 147.

6: COSTUME, DISGUISE AND SELF-DISPLAY

1. Peter Hyland, in *Disguise on the Early Modern English Stage* (Ashgate, 2011), 41, marks the few plays in the dramatic repertoire where this is not the case and where disguises fail: Shakespeare's *2 Henry IV* (2.4.256–7); Beaumont and Fletcher's *The Coxcomb* (2.3.49–50); Middleton's *More Dissemblers Besides Women* (1.2.201–6).

2. Hyland, 15, points to the moment near the end of Joe Orton's *Loot*, where the policeman Truscott declares that he is a master of disguise, then removes his hat with a flourish and the words 'Look, a complete transformation!'; the joke works for a modern audience because disguising oneself simply with a hat has become an implausibly silly idea. See also Victor Freeburg's conclusion to his survey of *Disguise Plots in Elizabethan Drama* (New York, 1915), 202, where he points out that 'in our theater the criterion of stage verisimilitude deprives us of the delightful improbabilities of romantic disguise plots'.

3. Contested particularly by Kevin A. Quarmby, in the thesis 'The "Disguised-Ruler" Plays in the Early Modern Repertory' (published as *The Disguised Ruler in Shakespeare and His Contemporaries* [Surrey, 2012]), where he argues against Leonard Tennenhouse's claim, now almost a critical commonplace, that the spate of Disguised Ruler plays that emerged soon after the accession of James I represented a coherent response to this event and staged 'new strategies' for 'authorizing monarchy' (Quarmby 11). Quarmby argues that to regard the motif as largely a product of James I's accession is to obscure its development over a longer period (Quarmby 15 and passim).

4. Dir. Frank Dunlop with Andrew Robertson, Young Vic, London, 1981.

5. Hyland, 55.

6. Dir. Roxana Silbert, Royal Shakespeare Company, the Swan theatre, Stratford upon Avon, 2011–12.

7. Dir. Greg Doran, Royal Shakespeare Company, the Swan theatre, Stratford upon Avon, 2005–6.

8. The same device is deployed in Thomas Middleton's *The Phoenix* (1603–4), in which Prince Phoenix disguises himself in order to discover the true, corrupt nature of many of his people, and in Shakespeare's *Henry V* (1599), in which the king mingles with his soldiers and discourses on kingship.

9. Hyland, 15.

10. Andrew J. Gurr, *Shakespeare's Opposites: The Admiral's Company 1594–1625* (Cambridge, 2009), 49.
11. Gurr, 50.
12. Gurr, 56.
13. Gurr, 51.
14. Dave Postles, '"Flatcaps", Fashioning and Civility in Early Modern England', *Literature and History*, 17.2 (October 2008), 1–13.
15. For reviews of sumptuary legislation, see Alan Hunt, *Governance of the Consuming Passions: A History of Sumptuary Law* (New York, 1996) and Frances Baldwin *Sumptuary Legislation and Personal Regulation in England* (New York, 1994).
16. Martin Ingram, 'Shame and Pain: Themes and Variations in Tudor Punishments', in *Penal Practice and Culture, 1500–1900: Punishing the English*, ed. Simon Devereaux and Paul Griffiths (Basingstoke, 2004), 36–63, 37, 38–9.
17. Ingram, 45.
18. Ingram, 43.
19. Extract from Thomas Platter's diary, 'Thomas Platter: a Swiss Tourist in London', *The Norton Anthology of English Literature*, http://www.wwnorton.com/college/english/nael/16century/topic_4/tplatter.htm, accessed May 2012
20. Ingram, 43.
21. The RSC 2011–12 production, mentioned on p. 123, had her jeered at as 'whore' from off stage and dressed in blue, with charivari-like devil horns to match.
22. Ingram, 47.
23. Hyland, 101.
24. The same device is deployed in *The Phoenix* in the play of that name by Thomas Middleton, written around the same time as Marston and Shakespeare wrote their disguised ruler plays to judge how they are ruled by a Deputy as in *Measure for Measure*; or to note their qualities and discourse on kingship, as King Henry does in Shakespeare's *Henry V* (4.1).
25. Thomas North's translation of Plutarch's *Lives of the Ancient Greeks and Romans*, in Geoffrey Bullough, *Narrative and Dramatic Sources of Shakespeare*, 8 vols (London, 1957–75), 5: 276.
26. Thomas North's translation of Plutarch's *Lives*, cited in Geoffrey Bullough, 5: 257.
27. North's *Plutarch* in Bullough, 5: 262.
28. North's *Plutarch* in Bullough, 5: 261. 'Marrying': Plutarch/North refers to Antony's attendance at the wedding celebrations of his favourite jesters and players; there follows the story of the morning after his jester Hippias'

wedding, when a friend is obliged to hold a cloak for him to vomit into at a Council meeting.

29. For a detailed history of the theory of the king's two bodies, see Ernst Kantorowicz, *The King's Two Bodies*, 1957 (Princeton, NJ), where he cites the 1571 'Plowden Reports' discussion on the theory, 7–9.

7: CHARACTER ACTING

1. W.B. Worthen, *Print and the Poetics of Modern Drama* (Cambridge, 2005).

2. Peter Thomson, *On Actors and Acting* (Exeter, 2000), 9.

3. T.W. Baldwin, *The Organization and Personnel of Shakespeare's Company* (Princeton, NJ, 1927), 183.

4. T.J. King, *Casting Shakespeare's Plays: London Actors and Their Roles, 1590–1642* (Cambridge, 1992).

5. *Actors and Acting in Shakespeare's Time: The Art of Stage Playing* (Cambridge, 2010), 37.

6. *Writing Matter: From the Hands of the English Renaissance* (Stanford, CA, 1990), 34–35.

7. *The First Part of the Elementarie Which Entreateth Chefelie of the Right Writing of our English Tung* (London, 1582), 49–50.

8. *The Art of Pronuntiation Digested into Two Parts* (London, 1617), sig. A4r.

9. John Brinsley, *Ludus Literarius: Or, The Grammas Schoole* (London, 1612), 151–2.

10. Leah Marcus, *Unediting the Renaissance: Shakespeare, Marlowe, Milton* (New York, 1996), 162.

11. See *The Early Comic Strip: Narrative Strips and Picture Stories in the European Broadsheet from c.1450 to 1825*, ed. David Kunzle (Berkeley, CA, 1973), 3.

12. R.A. Foakes, *Illustrations of the English Stage, 1580–1642* (London, 1985).

13. Holger Schott Syme, 'The Look of Speech', *Textual Culture*, 2 (2007), 34–60, esp. 37.

14. Bruce Smith, *The Acoustic World of Early Modern England: Attending to the O-Factor* (Chicago, IL, 1999), 125.

15. See esp. Sotaro Kita, *Pointing: Where Language, Culture, and Cognition Meet* (Mahwah, NJ, 2003); Jennifer DeVere Brody, *Punctuation: Art, Politics and Play* (Durham, NC, 2008).

16. Syme, 40.

17. See Don Weingust, *Acting from Shakespeare's First Folio: Theory, Text and Performance* (London, 2006). For an extensive critique of this approach, see Anthony Dawson, 'The Imaginary Text, or the Curse of the Folio', *A Companion to Shakespeare and Performance*, eds Barbara Hodgdon and W.B. Worthen (Oxford, 2008), 141–61.

18. Syme, 56.
19. Foakes, 99.
20. Foakes, 102.
21. *Shakespeare's Suspect Texts* (Cambridge, 1996), 148.
22. See Jeremy Lopez, 'From Bad to Verse: Poetry and Spectacle on the Modern Shakespearean Stage', forthcoming in *The Oxford Handbook to Shakespeare's Poetry*, ed. Jonathan Post; and Paul Menzer, 'Lines', forthcoming in *Twenty-First Century Approaches to Early Modern Theatricality*, ed. Henry Turner.
23. Astington, 141.
24. *Illuminating Letters: Typography and Literary Interpretation*, eds Paul C. Gutjahr and Megan Benton (Amherst, MA, 2001), 2.
25. Tiffany Stern, *Documents of Performance in Early Modern England* (Cambridge, 2009), 243.
26. Goldberg, 111.
27. Levin Schuking, *Character Problems in Shakespeare's Plays* (London, 1922), 113.

8: WITHIN, WITHOUT, WITHINWARDS: THE CIRCULATION OF SOUND IN SHAKESPEARE'S THEATRE

1. Paul Menzer, in his chapter in this book, notes how cartoons of actors speaking depict their speeches not in lines but in curves, creating a rounded effect, p. 149.
2. Stephen Handel, *Listening: An Introduction to the Perception of Auditory Events* (Cambridge, MA, 1989), xi.
3. David F. Armstrong, William C. Stokoe, and Sherman E. Wilcox, *Gesture and the Nature of Language* (Cambridge, 1995), 37.
4. To the best of my knowledge, I have been anticipated in this endeavour only by Carla Mazzio, 'The History of the Air: Hamlet and the Trouble with Instruments', *South Central Review*, 26.1–2 (2009), 153–96.
5. All quotations from Shakespeare's works come from *The Arden Shakespeare Complete Works*, rev. edn (London, 2001), and are cited in the text by act, scene and line numbers (plays) and line numbers (poems).
6. Francis Bacon, *Sylva Sylvarum: Or A Natural Historie* and *New Atlantis*, ed. William Rawley (London, 1626), 207.
7. Aristotle (attributed), *The Problemes of Aristotle with Other Philosophers and Physitions* [. . .] *Touching the Estate of Mans Bodie* (London, 1595), sigs. F5v–F6r.
8. Compare Helkiah Crooke in *Mikrokosmographia: A Description of the Body of Man* (London, 1615): 'in the day time the aire is dense, because it

is filled with light and the beames of the Sunne, but in the night more rare, because the fire and the beames are departed thereout' (sig. 3F3r).

9. Robert Boyle, *The General History of the Air* (London, 1692), sig. B1r.

10. Stage directions in original spelling from *The First Folio of Shakespeare*, ed. Charlton Hinman (New York, 1968), with act, scene and line numbers coordinated with *Arden Shakespeare Complete Works* 2001: *Romeo and Juliet*, 1.5.142; *Othello*, 2.1.95; *Antony and Cleopatra*, 4.13.1; *Macbeth*, 2.3.1; *The Tempest*, 1.1.1.

11. Lev Vygotsky, *Thinking and Speech* (1934), in *Problems of General Psychology*, eds Robert W. Rieber and Aaron S. Carton, trans. Norris Minick, vol. 1 (New York, 1987), of *The Collected Works*, 6 vols (New York, 1987–99), 1: 281, emphasis original.

12. As an example of the ambiguity between [!] and [?] compare *Macbeth* in *The Oxford Shakespeare: The Complete Works*, 2nd edn (Oxford, 2005): 'What hands are here! / Ha, they pluck out mine eyes' (2.2.57).

13. Thomas De Quincy, 'On the Knocking at the Gate in *Macbeth*', in *Collected Writings*, 14 vols, ed. David Masson (Edinburgh, 1889–90), 10: 389.

14. In chapter 2 of this volume, Gwilym Jones's highlights how the sound of thunder would have been created in the tiring house. p. 35.

15. The research is summarised in Stephen Handel, *Listening: An Introduction to the Perception of Auditory Events*, 2nd edn (Cambridge, MA, 1993), 73–112.

16. Bruce R. Smith, 'E/loco/co/motion', in *From Script to Stage in Early Modern England*, ed. Peter Holland and Stephen Orgel (Basingstoke, 2004), 131–50.

17. Tiffany Stern's chapter in this volume refers to the likelihood that Elizabethan amphitheatres were equipped with a bell for such sound effects, p. 29.

18. 'adíntra' in *Queen Anna's New World of Words* (London, 1611), sig. A5v. Florio's earlier dictionary, *A World of Words* (London,1598), sig. A4r, includes only 'adentro', 'deeply in, far in, inwardly'. Florio is cited in *OED*, 'withinward, -wards', *adv.*

19. Crooke, *Mikrokosmographia*, sig. 3T4v.

20. Crooke, *Mikrokosmographia*, sig. 3F3v.

21. Crooke, *Mikrokosmographia*, sig. 303r.

22. Crooke, *Mikrokosmographia*, sig. 303r.

23. René Descartes, *The Passions of the Soul* (1649), 1.31, in *Selected Philosophical Writings*, trans. John Cottingham and Robert Stoothoff (Cambridge, 1988), 230.

24. Crooke, *Mikrokosmographia*, sig. 3F3r.

25. Crooke, *Mikrokosmographia*, sig. 3F3r.

26. Crooke, *Mikrokosmographia*, sig. 2Q5r.

27. Michael Drayton, *Poems* (London, 1605), sig. 2C4v.

28. Martin Buzacott, *The Death of the Actor: Shakespeare on Page and Stage* (London, 1991), 51.

29. Charles Babbage, *Ninth Bridgewater Treatise*, 2nd edn (London, John Murray, 1838), 108–9.

9: 'AS DIRTY AS SMITHFIELD AND AS STINKING EVERY WHIT': THE SMELL OF THE HOPE THEATRE

1. Much debate surrounds the quarto and folio versions of this play. The quarto version does not include act or scene numbers. Alexander Pope is the first critic to label the opening scenes involving Christopher Sly as 'induction scenes'. See Elizabeth Schafer, 'Performance Editions, Editing, and Editors', in *Editing Shakespeare,* ed. Peter Holland (Cambridge, 2006), 198–212, 198.

2. All citations of Shakespeare's plays are from *The Arden Shakespeare: Complete Works*, ed. Richard Proudfoot, *et al* (Walton-on-Thames, 1998).

3. Peter Whithorne in *Certaine VVaies for the Ordering of Souldiours in Battelray, and Setting of Battailes, after Divers Fashions with Their Manner of Marching* (London, 1588) tells us dung is used in saltpetre, an ingredient of gunpowder.

4. All citations of *Bartholomew Fair* are from *Renaissance Drama*, ed. Arthur Kinney (Oxford, 1999), 490–555. For more on the 'humours' of the play, see Gail Kern Paster, '*Bartholomew Fair* and the Humoral Body', in *Early Modern English Drama: A Critical Companion*, eds Garrett A. Sullivan *et al* (New York, 2006), 260–286.

5. For a different reading of the play's references to Virginia, see Rebecca Ann Bach, *Colonial Transformations: The Cultural Production of the New Atlantic World, 1580–1640* (Basingstoke, 2000), ch. 3.

6. See Christopher T. Ball, John H. Mace and Hercilia Coronoa, 'Cues to the Gusts of Memories', in *Involuntary Memory*, ed. John H. Mace (Malden, MA, 2007), 113–126, 114.

7. See Mark Jenner, 'Civilization and Deodorization? Smell in Early Modern English Culture', in *Civil Histories: Essay Presented to Sir Keith Thomas*, eds Peter Burke, Brian Harrison, and Paul Slack (New York, 2000), 127–44; Jonathan Gil Harris, 'Smell of *Macbeth*', *Shakespeare Quarterly*, 58.4 (2007), 465–86; Holly Dugan, 'Scent of a Woman: Performing the Politics of Smell in Early Modern Culture', *The Journal of Medieval and Early Modern Studies*, 38.2 (2008), 229–52; Holly Pickett, 'The Idolatrous Nose: Incense on the Early Modern Stage,' *Religion and Drama: Studies in the Materiality of Performance*, ed. Jane Degenhardt

and Elizabeth Williamson (Farnham, 2010), 39–54, and Hristomir Stanev, 'The City Out of Breath', *Postmedieval*, 3.4 (2012), forthcoming.

8. See Janette Dillon, 'Clerkenwell and Smithfield as a Neglected Home of London Theater', *Huntington Library Quarterly*, 71.1 (2008), 115–35.

9. For more on the economic development of Smithfield market, along with tensions that arose from its incorporation into London and their effects on Jonson's *Bartholomew Fair*, see Adam Zucker, *The Places of Wit in Early Modern English Comedy* (New York, 2011), ch. 2.

10. See Thomas Dekker, *The Cold Yeare, 1614* (London, 1615), sig. C3v, and John Stow and Edmund Howes, *Annales; or A Generall Chronicle of England* (London, 1631), sig. 4Lr, both cited in Zucker, *The Places of Wit*, 79–80. See also Aubrey Wilson, *London's Industrial Heritage* (New York, 1968), 82.

11. See Zucker, *Places of Wit*, 90.

12. See Zucker, *Places of Wit*, 79–82.

13. See Frances Teague, *The Curious History of Bartholomew Fair* (Lewisberg, PA, 1985), 20.

14. See Henry Morley, *Memoirs of Bartholomew Fair* (London, 1859), 92.

15. See Morley, *Memoirs*, 42.

16. See Morley, *Memoirs*, 123.

17. The cloth fair's waning importance during Elizabeth's reign also led to changes in the Priory's space, as cheap tenements were built and rented out. See Zucker, *Places of Wit*, 78–9.

18. Most leather tanners worked in Southwark; however, a good number worked north of the city as well.

19. Eric Wilson, 'Plagues, Fairs, and Street Cries: Sounding out Society and Space in Early Modern London', *Modern Language Studies*, 25.3 (1995), 1–42, 23.

20. Morley, *Memoirs of Bartholomew Fair* (London, 1859), 146. See also William Blissett, 'Your Majesty is Welcome to a Fair', *The Elizabethan Theatre IV*, ed. G.R. Hibbard (Hamden, CT, 1974), 80–105, 90.

21. One example was the costly attempt to pave the field for £1,600. See Morley, *Memoirs of Bartholomew Fair*, 114.

22. See Sandra Billington, 'Butchers and Fishmongers: Their Historical Contribution to London's Festivity', *Folklore*, 101.1 (1990), 97–103, 98.

23. Dekker's *The Cold Yeare, 1614* refers to the large amount of money 'buried under that durtie Field by the hyring of hundreds of Labourers to reduce it (as it is reported) to the fairest and most famous Market-place that is in the whole new Kingdome' (London, 1615), sig. C3v, cited in Zucker, *Places of Wit*, 80. Dekker's text was not printed until 1615, suggesting that the paving began very late in 1614.

24. See Ronald Hutton, *Rise and Fall of Merry England* (Oxford, 1994), 44.

25. Dekker, *Cold Yeare*, sig. C3v. See also David Weil Barker, '"Master of the Monuments": Memory and Erasure in Jonson's *Bartholomew Fair*', *ELR*, 31.2 (2001), 266–288, 279.

26. See Zucker, *Places of Wit*, 144.

27. See Joan Thirsk, *Food in Early Modern England* (London, 2009), 241–2.

28. Thomas Firminger, Thiselton Dyer, *Folklore of Shakespeare* (London, 1884), 321.

29. Tobias Venner, *Via Recta Ad Vitam Longam* (London, 1620), sig. I1r.

30. William Rowley, Thomas Dekker and John Ford, 'The Witch of Edmonton', in *Three Jacobean Witch Plays*, ed. Peter Corbin and Douglas Sedge (Manchester, 1989), 143–210.

31. See Blissett, 'Your Majesty is Welcome to a Fair', 91.

32. See Paster, *'Bartholomew Fair'*, 260.

33. The theatre opened earlier that month when it hosted an expensive (and failed 'trial of wit' between the waterpoet, John Taylor, and a rival 'rhyming poet', William Fennor. When Fennor failed to appear, the audience rioted. See Tiffany Stern, *Documents of Performance in Early Modern England* (New York, 2009), 49.

34. See Kathleen Lynch, 'The Dramatic Festivity of *Bartholomew Fair*', *Medieval and Renaissance Drama in England*, 8 (1991), 128–45; Alison Chapman, 'Flaying Bartholomew: Jonson's Hagiographic Parody', in *Modern Philology*, 101.4 (2004), 511–41; Leah S. Marcus, 'Pastimes and the Purging of Theater', in *Staging the Renaissance*, eds David Scott Kastan, Peter Stallybrass (Routledge, 1991), 196–210.

35. For more on the doubled premiere of *Bartholomew Fair*, see Blissett, 'Your Majesty is Welcome to a Fair', 81–2, and Ian Donaldson, *The World Upside-Down* (Oxford, 1970), 48, 71–4.

36. See Lynch, 'Dramatic Festivity', 130–1.

37. See Chapman, 'Flaying Bartholomew', 515–16.

38. Chapman, 'Flaying Bartholomew', 515.

39. For more on the kinds of food sold in early modern theatres, see Natasha Korda, *Labors Lost: Women's Work and the Early Modern Stage* (Philadelphia, PA, 2011), 146.

40. Teague, *Curious History*, 35–6.

41. Lucy Munro, *Children of the Queen's Revels: A Jacobean Theatre Repertory* (New York, 2005), 49.

42. Curtis Perry, *The Making of Jacobean Culture: James I and the Renegotiation of Elizabethan Literary Practice* (Cambridge, 1997), 218.

43. See Blisset, 'Your Majesty is Welcome to a Fair', 83, Donaldson, *World*, 72–3.

44. See Harris, 'The Smell of *Macbeth*', 477–81.

45. Leah Marcus, *Politics of Mirth: Jonson, Herrick, Milton, Marvell and the Defense of Old Holiday Pastimes* (Chicago, IL, 1989), 40.

46. Since 1532, there had been a cockpit at Whitehall Palace; like Henry VIII, and Queen Elizabeth, James I was a fan of the violent 'sport', hosting numerous 'performances' at court. During James' tenure at Whitehall, the pit had, indeed, alternated between theatrical entertainments like *Bartholomew Fair* and baiting events. Glynn Wyckham cites two important royal baiting events: bear baiting and plays performed in Whitehall's Banquet House in 1608 and the baiting of 'white bears' in a masque at court in 1610. See *Early English Stages, 1300–1600*, 3 vols (London, 1972), 2: 63. Though most performances were in the Banqueting House or the Great Hall, it is plausible that Jonson's play was staged in the private, wooden cockpit, because renovations were taking place in both other spaces. See John Orrell, *The Theatres of Inigo Jones and John Webb* (New York, 2010), 91.

47. For more on the emerging link between class and olfaction in early modern London, see Holly Dugan, '*Coriolanus* and the "rank-scented meinie"', in *Masculinity and the Metropolis of Vice, 1550–1650*, eds Amanda Bailey and Roze Hentschell (Basingstoke, 2009), 139–59.

48. Ian Archer, *Pursuit of Stabilty: Social Relations in Elizabethan London* (Cambridge, 2003), 232.

49. The joke, of course, is that the most immediate olfactory smellscape to which he referred was not that of a 'sordid' inn, but of Blackfriars, where *The New Inn* debuted in 1629. Such a reference also subtly pokes fun at the olfactory world of other theatres, namely the Globe. The host's paraphrasing of Jacques' melancholy meditation on life and art in *As You Like It* (1599), one of Shakespeare's earliest plays to debut at the Globe, slyly references the material afterlives of past stages within the texts of plays.

50. See, for example, James E. Robinson, '*Bartholomew Fair:* A Comedy of Vapors', *Studies in English Literature, 1500–1900*, 1.2 (1961), 65–80.

51. Paster, '*Bartholomew Fair*', 266.

52. Paster, '*Bartholomew Fair*', 267.

53. The phrase 'turd i' your teeth' was a generic insult, though it obviously conjures forth a foul image and smell.

54. See Paster, '*Bartholomew Fair*', 267–8.

55. Turnbull street, now Turnmill street, was north of Smithfield and ran parallel to the Fleet sewer. For more on its associations with prostitution, see Darryll Grantley, *London in Early Modern English Drama: Representing the Built Environment* (Basingstoke, 2008), 120–1.

56. This had become the foulest part of the Fleet ditch as Middlesex justices, who were out of City jurisdiction, could not be compelled to clear it.

57. Ann Jennalie Cook, *The Privileged Playgoers of Shakespeare's London* (Princeton, NJ, 1981), 7–8.

58. Taken together, these two references to dunghills document that the city

(and its sewage system) was in transition. The first, Littlewit's reference to 'rakers', cites a long-established practice of dealing with London's waste by carting and removing it to the outskirts of the city. These were men hired by the parish, rather than City or Borough officials. The second reference, however, emphasises that by 1614, the amount of work required to maintain this system was almost insurmountable. Areas associated with noisome industry (like horse trading), tenement housing and prostitution were particularly dangerous and regulated: there would have been many such wheelbarrows in (and north of) Smithfield. There would also be plenty in Southwark. For more on this topic, see Rosemary Weinstein, 'New Urban Demands in Early Modern London', in *Medical History*, 11 (1991), 29–40.

59. Carol Chillington Rutter, *Documents of the Rose Playhouse* (Manchester, 1999), 33.

60. See Katherine Lynch, 'The Dramatic Festivity of *Bartholomew Fair*', 133.

61. For more on the phenomenological experience of London's crowd, see Ian Munro, *The Figure of the Crowd in Early Modern: The City and Its Double* (Basingstoke, 2008). For more on the role of the theatre in the expanding metropolis, see Jean Howard, *Theater of a City: The Places of London Comedy* (Philadelphia, PA, 2009) and Zucker, *Places of Wit*.

62. I would like to thank Farah Karim-Cooper, Dana Luciano, Samantha Pinto, Adam Smyth and Tiffany Stern for their helpful comments on earlier drafts of this essay.

10: TOUCH AND TASTE IN SHAKESPEARE'S THEATRES

1. Andrew J. Gurr, *Playgoing in Shakespeare's London*, 3rd edn (Cambridge, 2004), 86–7.

2. In the anti-theatrical treatise, *A Third Blast from Plaies and Theaters* (London, 1580), the author uses this term: 'it behoveth you to be verie warie, and circumspect how you thrust your selves into publique assemblies' (71).

3. A recent collection of extraordinary essays, Lowell Gallagher and Shankar Raman, eds, *Knowing Shakespeare: Senses, Embodiment and Cognition* (Basingstoke and New York, 2010), shows how 'early modern understandings of bodily sensation opened into the domains of affect, emotion, and social opinion', and describes the early modern understanding of psychology as a 'regulated chain of interactions linking sensations received from without to the so-called internal senses of common sense, imagination, memory' (4–5, 19).

4. Stephen Gosson, *The Schoole of Abuse* (London, 1579), sig. B6v.

5. Gallagher and Raman, eds, *Knowing Shakespeare*, 5.

6. See Marjorie O'Rourke Boyle, *Senses of Touch: Human Dignity and Deformity from Michelangelo to Calvin, Studies in Medieval and Reformation Thought* (Leiden, Boston, MA, Koln, 1998).

7. See '"O she's warm": Touch in *The Winter's Tale*', in *Knowing Shakespeare*, eds Gallagher and Raman, 65–81.

8. See *Sensible Flesh: On Touch in Early Modern Europe*, ed. Elizabeth D. Harvey (Philadelphia, PA, 2003).

9. See 'The Senses Divided', 85–103.

10. See *Phenomenal Shakespeare* (Malden and Oxford, 2010).

11. See *Dead Hands: Fictions of Agency, Renaissance to Modern* (Palo Alto, CA, 1999).

12. See Marjorie O'Rourke Boyle, *Senses of Touch*, 141.

13. Patricia Cahill, 'Take Five: Renaissance Literature and the Study of the Senses', *Literature Compass*, 6.5 (2009), 1014–1030, 1026.

14. Richard Brathwait, *Essaies Upon the Five Senses* (London, 1620), 49, 27, 30–1.

15. Brathwait, 31.

16. Brathwait, 44.

17. Thomas Wright, *The Passions of the Mind* (London, 1601), 110.

18. The *OED* provides two definitions for 'haptic'; the first, 'pertaining to the sense of touch or tactile sensations', is quite general, whereas the second definition refers to it as 'having a greater dependence on sensations of touch than on sight, especially as a means of psychological orientation'.

19. Helkiah Crooke, *Mikrocosmographia. A Description of the Body of Man* (London, 1615), 668.

20. Tanya Pollard, *Drugs and Theater in Early Modern England* (Oxford, 2005), 100.

21. John Baret refers to this metaphorical association with the word 'touch' when he glosses the phrase 'attestante omnium memoria' in *An Alveary or Triple Dictionary, in English, Latin, and French* (London 1574), 147: 'To touch one to the hart with remembraunce'.

22. Unless otherwise stated, all references to Shakespeare are taken from *The Arden Shakespeare Complete Works*, eds Richard Proudfoot, Ann Thompson and David Scott Kastan, rev. edn (London, 2001).

23. Andrew J. Gurr, *The Shakespearean Stage 1574–1642*, 4th edn (Cambridge, 2009), 176.

24. Dutch tourist Johannes De Witt noted that the Swan playhouse (1595) 'accommodates in its seats three thousand persons' (cited in Gurr, *The Shakespearean Stage*, 162).

25. Jenny Tiramani, 'Pins and Aglets', in Catharine Richardson and Tara

Hamling, eds *Everyday Objects: Medieval and Early Modern Material Culture and Its Meanings* (Farnham, 2010), 85–94, 85.

26. Ann Rosalind Jones and Peter Stallybrass, *Renaissance Clothing and the Materials of Memory* (Cambridge, 2000), 24.

27. Thomas Dekker, *The Seven Deadly Sinnes of London* (London, 1606), sig. C2r.

28. Anthony Munday, *A Third Blast from Plaies and Theaters* (London, 1580), 89.

29. Gosson, *Schoole of Abuse*, 17.

30. Stephen Gosson, *Playes Confuted in Five Actions* (London, 1582), sig. G6r.

31. William Shakespeare, *Coriolanus*, Arden 2nd Series, ed. Philip Brockbank (London, 1976, 2006).

32. Amy Cook, *Shakespearean Neuroplay: Reinvigorating the Study of Dramatic Texts and Performance Through Cognitive Science* (New York, 2010), 55.

33. The many synonyms (associated with the sense of touch) are illustrated in a search of Lexicons of Early Modern English. Randle Cotgrave's *A Dictionary of the French and English Tongues* (1611) provides, 'small pricke, sting, spurre, goad' as synonyms for *Piqueron*. http://leme.library.utoronto.ca/search/results.cfm, accessed 15 January 2012.

34. David Harris Sacks, 'London's Dominion', in *Material London Ca. 1600*, ed. Lena Cowen Orlin (Philadelphia, PA, 2000), 20–53, 23.

35. In his discussions about the sense of touch, Aristotle suggests that while all the senses can be assigned to a particular organ – sight, the eyes; sound, the ears; smell, the nose; taste, the tongue—touch is linked to the entire body which can experience tactile sensations: 'It is difficult to say whether touch is one sense or more than one, and also what the organ is which is perceptive of the object of touch' (Cited in Mazzio, 102). See Aristotle, *De Anima* II and *De Sensu*.

36. Karen Harvey, *The Kiss in History*, 9.

37. Harvey, 10.

38. Pollard, 102.

39. Farah Karim-Cooper, *Cosmetics in Shakespearean and Renaissance Drama* (Edinburgh, 2006), 80.

40. William Shakespeare, *Romeo and Juliet*, ed. René Weis, Arden 3rd Series (London, 2012).

41. Henry Crosse, *Vertues Common-Wealth or The High-Way to Honour* (London, 1603), sig. P4v.

42. See Pollard, 101, for a list of plays involving poisoned kisses.

43. Thomas Middleton, *The Lady's Tragedy*, ed. Julia Briggs, in Gary Taylor and John Lavagnino, eds *Thomas Middleton: The Collected Works* (Oxford, 2007).

44. Christopher Marlowe, *Dr Faustus* B-Text in David Bevington and Eric Rasmussen, eds, *Christopher Marlowe: Doctor Faustus and Other Plays*, Oxford World Classics (Oxford, 1995).

45. William Shakespeare, *A Midsummer Night's Dream*, ed. Harold F. Brooks, Arden 2nd Series (London, 1979). I am grateful to the wonderful insights of William Caldwell of Mary Baldwin College/The American Shakespeare Center and Shakespeare's Globe, whose helpful conversations about this phrase helped me to see its many possible meanings.

46. *OED* online http://www.oed.com/view/Entry/81765?rskey=Ns9GFg &result=4&isAdvanced=false#eid, accessed 1 August 2011.

47. Nancy Selleck, *The Interpersonal Idiom in Shakespeare, Donne and Early Modern Culture* (Basingstoke and New York, 2008), 58.

48. Selleck, 59.

49. For a good introduction to Galen, see Todd H.J. Pettigrew, *Shakespeare and the Practice of Physic: Medical Narratives on the Early Modern Stage* (Cranbury, NJ, 2007).

50. Munday, 95–6.

51. John Northbrooke, *A Treatise Against Dicing, Dancing, Plays, and Interludes with other Idle Pastimes* (London, 1577), 62.

52. John Fletcher and William Shakespeare, *King Henry VIII (All is True)*, ed. Gordon McMullan, Arden 3rd Series (London, 2000).

53. Charles Whitney, *Early Responses to Renaissance Drama* (Cambridge, 2006), 198.

54. William Shakespeare, *Hamlet*, eds Neil Taylor and Ann Thompson, Arden 3rd Series (London, 2006).

55. Harvey, 'The Sense of all Senses', in *Sensible Flesh*, 2.

56. Anthony Munday, *A Second Blast of the Retrait from Plaies and Theaters* (London, 1580), 11.

57. Gosson, *Schoole of Abuse*, sig. B7r.

58. Gosson, *Playes Confuted*, sig. D8r.

59. William Shakespeare, *Othello*, ed. E.A.J. Honigmann, Arden 3rd Series (London, 2001).

60. Ken Albala, *Food in Early Modern Europe* (Westport, CT, and London, 2003), 222.

61. Ben Jonson, *Volpone*, in *Ben Jonson: The Alchemist and Other Plays*, ed. Gordon Campbell (Oxford, 1995).

62. Munday, *A third blast*, 69.

63. Brathwait, 45.

64. See Ken Albala, *Food in Early Modern Europe*, for a discussion of early modern dietary practices, early modern ingredients and the nutritional theory that governed the composition of printed recipe manuals and nutritional guides in the period. Joan Fitzpatrick's *Food and Shakespeare: Early Modern Dietaries and the Plays* (Aldershot and Burlington, VT,

2007), a brilliant study of food and dietaries in Shakespeare, shows how people with particular humoral constitutions were advised in dietaries about the types of food to be avoided; for example, melancholic types should 'avoid excessive food and drink, especially "meats hard of digestion"' (3). See also *The Pleasures and Horrors of Eating: The Cultural History of Eating in Anglophone Literature*, ed. Marion Gymnich and Norbert Lennartz (Bonn, 2010).

65. C.M. Woolgar, *The Senses in Late Medieval England* (New Haven, CT, and London, 2006), 106.

66. Julian Bowsher and Pat Miller, *The Rose and the Globe—Playhouses of Shakespeare's Bankside, Southwark: Excavations 1988–90* (London, 2009), 146. Stephen Gosson recounts that apples or 'pippins' are consumed at the playhouses in London. See *Playes Confuted*, sig. G6r.

67. Bowsher and Miller, 146.

68. Bowsher and Miller, 152.

69. The work of Joan Fitzpatrick, Ken Albala and Norbert Lennartz is helpful in pointing to many references to food as well as explaining the cultural and moral significance of the use of food in theatrical and literary texts.

70. Gosson, *Schoole of Abuse*, sig. B6r.

71. Northbrooke, 64.

72. William Shakespeare, *Much Ado About Nothing*, ed. Claire McEachern for Arden 3rd Series (London, 2006).

73. Crosse, sig. Q3v.

74. Munday, *A third blast*, 69.

75. Munday, *A second blast*, 6.

76. William Shakespeare, *Love's Labour's Lost*, ed. H.R. Woudhuysen, Arden 3rd Series (London, 1998).

77. Gosson, *Schoole of Abuse*, sig. B6v.

78. William Shakespeare, *Julius Caesar*, ed. David Daniell, Arden 3rd Series (London, 1998).

11: 'SIGHT AND SPECTACLE'

1. Kestutis Kveraga, Avniel S. Ghuman, Moshe Bar, 'Top-down Predictions in the Cognitive Brain,' *Brain and Cognition*, 65 (2007), 145–68, 145.

2. Andy Clark, 'Do Thrifty Brains Make Better Minds?' http://opinionator.blogs.nytimes.com/2012/01/15/do-thrifty-brains-make-better-minds/, accessed 10 April 2012.

3. Jenn Stephenson, 'Singular Impressions: Meta-theatre on Renaissance Celebrities and Corpses', *Studies in Theatre and Performance*, 27, 2 (2007), 138.

4. Andrew Gurr, 'Meta-theatre and the fear of playing', in *Neo-historicism: Studies in Renaissance Literature, History, and Politics*, eds Robin Headlam Wells, Glenn Burgess and Rowland Wymer (Cambridge, 2000), 91–110, 91.

5. Andrew Gurr, *Playgoing in Shakespeare's London*, 3rd edn (Cambridge, 2004), 105.

6. Gurr, *Playgoing*, 105.

7. R.B. Graves, *Lighting the Shakespearean Stage 1567–1642* (Carbondale and Edwardsville, IL, 1999), 65.

8. Benedict Nightingale, review of *Henry V*, *London Times* (28 August 1997); see Cynthia Marshall, 'Sight and Sound: Two Models of Shakespearean Subjectivity on the British Stage', *Shakespeare Quarterly*, 51: 3 (Autumn 2000), 353–361.

9. See Gurr, *Playgoing*, 102–16, for a discussion of this issue.

10. Gabriel Egan, 'Hearing or Seeing a Play?: Evidence of Early Modern Theatrical Terminology', *Ben Jonson Journal*, 8 (2001), 327–47.

11. Bruce Smith, *The Acoustic World of Early Modern England* (Chicago, IL, 1999).

12. See Huston Diehl, *Staging Reform and Reforming the Stage* (Ithaca, NY, 1997) for an introduction to these issues within the context of the Elizabethan stage.

13. Antony Munday, *A Second and Third Blast of Retrait from Plaies and Theatres* (1580), sig. B1v.

14. Stephen Gosson, *The Trumpet of Warre* (1598) sig. C7v.

15. Thomas Platter, *Thomas Platter's Travels in England 1599*, trans. Clare Williams (London, 1937), 166–75.

16. Thomas Heywood, *Apology for Actors* (1612), sig. B3v-Clr.

17. Thomas Nashe, *Pierce Penniless His Supplication to the Devil* (London, 1592), sig. H2r, in Nashe, *The Unfortunate Traveller and Other Works*, ed. J.B. Steane (Harmondsworth, 1972), 112–13.

18. Susan Cerasano, '"Borrowed Robes", Costume Prices, and the Drawing of *Titus Andronicus*', *Shakespeare Studies*, 22 (1994), 45–57; see also Peter Stallybrass and Ann Jones, *Renaissance Clothing and the Materials of Memory* (Cambridge, 2000).

19. R.A. Foakes, *Henslowe's Diary*, 2nd edn (Cambridge, 2002); see also the digital archive of the manuscripts at: http://www.henslowe-alleyn.org.uk/index.html.

20. Foakes, *Henslowe's Diary*, 325, f. 45v.

21. Foakes, *Henslowe's Diary*, 325, 161,146; see also Hal Smith, 'Some Principles of Stage Costume', *Journal of Warburg and Courtauld Institute*, 25:3/4 (1962), 240–57; Jean McIntyre, *Costumes and Scripts in the Elizabethan Theatre* (Edmonton, 1992).

22. For a full discussion of scholarly disputes see Thomas Postlewait, 'Eyewitnesses to History: Visual Evidence for Theater in Early Modern England', in *The Oxford Handbook of Early Modern Theatre*, ed. Richard Dutton (Oxford, 2011).

23. Cerasano, '"Borrowed Robes"', 57.

24. Hal Smith, 'Some Principles of Stage Costume', 254.

25. All references are taken from *The Arden Shakespeare Complete Works*, eds Richard Proudfoot, Ann Thompson and David Scott Kastan, 3rd edn (London, 2011).

26. Frances N. Teague, *Shakespeare's Speaking Properties* (Cranbury, NJ, 1991).

27. Foakes, *Henslowe's Diary*, 319–20.

28. For a discussion of the connection between *The Tempest* and the Blackfriars, see Andrew Gurr, '*The Tempest*'s Tempest at Blackfriars,' *Shakespeare Survey*, 41 (1989), 91–102; see also Gwilym Jones' chapter in this collection, pp. 33–50.

29. William James, *Principles of Psychology*, 2 vols (Dover, 1950), 1: 404.

30. C.F. Chabris and D.J. Simons, *The Invisible Gorilla, and Other Ways Our Intuitions Deceive Us* (New York, 2010); see http://www.youtube.com/watch?v=vJG698U2Mvo.

31. Stephen L. Macknik *et al*, 'Attention and Awareness in Stage Magic: Turning Tricks into Research', *Nature Reviews*, 9 (2008), 871–9, 875.

32. Macknik, 'Attention and Awareness in Stage Magic', 875.

33. For a defence of this later view, see Amanda Barnier, John Sutton *et al*, 'A Conceptual and Empirical Framework for the Social Distribution of Cognition: The Case of Memory', *Cognitive Systems Research*, 9 (2008), 33–51.

34. For a full discussion of Iago's 'epistemological shell game' with the handkerchief, see Joel Altman, *The Improbability of Othello: Rhetorical Anthropology and Shakespearean selfhood* (Chicago, IL, 2011), 198ff.

35. Samuel Johnson, *Johnson on Shakespeare*, ed. Rubert Desai, 2nd edn (London, 1997), 174.

36. Katherine Maus, 'Introduction' to *Henry V* for *Norton Shakespeare* (London, 1997), 1449.

INDEX

Numbers in italic signify an illustration.

Abel, Lionel 14
actors
    illustrations of 149–158
    parts 159–65
    see also: character
Admiral's Men, The *see* theatre
    companies
Africanus, Leo, travel writer 41, 258*n*
air 172–4, 189–91
    see also: smell
Albala, Ken 231, 284*n*, 285*n*
Aldersgate 198
    see also: London
Alleyn, Edward, actor 91, 156, 160–2,
    164–5
amateur dramatists 82, 89
Anne of Denmark, queen 107
anti-theatre polemic 8, 96, 140, 205, 215,
    217–20, 222–32, 234–6, 240–1
Aristotle, philosopher 174–5, 215, 222
Armstrong, Archie 255*n*
Armstrong, David 172
Arras *see* stage architecture – curtain
Astington, John 143, 159
audience 11–14, 20, 31–2, 139, 177,
    192–4, 214, 218–21, 228–9, 238–9,
    247
    and imagination 11–13, 26, 32, 57, 64

Babbage, Charles, mathematician 193
Bacon, Francis, statesman 174

balcony *see* stage architecture
Baldwin, T. W. 142, 155
banderoles 149, 155–7
    see also: speech – graphic depictions
Bankside 198, 202, 205
    see also: London
Banu, Georges 60
Baret, John, lexicographer 282*n*
Barksted, William 87
Barnes, Barnabe
    The Divils Charter 21, 79
Bartholomew Fair 196–207, 210–12
    see also: London
Barton, Anne 76
    see also: Anne Righter
Bate, John 35
bear-baiting 202–6, 210, 280*n*
Beeston, Christopher, actor and
    impresario 103
Beevers, Geoffrey, actor 122
bell *see* stage architecture
Benfield, Robert, actor 142
Benton, Megan 159
Berkeley, William, governor and author
    Lost Lady, The 96, 113
Bird, William 87
Black Joan 87
blackface 104–117
    see also: stage paint
Blackfriars *see* playhouses
Blisset, William 202, 207, 278*n*, 279*n*

blood *see* stage effects
Blount, Thomas 23
Bourgy, Victor 53
Bowsher, Julian 218, 234
Boyle, Marjorie O'Rourke 215
Boyle, Robert 175–6
Brathwait, Richard, poet 160, 216–17,
    233, 255*n*, 282*n*, 286*n*
Brecht, Bertolt 14
Brinsley, John, schoolmaster 148
Brome, Richard, dramatist
    Late Lancashire Witches, The 88
Brook, Peter 179
Bulwer, John 17
Burbage, Richard, actor 18, 143, 192
Butler, Martin 92
Butterworth, Philip 80
Buzacott, Martin 192

Cahill, Patricia 216
cannibalism 73–6
    see also: staging – violence
Captain Thomas Stukeley 86
de Carles, Nathalie Rivere 4
Carnegie, David 52, 75
Carpenter, Sarah 103
Cathcart, Charles 132
Cerasano, Susan 242, 244
Chabris, Christopher 248
Chamberlain, John, letter-writer 254*n*
Chapman, Alison 203–4
Chapman, George, dramatist
    May-day 27
character 141–5, 159–65
    characterisation 145
    and handwriting 159–64
    types 142–4
    see also: actors
Charles I, king 103
Children of the Chapel *see* theatre
    companies
Children of the Queen's Revels *see*
    theatre companies
Chrysostom, John, church father 189
Churchyard, Thomas 259*n*
Clark, Andy 237
Claudius Tiberius Nero 73–6, 89

clothing 218–19
    see also: costumes
Cobb, Christopher 45
Cockpit, The *see* playhouses
Company of the Revels *see* theatre
    companies
Condell, Henry, actor 148
Cook, Amy 220
cosmetics *see* stage paint
costumes 80–1, 118–40, 242–4, *243*,
    245, 267*n*
    cost 125, 243, 286*n*
    and criminality 126–9
    disguise 118–26, 129–40
    doubling 125, 140
    see also: clothing
Cotgrave, Randle, lexicographer 283*n*
Coulthard, Ray, actor 122
Crane, Ralph, scribe 40
    see also: character – handwriting,
        scribal copy
Crooke, Helkiah, physician 175, 189–91,
    217
Crosse, Henry 224, 235
crowds *see* staging
curtains *see* stage architecture

Davenant, William 25
Davidson, Clifford 270*n*
Davies, John 230
Dawson, Anthony 101
decapitations 86–7
    see also: staging – violence, stage
        effects
Dekker, Thomas 17, 19, 254*n*, 255*n*
    Blurt Master-Constable 27
    Honest Whore, The 87
    *If this be not a good Play, the Diuell is
        in it* 36
    Seven Deadly Sinnes of London, The
        219
    Sir Thomas Wyatt 86
    Virgin Martyr, The 87
    Witch of Edmonton, The 157, 202
Descartes, Rene, philosopher 190
Dessen, Alan 52
dialogue *see* speech

dismemberment 86–91
  see also: staging – violence, stage
      effects
Donaldson, Ian 207
Donne, John, poet 111
Drayton, Michael, poet 192
dressers 25
  see also: clothes, costumes, tiring
      house
Drummond, William, poet 19
Dugan, Holly 7
dumb shows 85
Dunlop, Frank, director 272*n*
Dustagheer, Sarah 41

Edmond Ironside 86, 89
Egan, Gabriel 240
Elizabeth I, queen 199, 280*n*
Escolme, Bridget 5
extemporisation 145

Falconer, A. F. 42–3
Fair Maid of Bristow, The 81
Fenton, Geoffrey, politician 189
First Part of the Diall of Daies, The 258*n*
Fletcher, John, dramatist 89
  Bonduca 86
  Double Marriage, The 86–7
  Faithfull Shepheardesse, The 267*n*
  Henry VIII 11, 57–8, 228
  Maid in the Mill 27
  Pilgrim, The 118–120
  Prophetess, The 88
  Sea Voyage, The 44
  Sir John Van Olden Barnavelt 87
Florio, John, lexicographer 188
Foakes, R. A. 149, 156, 275*n*
food 234–5
  see also: taste
Ford, John, dramatist
  'Tis Pity She's a Whore 89
  Witch of Edmonton, The 157, 202
Fortune, The *see* playhouses
Foxe, John, historian 258*n*
frons scenae see stage architecture – scene
Fuller, Thomas, churchman and author
  Andronicus 89

Galen, physician 217
Gawdy, Philip, letter-writer 255*n*
Gayton, Edmund, physician 255*n*
ghosts 18, 21, 186
  see also: stage effects
Globe, The *see* playhouses
Goffe, Thomas, clergyman 261*n*
  Tragedy of Orestes, The 82
Goldberg, Jonathan 146, 163
Golding, Arthur, translator 259*n*
Gosson, Stephen, clergyman 215,
      219–20, 229, 240, 253*n*, 284*n*, 285*n*
Gouge, William, clergyman 254*n*
Graves, R. B. 239, 243
Greene, Robert, dramatist
  Looking-Glass for London and
      England, A 88
  Orlando Furioso 74, 77, 90–1, 93,
      160–2
  Selimus 88
Greene, Thomas, actor 151, 156
Greg, W. W. 77, 84
Guicciardini, Francesco, historian 189
gunpowder plot 207
Gurr, Andrew 40–1, 45, 56, 125–6, 130,
      214, 218, 238–9, 254*n*, 256*n*, 286*n*,
      287*n*
Gutjahr, Paul 159

Handel, Stephen 171
hangings *see* stage architecture – curtains
Harris, Jonathan Gil 102
Harvey, Elizabeth 215, 229
Harvey, Karen 222–3
Hazlitt, William, literary critic 14
heaven *see* stage architecture
hell *see* stage architecture
Heminge, John, actor 148
Henrietta Maria 103, 112
Henry V, Famous Victories of 243
Henry VIII, king 199, 280*n*
Henslowe, Philip, impresario 205, 242–3,
      246, 260*n*
Heywood, Thomas, dramatist 17, 114,
      241
  Apology for Actors 95–6, 241
  Appius and Virginia 75

Golden Age, The 89
Late Lancashire Witches, The 88
Love's Mistress, or the Queen's Masque
    96, 103–12
Holborn 200, 208
    see also: London
Hope, The *see* playhouses
Howes, Edmund, chronicler 255*n*
Husserl, Edmund 171–2
Hyland, Peter 119, 121, 125, 131

Ingelo, Nathaniel, author 255*n*
Ingram, Martin 126, 128

James I, king 207, 260*n*
James, William, psychologist 247
Jeamson, Thomas 108
Johnson, Samuel, lexicographer 251–2
Jones, Gwilym 4, 276*n*, 287*n*
Jones, Inigo, architect 103
Jonson, Ben, dramatist 7, 254*n*
    Bartholomew Fair 7, 196–7, 200–13
    Epicoene, Or the Silent Woman 232
    Every Man In His Humour 37
    Masque of Beauty 104–5
    Masque of Blackness 104, 107, 114
    New Inn, The 208
    Volpone 227, 232

Karim-Cooper, Farah 7, 107, 272*n*,
    281*n*, 283*n*
Kelly, Gene, actor 252
Kemp, William, actor 22
Killigrew, Thomas, dramatist 81
    Princess, The 81
    Thomaso, or The Wanderer 81
King Leir 264*n*
King, T. J. 142
King's Men, The *see* theatre companies
Kirkman, Francis, bookseller 261*n*
Kirschbaum, Leo 84, 264*n*, 266*n*
kissing *see* touch
Korda, Natasha 102
Kristeva, Julia 75
Kyd, Thomas, dramatist
    Spanish Tragedy, The 80, 89,
        151–7

ladders *see* stage architecture
Lamb, Charles, essayist 14
Lamentable Tragedie of Locrine, The 265*n*
leadership 124, 129–30, 133–5, 137–9
Lenton, Francis, poet 254*n*
Leslie, Alexander, army officer 1
lighting 238–9
    see also: air, stage effects
Lin, Erika 97
Lodge, Thomas, author
    Looking-Glass for London and
        England, A 88
London 199–202, 206–9, 212, 219, 222
    see also: Aldersgate, Bankside,
        Bartholomew Fair, Holborn,
        playhouses, Smithfield, Turnbull
        Street, Whitehall Palace
Look About You 96, 98–101
Lynch, Kathleen 203–4

Machin, Lewis 87
McMullan, Gordon 58
Maguire, Laurie 156
Mainwairing, Henry, author 43
make-up *see* stage paint
Mannering, Arthur 263*n*
Marcus, Leah 148, 203
Marlowe, Christopher, dramatist
    Doctor Faustus 34, 56–7, 74, 87, 88–9,
        226
    Massacre at Paris, The 89
    Tamburlaine 68, 95, 243
Marmet, Melchior de, author 255*n*
Marshall, Cynthia 239
Marston, John, dramatist
    Insatiate Countess, The 27, 87
    Antonio's Revenge 67–8, 89
    Malcontent, The 119, 130–4, 139
Mary I, queen 199
Massinger, Philip, dramatist
    Double Marriage, The 86–7
    Prophetess, The 88
    Sir John Van Olden Barnavelt 87
masques 104–5, 107, 110
Mazzio, Carla 214–16
medieval drama 100–1, 104, 198, 204
    Wisdom Who is Christ 107

Melton, John, politician 34
Menzer, Paul 6, 275*n*
metadrama 11, 14, 17–18, 26–7, 29, 31,
     38, 46, 97, 100, 126, 131
Middleton, Thomas, dramatist 19,
     224–5
  Blurt Master-Constable 27
  Changeling, The 88, 121
  Game at Chess, A 157
  Honest Whore, The 87
  Lady's Tragedy, The 225–6
  Phoenix, The 272*n*, 273*n*
  Revenger's Tragedy, The 76, 87–8
  Roaring Girl, The 156
Miller, Pat 218, 234
misdirection 247–9
  see also: stage effects
Montagu, Walter, courtier
  The Shepherd's Paradise 53, 104–5,
     112
More, Henry 255*n*
Morton, Timothy 43
*Most Pleasant Comedie of Mucedorus,
     A* 265*n*
Mulcaster, Richard, schoolmaster 146–7
Munday, Anthony, author 228–9, 235,
     240–1, 283*n*, 284*n*
  see also: anti-theatre polemic
Munro, Lucy 5

Nashe, Thomas, author 20, 241–2
North, Thomas, translator 136
Northbrooke, John, polemicist 228, 284*n*

Ovid 47, 262*n*
Owens, Margaret 74

Parks, Suzan-Lori, dramatist 98
Partiall Law, The 27
Paster, Gail Kern 209–10, 227
Peacham, Henry, poet 243–4
Peele, George, dramatist 77
  Battell of Alcazar, The 79, 84–5, 93,
     100, 265*n*
  Edward I 86
Perry, Curtis 207
Phoenix, The *see* playhouses

pillars *see* stage architecture
Pimlott, Steven, director 68
Platter, Thomas, diarist 127, 234, 241–2
playhouses 2, 13, 218–22, 234
  Blackfriars 13, 19, 21, 39, 41, 113,
     118, 131, 239, 247, 280*n*
  Cockpit, The 103
  Fortune, The 34
  Globe, The 1–2, 13, 20–1, 30, 56,
     132, 171, 173–7, 179, 190, 205,
     218, 234, 238–9, 280*n*
  Hope, The 196–8, 202–9, 211–2
  Phoenix, The 103
  Red Bull 33
  Rose, The 22, 125, 218, 234
  Swan, The 27, 205
  Theatre, The 21
  see also: London, smell
Plutarch 136–8
Pollard, Tanya 107, 217, 223
Postles, Dave 126
posts *see* stage architecture
Preston, Thomas, author 265*n*
  Cambises 80
print culture 141–67
  title pages 150–8
prompter 25
props 64–5, 86–7, 97–8, 101–2, 246
  blood *see* stage effects
  bodies 92
  cannonballs 36
  cauldrons 19
  clocks 29–30
  daggers 82
  hands 88
  heads 86–7
  ladders 27–8
  limbs 76–7, 84–6, 88–91, 93
  pigs and pork 199–203, 206–7,
     209–10
  skulls 87–8

Queen Anne's Company *see* theatre
     companies
Queen Henrietta's Men *see* theatre
     companies
de Quincy, Thomas, author 179

Rayner, Alice 97, 103
realism *see* staging
Rebellion of Naples, The 83
Red Bull, The *see* playhouses
Reynolds, Debbie, actor 252
Rich, Richard, lord chancellor 199
Righter, Anne 13, 14
Ripley, John 100
Robinson, Robert, linguist 146–8,
    156–7, 162
Rome 74–6
Rose, The *see* playhouses
Rowe, Katherine 74, 76, 215
Rowley, Samuel, dramatist 87
Rowley, William, dramatist
    Changeling, The 88, 121
    Witch of Edmonton, The 157, 202
Rylance, Mark, actor *123*, 124, *243*

Schafer, R. Murray 171
Scot, Reginald, author 79–80, 82, 87
scene *see* stage architecture
scribal copy 159–62
    see also: character – handwriting,
        speech, Ralph Crane
Selleck, Nancy 227
Seneca
    Hercules Furens 91
sensory experience 214–16
    early theories 215–16
    see also: air, sight, smell, sound, taste,
        touch
Serlio, Sebastiano, architect 256*n*
Shady, Raymond 103
Shakespeare, William, dramatist 2, 111
    All's Well That Ends Well 26
    Antony and Cleopatra 18, 29, 120,
        136–8, 184, 186, 252, 276*n*
    modern production 124
    As You Like It 15, 22, 142, 280*n*
    Comedy of Errors 17
    Coriolanus 79, 99–100, 184, 220–2, 246
    Cymbeline 19, 20, 30, 61–4, 78, 90,
        91–3, 173, 217, 246–7
    Hamlet 13, 17, 20–1, 22, 26, 29, 65–7,
        68, 87, 94–5, 145, 182–4, 186–7,
        229, 231, 233–4, 248–50

1 Henry IV 142
2 Henry IV 16, 182, 184
Henry V 8, 24, 80, 184, 196, 201,
    251–2, 271*n*, 273*n*
    modern production 239
1 Henry VI 56, 246
2 Henry VI 86
3 Henry VI 80, 184
Henry VIII 11, 57–8, 228
Julius Caesar 28, 37–9, 47, 75, 83, 93,
    99, 182–4, 189–90, 236
King John 29, 184
King Lear 22, 78, 120, 183, 187, 246,
    259*n*
Love's Labour's Lost 11, 114, 183–4,
    235
Macbeth 29, 30, 86, 94, 178–81, 183,
    186–8, 196, 248–51, 276*n*
Measure for Measure 24, 119, 121–2,
    124, 126–8, 130, 134–5, 139,
    185–6
    modern production 124, 273*n*
Merchant of Venice, The 16, 173
Midsummer Night's Dream, A 23, 26,
    31, 104, 175, 184, 226–7, 250
Much Ado About Nothing 235
Othello 21, 29, 104, 183–4, 187,
    230–1, 250–1, 259*n* 276*n*
Pericles 20, 47
Rape of Lucrece, The 53
Richard II 20, 173, 184
Richard III 30, 246
Romeo and Juliet 22, 24, 28, 180–1,
    183–4, 196, 224, 276*n*
Taming of the Shrew, The 195, 213
Tempest, The 19, 24, 39–49, 173,
    184–7, 193, 246–7, 276*n*
Timon of Athens 19
Titus Andronicus 17, 19, 74–6, 85, 88,
    89, 184, 196, 244, 245
Troilus and Cressida 24
Twelfth Night 121, 184–5, 187
Two Gentlemen of Verona, The 27,
    183, 258*n*
Winter's Tale, The 11, 47, 116, 173,
    196, 258*n*, 261*n*
ships *see* staging

Shirley, James, dramatist
  Bird in a Cage, The 112
  Politician, The 81, 279*n*
Sidney, Philip, courtier 24
Siege of London 246
sight 237–52
  and manipulation 247–51
  see also: sensory experience
Silbert, Roxana, director 272*n*
Simons, David, psychologist 248
smell 195–213
  and memory 197, 201
  of playhouses 204–9
  vapours209
  see also: sensory experience
Smith, Bruce 6, 150, 215, 240, 268*n*, 276*n*
Smithfield 196–204, 211–13
  see also: London
Sofer, Andrew 54, 74–5, 102
sound 171–94, 230
  early theories 189–91, 193
  soundscapes 184–5
  see also: sensory experience
speech 145–60
  aural characteristics 182–4
  graphic depictions 149–59
  memorising 147–8, 156
  production 176–7
  punctuation 154–5, 178
  scribal copy of 159–60
  see also: banderoles, sound
speech prefixes 157–8
Staell, Ioris 258*n*
stage architecture 15
  balcony 27
  bell 29
  curtains 12, 51–69
  and discovery 59
  and genre 55–6
  and metaphor 53, 66
  and time 60, 64, 66–7
  uses 51–2
  in visual culture 60
  ladders 27–8
  pillars 21–2
  heaven and hell 15–20
  scene 23–5

scene-board 24
tiring house 16, 25–7, 177–80
trapdoor 18–9
stage directions 73, 78–83, 90–1, 244, 246
stage effects 34–5, 246–7
  blood 74–81, 89–93, 98–9
  as disguise 99–103
  substitutes 79–81, 100–2
  body parts 76–7
  ghosts 18, 21, 186
  lighting 238–9
  supernatural 248
  thunder and lightning 35–8, 40–2
  and *Julius Caesar* 37–9
  and *The Tempest* 39–49
  see also: props, misdirection, sensory experience, stage paint
stage paint 95–107, 223, 225
  blackface 104–117
  and blood 97–103
  and gender 116–17
  vocabulary 269*n*
staging 12
  cannibalism 73–6
  crowds 244, 246
  realism 14, 43, 85, 102–3, 238
  ships 42–4
  storms *see* stage effects – thunder and lightning
  time 29–30, 57, 60, 64, 66–7, 99, 150
  violence 74–93
States, Bert O. 101
Stephenson, Jenn 238–9
Stern, Tiffany 4, 55, 160, 246, 255*n*, 279*n*, 281*n*
Stevens, Andrea 5, 80
Stockwood, John, author 254*n*
Stokoe, William 172
storms *see* stage effects
Stoughton, John 1, 17
Stow, John, historian 278*n*
Strachey, William, historian 47
Stubbes, Philip, pamphleteer 96
Suckling, John, poet 1
Sullivan, Daniel, director 267*n*

Swan, The *see* playhouses
Syme, Holger Schott 149, 155

Tailor, Robert, dramatist
    The Hogge hath Lost his Pearle 27
taste 231–6
    see also: food, sensory experience
Taylor, Gary 58
Taymor, Julie, director 85
theatres *see* playhouses
theatre companies
    Admiral's Men 86, 98, 125, 243
    Children of the Chapel 131
    Children of the Queen's Revels 40,
        131
    Company of the Revels 33, 50
    King's Men, The 113, 118, 131–2,
        134, 142, 205, 243, 247
    Queen Anne's Company 256n
    Queen Henrietta's Men 103
theatrum mundi motif 16, 20–1
Theweleit, Klaus 95
Thomas Lord Cromwell 86
Thomson, Leslie 38, 52
Thomson, Peter 274n
Tiberius, emperor 73
time *see* staging
Tiramani, Jenny, theatre designer 80,
    218
tiring-house *see* stage architecture
title pages 150–8
    see also: print culture
Tomlinson, Sophie 112
touch 215–36
    kissing 222–6
    see also: sensory experience
trapdoor *see* stage architecture
Tribble, Evelyn 8, 215
True Chronicle History of King Leir, The
    264n
Tryall of Chevalry, The 271n
Turnbull Street 211–2
    see also: London
Two Merry Milke-Maids, The 33–4
Twycross, Meg 103

typecasting 141–2, 162
    see also: character

Valefius, theologian 217
Vaughan, Henry, author 255n
Venner, Tobias, physician 279n
violence *see* staging
Vygotsky, Lev, psychologist 177, 188

Walter, Harriet, actor 124
Ward, Ned, satirist 201
Warning for Fair Women, A 56, 81, 99,
    265n
Webster, John, dramatist 96
    Appius and Virginia 75
    Devil's Law Case, The 87
    Duchess of Malfi, The 89
    Malcontent, The (Q3) 131–2
    Sir Thomas Wyatt 86
    Virgin Martyr, The 87
Wells, Stanley 58
Whetstone, George, author
    Promos and Cassandra 127–8
Whitehall Palace 197, 203, 206–9
    see also: London
Whithorne, Peter, military writer 277n
Whitney, Charles 228
Wilcox, Sherman 172
Wilkins, George, author 1, 265n
Wilson, Robert, dramatist
    Three Ladies of London 106
Wisdom Who is Christ 107
    see also: medieval drama
Wither, George, poet 255n
Witney, Geoffrey, poet 76
Witt, Johannes de, diarist 282n
Woolger, C.M. 233
Worthen, W.B. 141, 149
Wright, Thomas 217
writing 149–51
    see also: character – handwriting,
        scribal copy, Ralph Crane
Yarington, Robert, dramatist
    Two Lamentable Tragedies 74, 89,
        265n